Kathleen F. A

Problem-solving Discussions and Conferences: Leadership Methods and Skills

McGRAW-HILL SERIES IN MANAGEMENT
Keith Davis, *Consulting Editor*

ALLEN: *Management and Organization*

CALHOON, NOLAND, AND WHITEHILL: *Cases on Human Relations in Management*

DAVIS: *Human Relations at Work*

DAVIS AND SCOTT: *Readings in Human Relations*

FLIPPO: *Principles of Personnel Management*

GRIMSHAW AND HENNESSEY: *Organizational Behavior*

HARBISON AND MYERS: *Management in the Industrial World*

JOHNSON, KAST, AND ROSENZWEIG: *The Theory and Management of Systems*

KEITH AND GUBELLINI: *Business Management*

KOONTZ AND O'DONNELL: *Principles of Management*

KOONTZ AND O'DONNELL: *Readings in Management*

MAIER: *Problem-solving Discussions and Conferences: Leadership Methods and Skills*

MAYER: *Production Management*

PIGORS AND PIGORS: *Case Method in Human Relations*

SALTONSTALL: *Human Relations in Administration*

TANNENBAUM, WESCHLER, AND MASSARIK: *Leadership and Organization*

VANCE: *Industrial Administration*

VANCE: *Management Decision Simulation*

Problem-solving Discussions and Conferences:

Leadership Methods and Skills

Norman R. F. Maier

Professor of Psychology
University of Michigan

McGraw-Hill Book Company, Inc.

New York   San Francisco
Toronto   London

PROBLEM-SOLVING DISCUSSIONS
AND CONFERENCES

39715

Preface

Discussion leadership is becoming a science. It requires not only the knowledge of sound principles, but the skill, the insight, and the desire to put these principles to work. The principles are derived from research in experimental psychology, social psychology, and clinical psychology. Experimental psychology contributed to our understanding of problem solving, frustration, and attitudes; social psychology contributed to our knowledge of group processes, power relations, and interpersonal communication; and clinical psychology added to our understanding of adjustment and developed certain counseling procedures. All of these facets of human nature are set into operation whenever a group meets for discussion. Executives hold conferences at all levels in an organization; scientists work in teams; educators serve on committees; church workers hold conferences; parents serve on action groups; teachers educate by the use of participation methods; psychologists and psychiatrists practice group therapy; and teen-agers hold meetings. Everyone at some time or other finds himself working with others on some kind of project. Although the personal motivation of the leader of a group or the chairman of a committee may be questioned, the purpose of the meeting is to get a group organized to achieve a common objective. In practically none of the above meetings does the typical leader practice skills other than those that come naturally. The requirement for group leadership is primarily that of being in charge of a group.

Undoubtedly the reader will have experienced both satisfactions and disappointments at one time or another in connection with group meetings. Some groups work well together; others do not. Often participants blame one another for failures. The leader tends to take the bow for successes and blame some participants for failures. Since the reins are in the hands of the discussion leader, it is to him that we must look to make group effort both creative and satisfying.

The subject of methods and skills of conference and discussion leadership has been one of the author's central interests for a number of years. Much of his recent research deals with improving the effectiveness of a leader's performance in group problem solving and decision making. The present volume integrates these studies with his earlier researches on problem solving and frustration. The objective of skilled leadership is to dissipate the forces in a group that make for frustration and to utilize the group resources that make for cooperative problem solving. Groups have two assets that exceed those of any individual in the group: they possess more knowledge, and they can think in a greater variety of ways. These potential assets may cause the group to be in conflict, or they may lead to a superior product and increased satisfaction. For the latter to occur, the principles of group behavior must be skillfully used by the leader. What these principles are and how they may serve to improve meetings is the subject of this little book.

Much of the research reported in this volume was supported by USPHS grant No. M-2704 from the National Institute of Mental Health, United States Public Health Service. The author is indebted to his wife, Ayesha, to Professor A. R. Solem, and to Margaret Baksic, for many valuable suggestions in improving the manuscript, to Jewel Clabuesch Bos who carried the major burden of typing, and finally to hundreds of executives whose problems, interests, stimulation, and desire to improve management talents gave the author the stimulation and encouragement to develop the principles put forth in this volume.

Norman R. F. Maier

Contents

CHAPTER ONE

Improving decisions in an organization[1]

THE PRAGMATIC TEST OF DECISIONS

Most management situations are sufficiently complex so that solutions to problems or decisions that are to be made cannot be classified into correct and incorrect categories. Rather the alternative possibilities have relative merits, and the standards by which they are to be judged are not agreed upon. Frequently the criteria for judging them are unclear, or there is a lack of agreement on the correct standards to use. People may favor certain decisions because they fit the facts, because they like them, because they get support from those who must execute them, because they are the only ones that came to mind, because making a change in preference

[1] A modified version of this chapter has been previously published under the title Fit Decisions to Your Needs, *Nation's Business*, 1960, **48**, 48–52.

may cause them to lose face, because they like the person who suggested a particular decision, because the alternative favored is their brain child, because they participated in reaching it, and for a variety of other reasons. Some of these reasons may be of assistance in the reaching of effective decisions while others may be a hindrance.

Regardless of why people favor certain solutions or decisions over others, the test of a decision's value is quite a different matter. If the pragmatic test is to be used, an effective decision would be the one that produced the desired objectives most completely, achieved the desired objective most efficiently (costwise, energywise, and with the least undesirable side effects), and carried with it the most valuable by-products. These three measures of success might sometimes be in conflict, but in any event they would all be dependent on the outcome of the decision.

In other words, decisions can best be evaluated in terms of subsequent events, and unfortunately it is then too late to change the decision. For example, General Eisenhower's decision to invade the French coast at a time when the weather report was doubtful is regarded as a good one because it turned out that the weather did not interfere with the plans. Had the weather turned out to be sufficiently unfavorable and created great losses, his decision would have been open to criticism. In this instance the weather information indicated that invasion was risky on the date set for the invasion. However, the alternative was to set another date and go through the costly preparation process again.

Decisions of this sort may be regarded as lucky, or we might suppose that the decision maker has some kind of intuition, some special wisdom, or some special information that guides him. Regardless of how we view such decisions, the factor of chance plays a part. Some people are wealthy because their ancestors happened to settle along a river bank that later became a thriving city. Even if we view the ancestors as having the intuition to settle at the right place, the payoff on these decisions did not occur in their lifetimes. It seems unlikely that potential real estate values were factors influencing these decisions, and hence it would be more appropriate to attribute the successes of the decisions to luck than to wisdom.

Granting that chance plays a part in successful decisions, we also must concede that some people seem to be lucky more often than others and that the difference exceeds what one would expect from the laws of probability. Some executives seem to have an uncanny way of making decisions that turn out to be highly successful; others may go through several bankruptcies. Although the borderline between luck and decision-making aptitude may sometimes be narrow, it is important to do what we can to reduce the chance factors to their bare minimum if we are to examine the factors that make for decision-making ability.

Since the final evaluation of the decision is only possible some time after the decision has been made, and since the evaluation of alternatives is often not available, we must confine our speculation to the ingredients of decision that have high probabilities for success. In examining alternate decisions we may appraise them from the point of view of their probable effectiveness.

For example, if a first-place baseball team is to play the seventh-place team, an even-money bet placed on the first-place team would be wiser, even if it turned out that the seventh-place team won. One cannot take unknowns into account in appraising decisions before the actual test. However, failure to consider all the factors and influences that are available before the decision is made will reduce its possibility for success. Thus the illness of two star players on the first-place team should not be overlooked.

THE DIMENSIONS OF EFFECTIVE DECISIONS

Two different dimensions seem to be relevant in appraising a decision's potential effectiveness. One of these is the objective or impersonal *quality* of the decision; the other has to do with its *acceptance* or the way the persons who must execute the decision *feel* about it. The usual conception of effective decisions has emphasized the quality dimension. This approach leads to a careful consideration of the facts of the case. The advice is to "get the facts; weigh and consider them; then decide." It is this emphasis that causes one to assume that there is a correct answer to a problem, a right decision to make. Although this position is sound in technological matters that do not involve people, one cannot assume that it is universally sound. It is this position that causes us to concentrate on getting more information and to assume that when decisions do not work out there must have been some oversight. Thus nations may debate peace plans for the world, attempting to improve the decision, when the fault may lie elsewhere. It is quite possible that any number of plans would be adequate if they received international acceptance. As soon as the behavior of people is involved, opinions and feelings introduce a second dimension.

It is important to clearly separate these two dimensions since, as we shall see, the ways for dealing with them are very different. Failure to differentiate the dimensions leads to complications in discussion because one person may be using terms such as "good" to describe the quality of the decision, another to describe its acceptability; and a third may be thinking in terms of the outcome, which depends on both.

Decisions may have varying degrees of acceptance by the group which must execute them; and it follows that, quality remaining constant, the effectiveness of decisions will be a function of the degree to which the executors of the decision like and believe in them.

For example, let us suppose that there are four ways to lay out a job and that the quality of these methods, from best to poorest, is in the following order: method A, method B, method C, and method D. Suppose further that the persons who must use these methods have a preference order as follows: method D, method B, method C, and method A. It is conceivable under these circumstances that method B would yield the best results even though it is not the decision of highest objective quality. Naturally one must consider the degrees of difference between each alternative; nevertheless, the fact remains that an inferior method may produce better results than a superior one, if the former has the greater support.

The formula for an effective decision (*ED*) therefore would require consideration of two independent aspects of a decision: (1) its purely objective or impersonal attributes, which we are defining as quality (*Q*); and (2) its attractiveness or desirability to persons who must work with the decision, which we are defining as acceptance (*A*). The first depends upon objective data (facts in the situation); the second on subjective data (feelings which are in people). Simply stated, the relationship may be expressed as follows:

$$ED = Q \times A$$

This separation of quality and acceptance somewhat alters the meaning of such expressions as "good" decisions and "correct" decisions. The term "goodness" might be used to describe degrees of quality, acceptance, or effectiveness and hence has little meaning when applied to decisions. The term "correct" similarly has different dimensions and in addition is limited because it is an absolute term and suggests that there are no moderately effective decisions, medium-quality decisions, and partially acceptable decisions.

It must also be recognized that the effect of acceptance on performance will vary from one problem to another. It is clear that when the execution of a decision is independent of people, the need for acceptance is less than when the execution is influenced by the motivations and attitudes of the people who must carry it out. Nevertheless, a respect for acceptance may be a worthwhile consideration in all group problem solving since a concern for a participant's satisfaction may influence his motivations and attitudes, which in turn would influence his contributions. For example, a marketing plan may have high quality and still have poor acceptance by a group of persons involved in designing the visual appearance of a package. Since the execution of the design and its reception by the public are independent of the initial planning group, it can be assumed that the success of the decision will be independent of the degree of acceptance of the decision-making group. However, what effect will such a decision have on a group if it has been railroaded through? If some members of the planning group are dissatisfied with the decision, may not this make them less valuable participants in the future? When we take the long-range point of view, dissatisfaction with a perfectly good decision can depress a group's future performance; whereas, high satisfaction with a decision may serve to upgrade future performance.

If we can assume the position that the acceptance of a decision by the group that must implement it is a desirable ingredient, what are the problem issues? First of all, we must examine how this ingredient is related to the other desired ingredient—quality.

It is one thing to say that in striving for effective decisions two criteria must be satisfied, but can one achieve both of these objectives simultaneously? High-quality decisions, on the one hand, require wisdom, and wisdom is the product of intelligence and knowledge. Decisions of high acceptance, on the other hand, require satisfaction, and satisfaction is the product of participation and involvement in decision making. Thus the method for achieving *quality* differs from the method for achieving *acceptance;* as a matter of fact they are in conflict.

Figure 1A describes this basic problem in aiming at two objectives. If we aim for both objectives, we may achieve neither. The traditional leadership approach is to aim for quality first, as in Figure 1B. this means that the man responsible for decisions uses whatever resources he feels are needed in obtaining facts and opinions, and he may make free use of experts or consultants. However, the actual decision-making function resides in the leader who finally weighs the evidence and decides. Once a satisfactory quality has been achieved, the next step in this process is to obtain acceptance of the decision.

Traditional methods for achieving this secondary objective have ranged through (1) imposing the decision on subordinates who must execute it (dictatorial methods, using the motivation of fear); (2) playing the father figure and gaining acceptance through a sense of duty and trust (paternalistic methods, using the motivation of loyalty); (3) using persuasion types of approach which explain the virtues of the decision (selling methods, in which personal gains are stressed); and (4) using participative approaches which

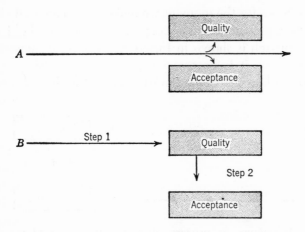

FIG. 1. Quality and acceptance as targets. (*A*) Aiming at both objectives achieves neither. This is particularly true when the aim is good. As one moves from left to right and approaches the objectives, the directions in which they lie become farther apart. When one is next to them, they lie in opposite directions. (*B*) The traditional approach is to aim at quality and so assure achieving it. Once this is accomplished, concern turns to acceptance, which thereby becomes a secondary objective.

encourage discussion of decisions by subordinates but leave the final decisions to the superior (consultative management, in which the motivation is based on a limited degree of participation in which there is opportunity to discuss but no right to make a decision). Although this evolution of the decision-making process reveals improvement, the change has been confined to the aspect that is concerned with obtaining acceptance of decisions by subordinates. Throughout the history of the decision-making process, the quality ingredient has remained in the hands of the top man or group leader. Management philosophy is that the person held accountable for the decision should be the one who makes it. The fact that changes in methods for obtaining acceptance have occurred, however, suggests that the adequacy of the acceptance ingredient still leaves something to be desired. Patching up an old method may improve things, but it lacks elegance.

Suppose for the moment we make a fundamental change in our thinking and regard acceptance as the initial objective. This approach is shown in Figure 2. To ensure success with this objective it is necessary to share the decision making with the subordinates who must execute the decision. Group

Fig. 2. Acceptance as primary objective. When acceptance is the initial target and is thereby assured, concern for quality is the major worry. Will quality suffer if it is made the secondary objective?

decision, a method in which problems are solved and group differences are resolved through discussion, now emerges as the appropriate approach. It immediately becomes apparent that in attempting to be sure of obtaining acceptance, one risks the ingredient of quality. At least, that is the first concern of leaders and superiors when the question of releasing the control of decision-making functions is raised. This notion of group decision becomes even more threatening when the leader discovers that he is to be held responsible for decisions made by his immediate subordinates. It is for this reason that he wishes to retain a veto power; yet such a safeguard tends to destroy the value of group problem solving. Yes-men are the products of a superior's tendency to disapprove of decisions made by subordinates.

It appears then that the second objective is endangered whenever the appropriate method for obtaining the first is used. If this conflict is inevitable, it may be well to conclude that there is no one best approach to the problem of effective decision making. Perhaps problems, as well as approaches, should be analyzed. It is possible that the best approach may be a function of the nature of the problem.

BASIC DIFFERENCES IN PROBLEMS

Problems may be examined with respect to the degree in which quality and acceptance are implicated. For example, in pricing a product it is apparent that a price may be so low that the loss will increase with the volume of business, or it may be so high that the company will be priced out of business. These two fates are possible, regardless of how acceptable the price is to the persons who make or sell the product. Establishing a proper price, therefore, is an illustration of a problem where the quality of the decision is a prime consideration. Although acceptance may influence the manufacture or sale of the product, it is quite clear that satisfaction with company decisions would not depend primarily upon problems of this type.

In contrast, let us select a problem involving the issue of fairness. What is fair is largely a matter of feeling, and it would be difficult for anyone to find an objective criterion that would ensure the achieving of fairness in a group. For example, when a new typewriter is introduced into an office group to replace an old one, who should get it? Should it be the person whose typewriter is replaced, the person with most seniority, the person who is most skilled, the person who is least skilled, the person who does the most work, or should some other criteria be found? Each member of the group might advocate a different scale of values, and invariably the criterion proposed is found to favor the person who advocated it. Thus when people want something, they select the facts and the values that tend to favor their feelings.

If a problem of this kind were solved by group decision,

the supervisor would hold a meeting and conduct a group discussion to determine the fair way to introduce the new typewriter into the group. Usually this type of discussion resolves itself into a reshuffling of typewriters so that several persons stand to gain. Furthermore, different groups will solve the same problem in different ways, and each group will be most satisfied with its own solution. Solutions of this kind cannot be generalized, and their merit lies in the fact that they are tailored to fit the groups who make them.

The question of quality is a minor one in such instances. The supervisor need not be concerned with which of several possible solutions is objectively the best; his primary concern is to have a decision that is acceptable. Future performance of the group will depend more upon the way the members accept decisions on such matters than upon their objective qualities. As a matter of fact, it might be difficult to find measures of quality that would be acceptable to everyone.

If we follow this approach to distinguishing between problems, the first step in decision making is to analyze the problem in terms of the important objective—quality or acceptance. Three classifications of problems would seem to emerge.

High-quality, low-acceptance requirement. These are problems in which the quality of the decision is the important ingredient and the need for acceptance is relatively low. Such problems can be solved effectively by the leader with the aid of experts. The ingredient of acceptance should come up for consideration only after concern with the quality of the decision has been satisfied. Thus the procedure for obtaining acceptance may be regarded as secondary, though necessary.

We shall see later that the quality of decisions often can be improved by the effective use of group participation. This use of the group has additional objectives and raises new problems. For the present we will confine the discussion to the types of problems that can adequately be solved by experts and do not create major acceptance problems. These include:

Decisions regarding expansion, new products, decentralization, plant sites, etc.

Problems concerned with setting prices, determining costs, etc.

Decisions regarding the purchase of materials

Solutions to problems requiring specialized or technical knowledge

Although persons may disagree on the relative importance of the *quality* and *acceptance* requirements, this evaluation must be made by the person who is responsible for the decision. If he feels that a particular decision is required, he is in no condition to permit participation without directly or indirectly imposing his views. In this state of mind he is in a better condition to supply the solution and make acceptance the secondary objective. When the leader strongly favors a particular decision, he is a more effective persuader than conference leader. Thus, regardless of whether quality is the most important factor in a decision or whether the leader thinks it is the most important, the procedure is the same— protecting quality by the effective utilization of the knowledge and intelligence of the decision maker.

Certain decisions that involve acceptance but for which there are no acceptable solutions may also be included in this classification of problems. For example, an airline had the problem of choosing a uniform for stewardesses when the company's new jet plane was introduced. The solution to this problem involves a quality aspect in that the uniform should artistically conform to the design of the plane's interior, and it involves an acceptance decision from the stewardesses, who would have to wear the uniforms. In this instance, the reaction of the stewardesses to the company-imposed decision was quite unfavorable, so that it seemed that the approach used may have been a poor one. On the other hand, could stewardesses have agreed on a solution even if effort had been made to hold group meetings with such a large population?

If we assume that blondes, brunettes, and redheads are favored by different color combinations, it is quite unlikely that all girls would be satisfied with the same uniform, so that any group decision would tend to favor the predominant group. Would such an outcome be a good group decision? Until we know more, it might be best to confine the group decision method to situations that permit a resolution of differences. However, it is important not to assume that all conflicts in a group resist resolution. It is conceivable that if group discussion had been used the girls would have:

1. Evolved a compromise that was artistic

2. Adopted a uniform that permitted variation in some part (such as a scarf) so that complexion differences would have been recognized

3. Been more satisfied because of having had some opportunity to influence the decision

Whether the cost of such meetings would offset the cost of the discontent, which would be temporary, is a decision that the responsible person must make.

High-acceptance, low-quality requirement. These are problems in which poor acceptance can cause a decision to fail and in which the judgment of quality is influenced by differences in position, experience, attitudes, value systems, and other subjective factors. Problems of this type can best be solved by group decision.

An illustration of a problem falling into this group arose when a supervisor needed two of the three girls in his office for work on a Sunday. He asked them individually, and each claimed that she had made a date that she could not break. The fact that Sunday work paid double did not interest them.

He decided to try the group decision method he had just learned about in the company training program. He asked the girls to meet in his office on Friday morning and told them about the emergency job. Since he needed the help of two of them, he wondered what would be the fairest way to handle it. The girls readily entered into the discussion. It turned out that all had dates, but one had a date with some other girls, and all three girls agreed that a date with other girls was not a "real" date. Thus this girl agreed that it was only fair that she should work.

One more girl was needed. Further discussion revealed that one girl had a date with the man to whom she was engaged, and the third had a date with a new boyfriend. All girls agreed that a date with a fiancé was a real date, but it was not a "heavy" date. It was decided that the third girl, who had the date with a new conquest, should be excused from Sunday work. Thus she was not required to work, even though she had least seniority, because this was considered fair.

The quality issue does not enter into this problem for two reasons: (1) All girls were qualified to do the work. Had this not been true, the supervisor might have been more reluctant to try out the method. However, it remains to be seen whether the girls would have placed an incompetent girl on the job. (2) The problem was stated in such a way as to limit it to the matter at stake. Had he posed the problem in terms of whether or not anyone should be forced to work on Sunday, the answer might have been "no." We shall see later that a problem should be so stated as to keep it within the bounds of the supervisor's freedom of action. If he has no authority to set such matters as pay rates, he cannot expect the group to solve this type of problem through group decision.

In using group decision the superior serves as the discussion leader and presents the problem to his subordinates. His objective is to have the group resolve their differences through discussion while he remains neutral. He confines his activities to clarifying the problem, encouraging discussion, promoting communication, supplying information that may be at his disposal, and making appropriate summaries. His objective is to achieve unanimous agreement on a decision that is the product of the interaction in a group discussion.

Problems that fall into the high-acceptance category have to do with:

The fair way to distribute something desirable, be it a typewriter, a truck, office space, office furniture

The fair way to get something undesirable accomplished, be it unpleasant work, unattractive hours or shifts

The scheduling of overtime, vacations, coffee breaks, etc.

The fair way to settle disciplinary problems that involve violations of regulations, lack of cooperation, etc.

High-acceptance, high-quality requirement. These are the problems that do not fall into the other two categories. At first this may seem to be the largest category of all, so that little seems to have been achieved by extracting the other two. However, in working with group problem solving, it soon becomes apparent that group decisions are often of surprisingly good quality. It is not uncommon for a supervisor to volunteer the information that the group's solution surpassed not only what he had expected, but what he could have achieved by himself. The fear that group decisions will be of poor quality appears to be greater than the hazard warrants. However, if the supervisor is anxious about the outcome, he is likely to interfere with the problem-solving process, rather than facilitate it. For this reason this category of problems should be handled by group decision only when the leader is experienced. Thus it is a category for which either group decision or leader decision is recommended, depending upon the supervisor's skills.

The fears of people frequently determine the motives they ascribe to others, particularly if they are members of an opposition group. For example, if a manager fears a drop in production, he unjustly assumes that his employees are motivated to produce less. Actually the motivational forces in employees form a complex pattern. They include not only what the employees want, but ways of protecting themselves from what they fear management wants to accomplish. With fear removed by the opportunity to participate, the outcome of a discussion often differs greatly from what is anticipated. Obstacles that seem insurmountable frequently disappear in thin air.

THE DYNAMICS OF GROUP PROBLEM SOLVING

In order to illustrate the types of forces at work in a problem-solving interaction, it may be best to describe a case in the use of group decision. Specific incidents serve to bring theories and generalizations in closer contact with reality.

This case is selected because it is characteristic of the manner in which men solve problems involving attitudes toward prestige and seniority rights. At the same time it illustrates how the men on the job are aware of company objectives and do not take advantage of the company or of each other when the need for protective behavior is removed.

The problem arose because repair foremen in the telephone industry had a persistent problem in getting their men to clear "wet-weather drops."[2] A wet-weather drop is a defective line that runs from a pole to a building. These lines have to be replaced from time to time because water can seep through a break in the insulation and create a short. After a heavy rain there are reports of trouble, but since the difficulty is present only when the line is wet, the problem is a purely temporary one. During periods of expansion or when replacement material is at a minimum, many lines suffer from this wet-weather difficulty. If a station is out of order for this reason, the loss of service corrects itself and is not as serious as if the station were completely out of order. Hence the company, as well as the men, regards wet-weather drops to be minor and routine jobs in contrast to emergency jobs. Furthermore, repair men do not like to do this unimportant work, and they feel that anyone can do it without thinking. As a consequence, the men make little effort to get these jobs done. If the foreman decides to pressure men into bringing in a few wet-weather drops, he finds himself at a disadvantage. The men may promise to pick up one or two and then fail to do so. When asked why, they can claim that

[2] Taken from N. R. F. Maier, *Principles of Human Relations.* John Wiley & Sons, Inc., New York, 1952.

they ran into extra difficulty on an emergency job and say, "You wanted me to do a good job on the other first, didn't you, boss?" Although the foreman may know the men are shirking, he never knows on what occasion the excuse is justified. It thus comes about that wet-weather drops are a headache to the foreman. When he gets far enough behind, he puts one man on the job full time and lets him clear wet-weather drops. The man in question feels degraded and wonders why he is picked on. To be as fair as possible, this job is usually given to the man with least seniority. He may complain violently, but invariably the man with least seniority is in the minority. Among supervisory groups this practice is considered the fairest way to handle the situation, and they believe that the men want seniority to be recognized this way. They are completely unaware of the fact that this practice turns an undesirable job into one that has low status as well.

In a particular crew of twelve men the number of wet-weather drops was gradually increasing, and the time was approaching when something would have to be done about the matter. The foreman decided that this was a good problem on which to try group decision. He told his men that he realized no one liked to clear wet-weather drops and that he wanted to have their reactions on how the problem should be handled.

Of interest is the fact that no one in the group felt that the man with the least seniority should do the whole job. The man with most seniority talked against the idea of picking on the fellow with least seniority, saying that he had hated being stuck with the job when he had the least seniority and that he couldn't see why everybody shouldn't do a share of it. It was soon agreed that the job should be evenly divided among the crew. This crew divided up the job by assigning a work area for each man. In this way each man was to be responsible for the wet-weather drops in his area, and he was to be given a list of those. Each morning the local test desk was to designate for each man the wet-weather drop most in need of replacement. It was understood that he was to clear this one, if at all possible. This condition took care of clearing up the drops that were most essential from the point of view of the office. In addition, all agreed that each man should clear as many additional drops as his load permitted. However, when a man had cleared up all the wet-weather drops in his area, it was specifically understood that he should not be asked to help out another. This last condition clearly reveals an attitude built up over the years. It is evident that the reluctance to clear wet-weather drops hinged on the idea that when a man was conscientious, advantage was taken of him. Soon he got to be the "sucker" in the group or perhaps the foreman's pet. It was evident that all men were willing to do their parts, but they did not wish to run the risk of being made a sucker. (Other foremen have testified that this defensive reaction made sense from the manner in which the job is frequently handled. The foreman wants to get the job done, and he begins to rely on those individuals who have cooperated in the past. Soon these men find they are doing all the undesirable jobs. It is just a matter of how long it takes a man to find out that he is losing out with the group.)

The results of this solution were immediately apparent. During the three-month period previous to the discussion, a total of eighty wet-weather drops had been cleared; during the week following the discussion, seventy-eight wet-weather drops were cleared and without any letup on the rest of the work. Within a few months the problem was practically nonexistent. The reaction of the men also bore out the effectiveness of the decision. Men discussed the number of drops they had cleared and showed a friendly competitive spirit. They discussed the time when they expected to be caught up and would only have to take care of wet-weather drops as they arose.

It should be noted that the men's notion of fairness was quite different from what the supervisor had anticipated. Although men strongly urge seniority privileges, they do not wish to give junior men a hard time. Rather, advantage is taken of junior men only when seniority rights are threatened. It is of special interest to note the protective reactions against the possibility that cooperation will lead to abuse. Once the protection was ensured, the men considered customer service. This recognition of the service is apparent from the fact that the crew wanted to clear the drops in the order of their importance. With defensive behavior removed, it is not uncommon for good quality solutions to emerge.

DEPENDENCE OF THE SOLUTION'S QUALITY ON THE LEADER'S SKILLS

The quality of group decisions can further be enhanced by improving the skills and the attitude of the discussion leader. Even with a minimum of skills the group decision approach can be effective with problems such as the following:

Setting standards on tardiness and absenteeism

Setting goals for production, quality, and service

Improving safety, housekeeping, etc.

Introducing new work procedures, changing standards, introducing laborsaving equipment, etc.

It is apparent that both quality and acceptance are needed in solving problems of this type, and for this reason they are the areas of greatest conflict in labor-management relations. However, the requirement of skill is more than methodology because it is something that cannot be decided, adopted, or purchased. It requires additional training in conference leadership, and this means an increase in a company's investment in management talents.

CONCLUSIONS

Problems may be divided into the following three types:

Type 1. $\frac{Q}{A}$ problems: those for which the quality of the decision is clearly a more important objective than its acceptance. These may be successfully solved by the leader.

Type 2. $\frac{A}{Q}$ problems: those for which acceptance of the decision is clearly a more important objective than its quality. These may be successfully handled by the group decision method in which the decision is made by the subordinates with the superior serving as a discussion leader.

Type 3. Q-A problems: those for which both quality and acceptance of the decision become major objectives. These problems may be handled in either of two ways, each requiring a different set of skills on the part of the leader. The alternatives are as follows:

Leader decision *plus* persuasive skills to gain acceptance or

Group decision *plus* conference leadership skills to gain quality.

The emphases in this book are on the second alternative because conference skills permit the effective use of a greater range of intellectual resources, thereby achieving high-quality decisions as a by-product.

CHAPTER TWO

Conference leadership

LEADERSHIP METHODS VERSUS LEADERSHIP SKILLS

Skills associated with authoritarian methods. Research in our laboratory on group problem solving has demonstrated the need to distinguish between leadership methods and leadership skills. When a supervisor makes a decision that affects his subordinates, he must gain their acceptance of any changes in the procedure which the decision introduces, if it is to be effectively implemented. Obtaining satisfactory acceptance requires not only time but considerable persuasive skills. Two supervisors differing in the degree to which they possess these skills might achieve quite different amounts of acceptance. The amount of acceptance that differing degrees of persuasive skills might achieve can range from enthusiastic acceptance to complete rejection of the decision, i.e., a walkout.

If a leader wishes to follow the authoritarian method, his success will depend not only upon his ability to make high-quality decisions but also upon his ability to persuade and inspire subordinates. People differ in the degree to which they possess these abilities, and undoubtedly both abilities could be improved through training.

Training programs designed to improve the leader's ability to make decisions would be oriented toward obtaining facts, evaluating information, utilizing advisors, developing self-confidence, etc. Such training would be based on the assumption that the nature of the decision is highly important to its success. Case studies requiring the integration and appraisal of complex patterns of information, business games, and training in logic and decision theory might be considered appropriate.

In order to improve a leader's persuasive talents the study of motivation and attitudes, as well as practice and training in public speaking, would undoubtedly be an important asset. Opinion surveys and counseling skills also might be regarded as appropriate in such training programs.

Skills associated with the group decision method. The group decision method as a way of management creates quite a different situation. Suppose a superior wishes to follow this approach and takes a problem regarding some change of work procedures to his group. The possible outcomes are (1) the decision that the leader would have made himself had he followed the authoritarian method; (2) the decision to continue as before; and (3) the discovery of a procedure that is different both from the old method and from the one management might have proposed. It is this third possibility that tends to be excluded when the superior makes a decision himself and then tries to sell it. Yet this is the very solution that frequently has the greatest acceptance. However, the quality of the third type of decision depends not only upon the thinking ability of the participants, but upon the skill of the leader.

When using the group decision method on problems of this nature, it appears that the *skill* of the discussion leader tends to upgrade the quality of the decision, while the *method* tends to ensure acceptance. When the leader makes the decision himself, his skill in persuading the group tends to upgrade *acceptance,* while the quality of the decision depends upon his intellectual ability.

Improving skills in group decision requires the ability to locate problems and to involve the group in cooperative problem solving. The remaining chapters of this book are concerned with the various skills that may be developed for handling meetings which have as their objective the improvement of the quality of *group decisions.* Needless to say, the leader who tries to impose his thinking on the group to improve quality is not following the group decision procedure.

Underlying the training in group decision is the assumption that the success of a decision depends not only on the nature of the decision, but also upon the process by which the decision is reached. Thus there are two sources of satisfaction and dissatisfaction: the nature of the decision and the kind of process that leads to the decision.

In comparing discussion time one should not only consider the time required to reach a decision but also the time required to communicate it and to gain acceptance of it. Authoritarian decisions, on the one hand, usually require little time in decision making but considerable time in communicating them and gaining acceptance for them. Group decisions, on the other hand, require considerable time in the decision making but require little or no time in gaining the understanding and acceptance of the group. Table 1 shows how these times may be distributed for a relatively simple decision. Whether the overall time for one method

TABLE 1. *Comparison of Time Requirements for Decisions Made by Leader versus Those Made by Groups*

Source of decision	Time to reach a decision	Time to obtain full understanding by subordinates	Time to gain adequate acceptance by subordinates
Leader	Few minutes	Approximately half hour	Approximately half hour
Group	Half hour or more	Zero	Zero

exceeds the other will vary with the problem. The important point is to recognize that a comparison of the decision-making times is an incomplete measure even when time is the only consideration.

Controlling skills through refinement of methods. Before turning to the subject of problem-solving conference *skills,* it is desirable to explore the part that conference *methods* play in influencing outcomes. If the authoritarian method yields results different from the group decision method, it may be possible to find alternative procedures within each of these general methods and through refinements along these lines to achieve additional gains. For example, it will be apparent that the authoritarian leadership method suggests two alternative ways by which the acceptance of a decision may be gained. One way is through the use of fear (negative motivation); the other is through some form of persuasion (positive motivation). There is ample reason to believe that these two more specific approaches would yield quite different results. Following this lead, it may be assumed that within the frame of reference of group decision there are varieties of choices in method that are likely to yield differences in outcome. The value of a general method therefore will undoubtedly depend on the degree to which it has been refined.

Since skills are closely linked with methods, success or failure may depend on whether the proper method was used as well as upon whether the leader possessed the adequate skills. A surgeon may fail to cure a patient either because of his choice of method or because of his lack of skill. In so far as the contribution of method is not fully understood and explored, results of conference outcomes will show an inconsistent relationship with skill training as well as with autocratic and group decision forms of leadership.

The advantage of isolating a method becomes apparent as soon as an attempt is made to refine skills. When a method is isolated, the objective becomes clarified, and a specific mental set or attitude is supplied. For example, the reader may decide to avoid getting into an argument with another person and before long find himself tricked into one. Persons in management training programs resolve to listen more in the future and then shortly thereafter find themselves doing most of the talking. Why does one fail to practice these simple skills even when he has the best intention of trying them out? Is it because the skills are too complex to control or because of interfering habits and attitudes?

Continued practice under supervision may successfully reduce a person's failures in this area, but it seems that the isolation of a method may assist further by controlling the attitude. Suppose the reader is asked to imagine himself a newspaper reporter who was assigned the task of interviewing a person in order to learn his views regarding a particular controversial issue. In the position of a reporter, the reader is less inclined to express his own views and more inclined to ask questions to draw out the person he is interviewing. The mental set of the reporter is therefore one of listening and understanding so that he can write about the material he gathers in his interview. In this capacity he is less inclined to evaluate and hence to disagree or enter into a discussion. Thus by asking the reader to play the role of a reporter, certain skills already in his possession are selected from his many abilities. Asking the reader to play the role of an opponent in a debate would tend to select a different set of skills.

Even though the skills selected by this role process may be imperfect, it is nevertheless apparent that any control of the selection process may be expected to facilitate the acquisition of skills.

The purpose of methods or techniques is to function in this selection process. In order to measure the contribution of methods to success in conferences, it is important to keep the skill level constant while trying out different methods.

If both skills and methods contribute to the success of a conference, it is important that they be studied separately, since a good method with the inappropriate skills may yield unsatisfactory results even though each may be effective when used in a proper combination. The fact that skills vary with method may explain why many training programs fail to live up to expectations.

METHODS AS DETERMINERS OF CONFERENCE RESULTS

Selling a decision versus group decision. Experimental evidence is available to support the view that the method of group discussion will influence the outcome. A case known as the Change of Work Procedure was used in one of these studies.[1] It dealt with a situation in which the foreman wished to change the procedure of work of three men performing a subassembly operation. The job was a simple routine operation in which each man worked in a given position and added certain parts to a casting. When each worker had done his part, the product was a completed fuel pump. Pay was based on a group piece rate. Because the work was simple and monotonous, the men exchanged work positions every hour.

A problem arose when the foreman was supplied with facts by the time-study department. The data furnished him showed that each man was most proficient at one of the three positions. It followed quite naturally that if each man worked at the position on which he did his best work, production, and the resulting pay, would be materially increased. The amount claimed was 17 per cent. In order to simulate a real-life problem situation, this information was supplied to persons who were to take the part of the foreman. The persons who were to take the part of the three men also received instructions. These pointed up boredom, distrust of any production increases, and dislike of time-study experts. After both foreman and workers had read their instructions, they met as a group to discuss the problem confronting the foreman. The foreman presented the problem and conducted the discussion.

It is apparent that this situation creates an acceptance problem for the foreman since he knows that imposing a

[1] N. R. F. Maier, An Experimental Test of the Effect of Training on Discussion Leadership. *Human Relat.*, 1953, **6**, 161–173.

change in work methods may cause the men to retaliate with a work slowdown. At the same time he is under pressure to get a good decision.

Two sets of approximately forty groups were used in this experiment. One set of groups was made up of management personnel who had no training in group decision but who nevertheless had training in other human relations concepts and were well aware of the need to get men to go along with changes in work procedures. The other set of groups had additional training which dealt with the concept of group decision.

Generally speaking, the first set of foremen will confront their men with the notion of adopting the new method to increase production and pay. Thus they present their groups with the solution; usually they try to sell the new method, and when this fails, they may become somewhat threatening.

The second set of foremen ideally should go to their groups with facts and the *problem* of how to use them. Because the solution is so clear to them, many foremen in this group also presented the solution and tried to sell it. However, when they were confronted with opposition, they were more inclined to encourage discussion and approach the group decision type of leadership.

The results of these two sets of groups are shown in Table 2. It will be seen that the selling approach used by the untrained leaders accomplished change in half the groups, whereas the other half of the groups refused to change. This

TABLE 2. *Results of Acceptance of Change Obtained among Leaders with and without Training in Group Decision*

	Percentage of groups that:		
Groups	Refused to accept change	Accepted the desired change	Accepted other changes
Without training (36 groups)	50	50	0
With training (44 groups)	4.5	59	36.5

choice situation seems to be the outcome when the solution to a problem is supplied by the discussion leader and when men initially do not want change. Only the alternatives of accepting or rejecting come up for consideration. However, with the group receiving some training in group decision, a third set of possibilities comes up for consideration and these seem to be the product of discussions in which the leader is more inclined to pose problems than solutions. Solutions under the heading "Other Changes" include (1) two men periodically trading jobs while the third works on his best position; (2) all men rotating between their two best positions; and (3) all men rotating as formerly, but spending a longer period at their best position than at the other two. It should be noted that this group of solutions replaced the failures rather than reducing the number of solutions that conformed with what management had in mind.

These findings show that acceptance of change was increased by some familiarity with the method of group decision. It may be assumed that increased skill either in selling or in group discussion leadership would have produced greater acceptance in each set of groups.

The question of the decision's *quality* may be difficult to demonstrate in this case. It seems that the solutions described as "other" may be the best since they incorporate consideration of boredom as well as the time-study data. However, the production outcome will depend not only upon the decision reached but upon the degree of worker acceptance.

These results are presented to demonstrate that the method a leader uses does influence the type of solution reached. The skill factor in this instance would tend to favor the untrained groups, since they felt free to practice the method to which they had been accustomed. The groups trained in group decision had learned about the method but had not received training in the various skill areas. These include methods of (1) introducing information; (2) stating the problem; (3) conducting discussions so as to draw out various attitudes and ideas; and (4) summarizing. Any skills they may have used would be those common to the two methods. It seems safe to conclude therefore that since skill training was not involved and only the method was experimentally varied, the difference in solution outcomes obtained must be attributed to the method.

The dependence of the degree of acceptance of a solution on the method followed by the leader will be discussed later in the chapter. For the present, it may be assumed that acceptance will also be affected. However, our immediate concern is the extent to which the solution to a problem hinges upon the method practiced by the leader when the facts of the case remain the same.

Two group decision methods—free discussion and developmental discussion. Methods which are as different as that of a leader attempting to get acceptance of his decision and conducting a group decision conference may be expected to yield different outcomes. Suppose, however, that two group decision methods are compared and the facts are presented in exactly the same manner. Will the method then be sufficiently important to influence the outcome?

The *free* and the *developmental* discussion methods previously described by the author [2] are used for this experimental comparison.[3]

The problem used was the "Case of Viola Burns." [4] In the case, Viola is a young office worker who is being considered for promotion to a position as private secretary to a sales executive. A general description of Viola, an interview between Viola and the personnel manager, and a second interview between Viola's boss and the personnel manager provided information to all group members about (1) Viola's

[2] N. R. F. Maier, *Principles of Human Relations.* John Wiley & Sons, Inc., New York, 1952.

[3] N. R. F. Maier and R. A. Maier, An Experimental Test of the Effects of "Developmental" vs. "Free" Discussions on the Quality of Group Decisions. *J. appl. Psychol.,* 1957, **41,** 320–323.

[4] P. J. Pigors, L. C. McKenney, and T. O. Armstrong, *Social Problems in Labor Relations.* McGraw-Hill Book Company, Inc., New York, 1939.

personality, appearance, intelligence, relations with other workers, job duties, and job performance; (2) her boss's favorable attitude toward her; (3) a description of the new job and the importance the new boss attaches to having it properly filled; and (4) Viola's indecision about accepting the new offer. This indecision serves as the basis for the problem given to the groups: Should Viola be encouraged or discouraged from taking the new job? In order to rule out the possibility of conflicting interests, the decision to encourage or discourage Viola was made first from the point of view of the good of the company and then from the point of view of what is best for Viola. Although a majority of people usually vote to encourage her from both points of view, the data really indicate that her personality and ability to relate to other people would make her unable to do the job effectively. Thus the decision to discourage Viola from accepting the new job was considered to be of higher quality than the one to encourage her.

The developmental discussion method was designed to improve the quality of group decisions by breaking the problem into steps so that the discussion would not spread to many aspects of the problem. By dividing the discussion into smaller parts, it was felt that participants would be encouraged to think about the same questions simultaneously and that a more systematic coverage of the whole problem would be assured.

A leader was assigned to each small discussion group (from four to five persons). A total of forty-one leaders (the free discussion groups) were given the following general instructions.

You are meeting to decide whether or not Viola should, in the next interview, be encouraged or discouraged about taking the new job. The case as presented gives all the known facts. This instruction sheet tells you how to conduct this meeting. In general:

A. Try to get everyone to voice their views and to give reasons for their ideas. Encourage interaction of ideas.

B. Do not impose your views on the group. Be as permissive as you can.

C. See if you can get agreement on the recommendations made.

D. Get a final vote on the recommendations and be ready to report them to the class.

Lead the discussion to decide the following:

1. From the point of view of the good of the company, we recommend that Viola be (discouraged from taking) (encouraged to take) the new job.

2. From the point of view of Viola's best welfare, we recommend that she be (discouraged from taking) (encouraged to take) the new job.

The forty-five leaders who were to conduct the developmental type discussions were given the above instructions with the following additions.

To assist in making the final decision, try to obtain unanimous agreement on each of the preliminary problems below.

Problem 1. Develop a list of Viola's activities on her present job.

Problem 2. Grade Viola's proficiency on each, with letters A, B, C, D, or E, and write the grade after the activity.

Problem 3. Develop a list of activities Viola would be expected to perform on the new job.

Problem 4. Grade how well your group thinks Viola will do on each.

Problem 5. Select the three activities Viola's new boss will consider most important for the success of his office.

A total of 374 college students participated in the experiment. The results show a distinctly different trend in the decisions reached with the two methods. Table 3 shows that persons participating in the developmental discussion

TABLE 3. *Effects of Development versus Free Discussion on Decision Reached*

Viewpoint	Decision	Developmental discussion, %	Free discussion, %
Interest of company	Discourage	39.7	18.9
	Encourage	60.3	71.1
Interest of Viola	Discourage	39.7	20.6
	Encourage	60.3	79.4

reached the higher-quality decision (discourage) in 39.7 per cent of the cases, whereas only 18.9 per cent of the persons participating in the free discussion reached this decision. Consideration for Viola's welfare seemed not to be a factor in the outcome, since the decisions were affected very little by a consideration of the decision in terms of the company's versus Viola's interests. It cannot be claimed therefore that the free discussion makes for a more considerate attitude toward Viola; rather, the method seems to protect participants from faulty assumptions or oversights.

The results were also studied from the point of view of whether or not each group reached a unanimous decision. Table 4 shows the results of this analysis. It is apparent that

TABLE 4. *Effects of Development versus Free Discussions on Unanimity of Decisions*

Viewpoint	Degree of agreement	Developmental discussion, %	Free discussion, %
Interest of company	Unanimous	64.4	80.5
	Split	35.5	19.5
Interest of Viola	Unanimous	60.0	78.0
	Split	40.0	22.0

the majority of the groups reach unanimous decisions even though different groups using the same method might reach opposite decisions. Discussion, therefore, tends to resolve difference. However, in the case of free discussion, unanimous agreement occurs in approximately 80 per cent of the cases, whereas in the developmental discussion this degree of agreement is found in approximately 60 per cent of the groups. This difference suggests that agreement or acceptance of a decision is somewhat easier to achieve in free than in a developmental discussion. Apparently the developmental type of discussion requires somewhat more skill if acceptance is the primary objective. Since the developmental discussion restricts procedure but not the decision-making function, it seems that procedures that limit freedom are the more difficult conference assignments.

Comparison of method by instructing group. In the above experiment, the skill requirement was not experimentally manipulated, so the leadership skills exhibited were those of untrained individuals. Despite this fact, the introduction of a new method clearly influenced the outcome.

When using a new method, it is possible that the leader may be unsuccessful in getting his group to follow the procedure. In order to ensure more appropriate utilization of the two methods, it seemed desirable to expose not only the leaders but also the participants to the two sets of instructions. Furthermore, in order to remove opposition to the leader's attempt to control the procedure, it seemed appropriate to compare the two methods without appointing a discussion leader. Thus, the leadership functions would not be imposed from the outside.

For this experiment [5] the case of Viola Burns was used with a group of teachers working in the field of executive development (European Productivity Agency Seminar in Stockholm, 1960). Ten 3-person groups were used, half being instructed to follow the free discussion procedure described, and the other five the developmental discussion procedure. All groups were asked to decide whether Viola should be encouraged or discouraged from taking the job when next interviewed. If, however, it was felt that more information was needed to make this decision, the group might decide that insufficient information had been given for reaching an intelligent decision.

Table 5 shows a dramatic contrast in outcome. Only one of the free discussion groups reached the high-quality decision, whereas three groups (nine persons) reached the low-quality decision, with one group abstaining. However, all groups (fifteen persons) in the developmental discussion groups reached the high-quality decision, and none felt that the facts supplied were inadequate.

The author has repeated this procedure many times with middle management groups, and the results always strongly favor the developmental discussion. However, a more typical

[5] This experiment has not been previously published.

result obtained from forty such persons is that in which the developmental discussion caused 70 per cent to decide to discourage, 15 per cent to claim insufficient information, and the other 15 per cent to decide to encourage. The corresponding figures for the free discussion are 10, 15, and 40 per cent.

Of interest too is the fact that groups almost invariably reach unanimous agreement even though three different outcomes were represented. The occasional groups that are not in full agreement are more likely to appear from free discussion. The fact that discussion makes for agreement, and

TABLE 5. *Comparison of Groups of Management Teachers Instructed to Follow Free versus Developmental Discussion*

	Free discussion				Developmental discussion		
Group	Dis- courage	Insufficient information	En- courage	Group	Dis- courage	Insufficient information	En- courage
A	0	3	0	B	3	0	0
C	3	0	0	D	3	0	0
E	0	0	3	F	3	0	0
G	0	0	3	H	3	0	0
I	0	0	3	J	3	0	0
Total ..	3	3	9	Total ..	15	0	0

not necessarily high quality, becomes quite clear from these results.

This degree of consensus also indicates that when the groups are instructed to follow a procedure, they are more inclined to accept the restrictions than when the leader tries to impose them. It appears that even when the leader is willing to accept a group's decisions, his mere attempt to control the type of discussion creates some degree of resistance.

Using methods as guides to skills. The superiority of the developmental discussion seems to be due to two factors: it assures systematic coverage of the topic and synchronizes the discussion so that all members tend to talk about each aspect of the problem at the same time. Both of these advantages favor the quality of the decision. In the light of our present knowledge, it seems that the free discussion would tend to have its greatest advantage for problems in which acceptance of the decision was important and in which the emotional involvement of the participants was high.

The distinction between the free and developmental discussion and a knowledge of their specific merits can contribute greatly to the skill of the leader for a number of reasons. These include the following:

1. Deciding on the kinds of problems that profit from or can be hindered by structuring the discussion

2. Being more sensitive to a group's reaction to structuring

3. Being able to get known facts introduced into the discussion without suggesting the facts or hinting at the solution

4. Having a specific target to guide the discussion; either drawing relevant information from the group and remaining in the center of the discussion, or letting the group interact freely and staying in the background

The latter point is especially important because the discussion leader often wishes to know when he should guide the discussion and when he should carefully avoid such guidance. Each of these types of activity requires skill, but helpful knowledge of when to use them assists in the development of both. The isolation of methods therefore becomes a way of improving skills by setting up specific and short-range objectives.

Objectives as determiners of method. In order to appreciate the extent to which an objective will influence outcome, let us consider the problem of disciplinary action. In an experimental test of this kind, a role-playing situation was used in which a worker was laid off for violating a no-smoking regulation.[6] In this case, the *facts* clearly favored the foreman's decision to use discipline; whereas the *feelings* of the worker opposed discipline, and he had the support of the

[6] N. R. F. Maier and L. E. Danielson, An Evaluation of Two Approaches to Discipline in Industry. *J. appl. Psychol.*, 1956, **40**, 319–323.

union steward. For the foreman, two objectives are possible in such situations: determining the innocence or guilt of the man or preventing future violations. One approach leads to controversy, the other to problem-solving activity, regardless of the interviewing skills of the foreman. The first is the legalistic way of reaching a decision and concerns itself with the facts of the case. Before the law the foreman would be assured of winning. The second is the human relations approach and takes feelings into account because acceptance is needed if a decision is to be supported.

A total of 52 per cent of the foremen followed the human relations approach and resolved the difference by either eliminating or reducing the layoff; 35 per cent followed the legalistic approach and insisted on the full penalty, while 13 per cent failed to settle the matter in the time allowed. The first approach resulted in laying the groundwork for future control of smoking—with the steward's cooperation; the second resulted in poor relations—with all parties dissatisfied and little prospect of reduced smoking unless the job was policed. In another experiment, utilizing a different disciplinary problem, similar results were obtained.[7] It appears that various factual details have little effect on the way that the two different objectives influence outcomes.

Which of these objectives is regarded as proper and just is not relevant for our present purposes. The finding that the objective determines the supervisor's method, that this method, and not just the facts of the case, influences the outcome, is something that must be faced.

The experimental evidence cited illustrates how methods, as distinct from skills, may contribute to the outcome of a conference. These outcomes include not only the satisfactions and motivations of the participants, but also the quality of the final product. The value that locating methods and objectives have for conferences is similar to certain training aids or principles in sports. For example, telling a person what to attend to when returning a ball in a tennis

[7] L. E. Danielson and N. R. F. Maier, Supervisory Problems in Decision Making. *Personnel Psychol.*, 1957, **10**, 169–180.

match, where to fixate the eyes when putting in golf, or how to distribute his weight when swinging at a baseball, improves performance by selecting behavior from skills already present. Doing each of these things properly may require good judgment, but rules and targets serve as valuable guides. The more of these guides one can develop, the more the training becomes a science and less an art. The transition from art to science is similar to what has occurred in medicine. Gradually the art aspect of practicing medicine is replaced by the science of medicine, and the good diagnostician supports his conclusions with principles rather than with hunches. The art of conference leadership too can move in the direction of a science. Methods and objectives serve as guides. However, they are not substitutes for skills, even though they facilitate them as well as select from among those already in the conference leader's possession. And no objective or method can select what is not already there.

SKILLS AS DETERMINERS OF CONFERENCE RESULTS

Problem solving with subordinates. The skill of a conference leader can reveal itself in a variety of ways. In the change of work procedure experiment (pages 25 ff.) there were differences not only between the trained and the untrained groups, but marked differences within each of these groups. Some leaders who used the method of persuasion succeeded in getting a decision accepted and others failed. Likewise, among groups that were persuaded to adopt the new method, there were differences in the degree to which members were satisfied with the decision. Although some of the differences in group results must be attributed to the personalities of the group members, it seems one must also concede that the leader's skill played a part.

This fact becomes very apparent if one questions participants after discussions regarding their satisfactions and dissatisfactions. Invariably the discussion leader is mentioned for having done something that contributed to either their positive or negative feelings. However, it is always possible to claim that the differences obtained by various leaders may have been in method rather than in skill.

In order to obtain some objective measures of the effects of skill training it is feasible to compare results when the same method is used after different degrees of training. In one experiment of this type the quality of the end product was compared when all leaders were asked to follow the group decision method.[8]

Three levels of conference leadership training were distinguished: little or none, moderate, and high. Since the problem was one in which the leader had little or no emotional investment, it was not difficult for him to accept the philosophy of the group decision method. The leader was not threatened so he did not have to protect his rights, and since he did not know a good solution to the problem, he had little inclination to sell one. Under such conditions a leader will permit a group considerable freedom for discussion.

His problem was to find a way to reduce a bottleneck on the production line. Since men differ in their aptitudes and no amount of experience makes them equal, a piling up of work must develop in every assembly line unless, of course, fast workers slow down.

A rather creative solution to the problem in this case is for the workers to rotate positions periodically so that any pileup of work will be inherited by the next occupant of the position. If he is a faster worker, he reduces the backlog; if slower, he adds to it. Eventually the pace will become one which suits the average worker. However, to be effective this solution must be accepted by the workers.

The three levels of training were compared on the basis of the frequency with which the creative solution was developed by the three groups. Table 6 shows that this solution was reached by only 3.4 per cent of the groups with untrained leaders, by 63.6 per cent of the groups with moderately trained leaders, and by 83.3 per cent of the groups with highly trained leaders. It goes without saying that the leader

[8] N. R. F. Maier, The Quality of Group Decisions as Influenced by the Discussion Leader. *Human Relat.*, 1950, **3**, 155–174.

did not supply or suggest the solution in any of the cases. However, the most skilled leaders were familiar with the solution, which knowledge helped them to ask thought-provoking questions. In other tests where a leader suggested the creative solution, the chances of its acceptance were actually reduced. When subordinates have no motivation to agree with a discussion leader, it is the rule rather than the exception for them to become critical of his contribution.

Satisfaction with the solution reached by each group was also determined in this experiment. The last column of Table 6 shows that the percentage of persons satisfied with the solution reached was 62.1 for those with the untrained lead-

TABLE 6. *Effect of Leader's Skill on Group Performance*

Amount of training	Percentage of creative solutions	Percentage satisfied with solution
Little or none	3.4	62.1
Moderate	63.6	72.7
A great deal	85.3	100.0

ers, 72.7 for those with moderately trained leaders, and 100 for those with the highly trained leader.

This experiment demonstrates that a skillful supervisor can upgrade the thinking of a group of subordinates and thereby cause the quality of his group's solution to improve. Although the group decision method results in a high degree of acceptance and satisfaction with the decision reached, even this facet of group interaction can be bettered by training discussion leaders.

Relation between leader skill and satisfaction. The contribution of skills may be measured either by comparing groups with different amounts of training or by classifying individuals according to their skills. This latter approach was used to explore the influence of a leader's skill on the satisfaction of participants. The New Truck problem [9] was used

[9] N. R. F. Maier and L. F. Zerfoss, MRP: A Technique for Training Large Groups of Supervisors and Its Potential Use in Social Research. *Human Relat.*, 1952, **5**, 177–186.

in this experiment. In this situation, the foreman gets a new truck that he must give to one of his five truck drivers as a replacement. Since he has had trouble in the past in introducing a new truck into the group, it is suggested that he put the problem to the men to decide.

General information is supplied to all participants regarding the territory in which they drive, the years of service each has in the company, and the ages of the various trucks in use. In addition, each driver has individual instructions which give him a rationale for getting the next new truck. These rationales include seniority, care of truck, accident record, condition of present truck, amount of driving, make of truck, personal health, and personal preferences.

This problem creates a lively discussion in which all are in conflict. Usually it requires about twenty-five minutes to resolve the conflict and reach a decision. The results show a great variety of solutions, there being variations with respect to (1) who gets the new truck, (2) how many persons obtain a different truck, (3) the pattern of exchanges, (4) who is dissatisfied, and (5) the number of dissatisfied persons.

One of these studies is relevant for our present purposes.[10] All groups tested had received some training in group decision, and the instruction to the foreman was that he put the problem to his men. Despite this training and these suggestions, leaders differ in the skill they show in following the instructions. In order to appraise this skill, each group was asked to evaluate its foreman's performance and to decide whether the decision was dominated by the foreman, whether it was a true group decision, or whether it was a mixed influence. In the event members of a group disagreed on the classification, the situation was classified as mixed. Thus, the foreman-domination and group-decision classifications were given only when the five participants agreed on the foreman's handling of the discussion.

Results were obtained from ninety-eight groups, sixty-two of which were classified as having a foreman who fol-

[10] N. R. F. Maier and L. R. Hoffman, Group Decision in England and the United States. *Personnel Psychol.*, 1962, **15**, 75–87.

lowed group decision, twenty-four of which were classified as having foremen who dominated the decision, and only twelve had the mixed style of leadership. The high frequency with which leaders followed group decision is largely due to the fact that the foreman doesn't have a particular solution in mind; this fact tends to make him quite acceptant at the outset. Yet many leaders do find ways of restricting or controlling a discussion and developing preferred solutions.

The results of this experiment are shown in Table 7. The satisfaction pattern is clear. Nearly 76 per cent of the foremen who were regarded as letting the group decide reached decisions in which all drivers were satisfied, and only 3.2

TABLE 7. *Discussion Leadership Skill and Satisfaction*

Reported method used	No. of groups	Groups with all satisfied, %	Groups with one dissatisfied, %	Groups with two or more dissatisfied, %
Group decision	62	75.8	21.0	3.2
Mixed	12	16.7	66.7	16.7
Foreman dominated	24	4.2	54.2	41.7

per cent had two or more dissatisfied. In contrast, only 4.2 per cent of the foremen who were inclined to dominate or influence the decision had all members of their groups satisfied, and 41.7 per cent of the groups had two or more dissatisfied. The results for the groups where the influence is mixed fall between these.

Satisfaction seems to depend on the foreman's conduct of the discussion more than on any other single factor. There is no one solution that tends to be associated with satisfaction, and even the number of exchanges of trucks seems to be of minor importance. It might be supposed that the more the trucks are shifted around, the more individuals profit from the introduction of a new truck. However, Table 8 shows that low satisfaction occurs only when the solution is one in which only one person gets a different truck. When from two to five men receive a different truck, the groups with all satisfied members range from 50 to 66.7 per cent, with no trend in evidence. It appears that satisfactions depend more on the process by which the decision is reached than upon the decision as such, and this process depends upon the skill of the leader.

Training in developmental discussions. The superiority of the developmental discussion method over the free discussion method for increasing the quality of decisions has already been described (pages 28 ff.). The question now

TABLE 8. *Satisfaction with Solution and Number of Crew Members Receiving a Different Truck*

	Different trucks to:				
	1 man	2 men	3 men	4 men	5 men
Number of groups	7	41	30	12	8
Per cent of groups with all satisfied	28.6	51.2	50.0	66.7	50.0

raised is whether this superiority can be increased further with training. In order to test this question, three levels of training were compared, using the case of Viola Burns. It will be recalled that this is not a role-playing case, and the purpose of the discussion is for a group of persons, led by a discussion leader without any rank or authority over the group, to decide whether Viola should be encouraged or discouraged with regard to her indecision to take a new job. In this experiment groups were required to reach a decision and could not plead insufficient information.[11]

The minimum training condition was to give the leaders the instruction only. This means that they were given the descriptions of either the free or the developmental procedures as outlined on pages 29 ff. Since the subjects were recruited from a human relations course, the group leader may have been more considerate and less dominating than the average college student. The second level of training condition was

[11] N. R. F. Maier and L. R. Hoffman, Using Trained "Developmental" Discussion Leaders to Improve Further the Quality of Group Decisions. *J. appl. Psychol.*, 1960, **44**, 247–251.

made up of leaders recruited from an advanced management course in which discussion leadership was emphasized. In addition to receiving the above descriptions, these leaders were given a demonstration of the developmental discussion procedure showing how to get participants to use the various steps in drawing out the group, but stopping short of reaching any conclusions as to the action to take. These leaders did not know the correct answer.

The highest level of training condition also utilized leaders from the advanced management course who received the above-mentioned demonstration in the use of the developmental discussion. In addition they had completed a previous semester of skill training in both leadership and interviewing. Furthermore, they were familiar with the case and knew the correct answer.

The results of these three training conditions are shown in Table 9. There is a highly significant trend in the direction

TABLE 9. *Effects of Training on Use of Developmental Discussion*

		Type of training given leader		
Viewpoint	Decision	Undergraduate with instructions only (194 persons), %	Advanced student instructions and demonstration (88 persons), %	Two courses instructions demonstration and knowledge of cases (79 persons), %
Interest of company	Discourage	39.7	61.4	74.7
	Encourage	60.3	38.6	25.3
Interest of Viola	Discourage	39.7	55.7	73.4
	Encourage	60.3	44.3	26.6

of obtaining better decisions (discourage Viola) with increased training. With the minimum training only 39.7 per cent of the individuals favor discouraging Viola both from the company viewpoint and her own. Although this number of correct answers is twice as great as is produced by the free discussion, it still represents a minority opinion. The reason for the majority of discussants reaching a poor solution seems to be due to a desire to reward Viola for her past performance and to the fact that the description of her creates a favorable impression. The developmental method tends to reduce these influences. With the advanced discussion leaders, further improvements were made: the correct decision was reached by a majority for the first time, 61.4 per cent favoring "discourage" from the viewpoint of the company and 55.7 per cent favoring this conclusion for Viola's sake. The leaders themselves were more often wrong than their participants and hence could not have contributed valuable ideas.

Additional training and a knowledge of the correct answer caused the proportion of good decisions to be increased further, but not sharply (to 74.7 per cent). It is quite unlikely that the leaders attempted to influence the outcome of the decision, and, if the writer's experience is typical, such an attempt would have turned the group opinion against them.

This experiment demonstrates that a good method is favored by skills. In a case of this kind, when a majority opinion is misled by thinking of promotion as a kind of reward for a deserving person, it may take considerable skill with a good method to turn the majority opinion in the direction of a practical evaluation. Many problems are of this type, and the skill of a leader would reveal itself in three ways: (1) his ability to select problems in which the developmental type of discussion would be valuable, (2) his ability to break the problem into logical parts, and (3) his ability to conduct the discussion without manipulating the thinking or introducing his own bias.

It will be recalled that when groups were instructed to follow the developmental discussion pattern (pages 42 ff.), the skill requirements of the leader were greatly reduced. A method, therefore, is more effective when all participants understand and accept it. Although the results of these two studies are not directly comparable, because the groups reported in Table 9 had no opportunity to plead insufficient information, it must be conceded that this category was selected primarily by groups using the free discussion.

Value of training in listening skills. Still another way to measure skill is to test the frequency with which a leader violates known skill principles. In an experiment of this kind, groups of persons were trained to listen and draw out the views of another person rather than to disagree or impose different viewpoints. These *permissive* skills are essential for avoiding arguments and for demonstrating an *accepting* state of mind.

The case on which this approach to measuring the value of training was used is known as "A Problem with 'Old' Girls." [12] Mr. Jones, the personnel director, is in an interview situation with Mr. Smith, an office manager who has a very unfavorable attitude toward older women working in his department. It is Mr. Jones's objective to try to change Mr. Smith's attitude.

The values of listening and drawing out the feelings of a biased person and the importance of avoiding an argument are known to the participants. However, Mr. Smith's role makes him very unreasonable since he selects only the unfavorable facts about older women in order to defend his point of view. This bias traps Mr. Jones into pointing to the favorable facts, and before long he tends to sell Mr. Smith on their merits. Unless Mr. Jones is skilled, the interview is likely to turn into an argument, resulting in hard feelings rather than improved relations.

Three levels of training were used in this experiment.[13] Students in a course in human relations were used as subjects. The course involved subject matter, practice in role playing, and participation in discussions. The first group was tested after the second week, the second group after the tenth week, and the third group during the thirteenth week, which was immediately preceded by exercises in nondirective counseling. The numbers of interviewing pairs were

[12] N. R. F. Maier, *Principles of Human Relations.* John Wiley & Sons, Inc., New York, 1952.

[13] N. R. F. Maier, L. R. Hoffman, and L. M. Lansky, Human Relations Training as Manifested in an Interview Situation. *Personnel Psychol.*, 1960, **13**, 11–30.

sixty-seven, seventy, and fifty-three respectively, for the three groups compared.

The case material included four facts favorable to older girls, four facts unfavorable to them, and two ambiguous facts, e.g., production was the same for old and young girls, a fact which could be treated as favorable or unfavorable depending on the attitude. These same facts were supplied to both members of each pair but given against a background of either a favorable or hostile attitude toward old girls.

Since the purpose of the training dealt with the need for the interviewer to elicit information from the interviewee, the effect of the training may be examined from the point of view of how many of the facts were introduced into the conversation by each participant. Table 10 shows the percentage

TABLE 10. *Total Percentage of Facts about Old Girls First Mentioned by Joneses and Smiths in Each Training Group*

	Per cent of facts mentioned by:		
Training group	Jones	Smith	Neither one
Group 1	41.0	42.4	16.6
Group 2	35.1	46.0	18.9
Group 3	27.4	42.2	30.4

Note: Chi-square test of this relationship is significant at the .001 level of confidence.

of the facts introduced by Jones, the interviewer, and Smith, the interviewee.

It will be seen that with increased training, Mr. Jones introduced a smaller percentage of facts, dropping from 41 to 27.4 per cent and a greater number of facts were left unexpressed, 16.6 rising to 30.4 per cent. Mr. Smith contributed about the same percentage of facts in the three groups, which is to be expected since he was not supposed to control the interview. Whether he argued or was drawn out, it was his inclination to introduce the unfavorable material and to make ambiguous facts appear unfavorable. When pairs receive little training (group 1) and have been taught no prescribed method to follow, Jones and Smith tend to introduce an equal percentage of facts.

The effect of the training is primarily one of causing Jones to be less inclined to argue in favor of old girls. This fact is apparent from the trend in Table 11, which shows a decline from 73.1 to 51.4 per cent in the number of facts that Jones introduces favorable to old girls. However, it will be noted that the interviewers' skills have not progressed to the point where they cause Smith to introduce an increasing

TABLE 11. *Number and Per Cent of Facts Favorable to Old Girls First Mentioned by Joneses and Smiths in Each Training Group*

Training group	Jones N	Jones %	Smith N	Smith %	Neither one N	Neither one %	Total N	Total %
Group 1	196	73.1	24	9.0	48	17.9	268	100
Group 2	179	63.9	40	14.3	61	21.8	280	100
Group 3	109	51.4	21	9.9	82	38.7	212	100

Note: Chi-square test of this relationship is significant at the .001 level of confidence.

number of favorable facts. Rather the favorable facts go unmentioned. Despite this fact, the interviews become more friendly, and there is more problem solving in the groups where training has been more complete.

Avoiding defensive behavior and argument is a difficult skill, and even though interviewers and discussion leaders enter an interview or a conference with a determination to do a good job of listening, they find themselves maneuvered into a defensive position. The skill requirements in this area are very great, and the preceding experiment demonstrates only that the more elementary skills have been acquired. The skills in avoiding defensive behavior are equally relevant to interviews and conferences.

The remaining chapters of this book are devoted to a discussion of the various skills that may be utilized in reducing the emotional problems in conference leadership so that the discussion may proceed to constructive problem solving.

THE PROFESSIONAL MANAGER'S NEED TO IMPROVE BOTH METHODS AND SKILLS

Both the methods and the skills of a discussion leader appear to play a predominant part in determining the *quality* as well as the *acceptance* of decisions. It appears that group discussion not only is a way to develop a sense of responsibility for, and an interest in, the success of decisions, but also can serve as a means for improving the quality of decisions. A great deal of potential talent appears to lie dormant in lower levels of management because supervisors are unable to draw upon it. A knowledge of various methods may be very helpful in capturing some of the latent talent, but the skill requirement demands more concentrated and persistent effort.

If one regards management as a profession, the skill requirements are less likely to appear as an unreasonable demand to make of a manager. All professions require both knowledge and skill. Once the management of people is regarded as having a scientific basis, problems involving people become a challenge rather than a headache. The desire to substitute machines for people will only remove some of the problems that people introduce, and even though this trend reduces the work force, it is unlikely that middle management will be reduced to automation. It is in middle management that some of our greatest talents are wasted because creative individuals are unable to contribute to important decisions. Subordinates would welcome the opportunity to contribute more creative effort and become more emotionally involved in the success of the business. At present, much of their emotional involvement is in the form of frustration and fear.

Unfortunately, a written treatment of skills can only serve as a guide in directing leadership training; it can never be a substitute for practice. In order for the reader to profit from the skill principles discussed in the following chapters, he may wish to make an analysis of different phases of his performance to see which principles he has used and which he has violated. The objective is not to expect perfection since this becomes discouraging, but to reduce the number of violations. When perfect performances become common occurrences, it is likely that standards have been lowered. Such are the skills in conference leadership at the present time. Steady and persistent improvement will put most managers ahead of prevalent practice.

CHAPTER THREE

Locating the problem

THE PROBLEM AS THE STARTING POINT

One important area of conference skill resides in the matter of locating the problem. Suppose a company has a need for getting more creative talent and has the problem of how to increase it. This looks like a pretty definite and clear-cut problem. However, the statement actually contains a number of more specific problem locations of which the following are representative.

How to do a better job of college recruiting

How to attract talent from other companies

How to keep our best talent from leaving

How to locate talent in other departments of our company

How to increase the talents in our present force

How to divide up the job so as to distribute work according to the talents now available

Some of these specific problems may be readily soluble, some might be solved with difficulty, and still others may be insoluble. It follows, therefore, that successful problem solving depends, in part, upon the location of the specific problem that is selected from the general problem area. This location of the problem influences the approaches that are made, and it is important to find the feasible approaches.

The leader of a problem-solving conference or the individual problem solver, however, is prone to take his first conception of a problem as the starting point and move toward the desired goal. Thus the first group of skills in problem solving demands that considerable time be spent on exploring, choosing, and isolating a starting point. In order to develop these skills, it is necessary to suppress an interest in *solutions* and develop a greater interest in exploring the *problem*.

THE IMPORTANCE OF THE LOCATION OF THE PROBLEM

To get a better appreciation of the way the location of a specific problem or obstacle influences the thinking process, it is desirable to analyze a general problem situation in detail.

Figure 3 shows a person trying to solve the problem of tying together the ends of two strings which are attached to the ceiling some distance from each other. The strings are so spaced that he cannot reach the second string while holding the end of the first one. Initially a person tries out activities without too much thinking. He takes the end of one string, and while holding onto it, tries to reach the second. When this fails, he takes the end of the second string and tries to reach the first. This initial exploration is called trial and error and precedes any attempts at locating an obstacle or a more specific problem. Only after rather random trial and error has failed to produce results does the person become aware of obstacles.

The obstacles that a person may experience in this situation often have quite different natures, and each will suggest its appropriate remedies. We will differentiate between these various obstacles by regarding them as different locations of the problem.

The first problem that comes to the mind of a person placed in this situation is "arm is too short." This location of the problem occurs to him when he finds that extending his

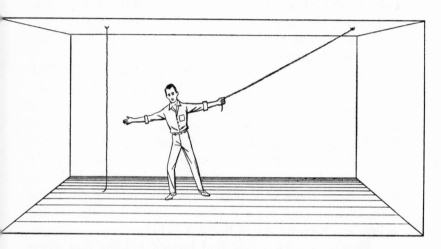

FIG. 3. Two-string problem. This situation was used to investigate how the location of the obstacle in a problem influences the solution. Two strings hang from the ceiling, spaced so that a person holding the end of one cannot reach the other. The problem requires that the person tie the ends of the two strings together.

The person may see the obstacle location as follows: (1) my arm is too short; (2) the string I'm holding is too short; (3) the string won't stay in the center position while I leave it to fetch the other; and (4) while I hold one of the strings, the other won't come to me when I want it to. Each of these locations suggests its class of solution. These are respectively: (1) extending the reach with appropriate tools; (2) lengthening the string with certain accessories; (3) anchoring one string in a position between the two cords (with a chair, for example); and (4) attaching a weight to one string to turn it into a pendulum so that it can be reached while holding the end of the other string. The latter is an elegant solution and is the only one possible if the available tools are such things as a bolt or a pair of pliers. (*Taken from N. R. F. Maier, Reasoning in Humans: II. The Solution of a Problem and Its Appearance in Consciousness. J. comp. Psychol., 1931, 12, 181–194.*)

reach for the free string is inadequate. Finding his arm too short, he turns to the use of tools. His selection of tools will be those which increase the reach and may include such things as window sticks, brooms, and even chairs.

A second location of the problem, which is also very common, is "string is too short." The awareness of this difficulty or obstacle causes our problem solver to think of ways to increase the length of the string. He may observe pull cords on window shades, electric cords, and even consider the use of his own belt.

Still another location is experienced when a person realizes that, since the strings just reach from the ceiling to the floor, they cannot be brought toward each other without holding or anchoring one of them. The "lack of an anchor" thus becomes the third location of an obstacle. This location is less obvious than the other two, and a fair number of problem solvers do not hit upon it. Persons who try to deal with this obstacle think of various ways of weighting down the cord, or they may place a piece of furniture between the strings and then tie one of the strings to it.

Finally, a person may find himself holding one string and looking toward the other. Since he cannot go to it without letting go of the one he is holding, he might consider the possibility of the string coming to him. Since he is not allowed to have the help of an assistant, he may think of having the wind blow the string toward him. The sometimes-expressed wish for an electric fan reveals that the obstacle is seen as "the string won't come to me when I need it." This location of the problem is the least frequent and is discovered by less than 40 per cent of a college population.[1] The solution to which this location of the problem leads is that of making a pendulum out of one of the strings by fastening a weight to it.

If all of the materials mentioned above are available, the ends of the strings can be tied together by overcoming

[1] N. R. F. Maier, Reasoning in Humans: II. The Solution of a Problem and Its Appearance in Consciousness. *J. comp. Psychol.*, 1931, **12**, 181–194.

any of the four obstacles, i.e., by approaching the problem through any of the four locations. It is to be noted, however, that the solutions would be distinctly different in type. Similarity in solutions, therefore, depends upon the obstacle that is overcome. For example, even if a particular obstacle or difficulty were overcome by the use of a variety of tools, the solutions would be equivalent because the function of the tools would be the same.[2] Even an extension cord if used as a lasso would be recognizable as one of extending the reach. Creativity is indicated by the ability to shift the thinking from one obstacle to another rather than finding various ways to overcome the same obstacle.

Actually, a single tool might be used in four different ways to overcome each of the four different obstacles. For example, a pair of pliers might be used to extend the reach. In this instance one string would be held in one hand while the pliers would be held in the free hand to extend the reach for the other string. If, however, the obstacle was "string too short," the pliers would be utilized to hold onto the first string and permit the problem solver to get closer to the second string so he could reach it with his free hand.

In the event that an anchor solution were sought, the pliers would be used to anchor one of the strings as close to the other as possible. In this case, the person would carry the free string as far toward the anchored one as possible and then try to get hold of the anchored string with his foot. Since the strings just reach the floor, the pliers would not serve this purpose well.

Obviously the function of the pair of pliers would be most elegant when used as a weight for the pendulum solution. By putting one string in motion, the problem solver could stroll toward the other, carry it back toward the center, and grasp the swinging string as it came toward him.

By limiting the available equipment and by spacing the

[2] B. J. Sherburne, Qualitative Differences in the Solution of a Problem Involving Reasoning. Doctoral Dissertation, University of Michigan, 1940. Available through University Microfilms, Inc., Ann Arbor, Mich.

strings in a certain way, all solutions, excepting the pendulum solution, can be excluded at will. In other words, the success of the problem-solving process could be limited to one approach. Success or failure in problem solving would then depend directly upon whether or not the obstacle that was located could be circumvented. Finding such obstacles thus becomes a key process in successful problem solving.

LOCATING OBSTACLES THAT CAN BE OVERCOME

If success in problem solving depends upon the locating of obstacles that can be overcome, one might suppose that such success is largely a matter of good fortune or chance. However, further exploration reveals that certain principles can serve as guides.

Suppose that it is possible to locate many obstacles or approaches to the solution of a problem. This condition would prevail in the string problem just discussed if a great variety of materials were available. Thus the problem could be solved by extending the reach, lengthening one of the strings, or by anchoring; and several methods for doing each of these would be possible.

When faced with a situation that is rich in solutions, the essence of problem solving really becomes one of selecting the solution that is best for a given occasion. This process would require an evaluation of the several solutions in terms of other criteria such as cost, ease of execution, personal preference, etc. The purpose of seeking out as many different locations as possible would not be to solve the problem, but to find the most desirable solution. This objective would most readily be achieved if the list of possibilities were a long one.

The opposite condition is one in which there is a deficiency in solutions. This is always the case when the problem is a difficult one. Such a condition would prevail in the string problem if the only materials available for solving the problem were a pair of pliers and if the distances between the strings were such as to make the pliers useful only as a pendulum weight. Under these circumstances, the pendulum solution would be the elegant one, but it would be a difficult problem because the obstacle of "how to make the string come to me" is not readily located. Certain problem locations are out of the ordinary stream of experience and therefore are either overlooked or not discovered by most problem solvers. It is by the locating of new or unusual obstacles that inventive and creative solutions are facilitated.

The following instructions or problem-solving principles are relevant under these circumstances and were developed in connection with research on creative thinking.[3]

Seek unusual obstacles to overcome or new approaches to follow. The usual way of looking at a problem that is known to be difficult obviously does not apply; otherwise the problem would have a ready solution. From the mere fact that a problem is difficult one may infer that most people cannot solve it, which means that the usual ways of approaching the problem are inadequate.

Often this means doing something quite different from what common sense and experience may dictate. In attempting to solve such a problem as the control of yellow fever, many scientists approached it by trying to make man immune to the germ. However, posing the problem in terms of how to keep the yellow-fever germs from reaching man, which seemed somewhat absurd at first, led successfully to the solution, i.e., destroying mosquitoes that transport the germ.

In many instances one must think of a way that is exactly the opposite of tradition. In the string problem, discussed in the preceding section, there is the tendency for the person to pose the problem in terms of "how to get to the other string," yet the elegant solution depends upon formulating the problem in terms of "how to make the other string come to me." Many instances of scientific discovery hinge upon such reversals in viewpoint. In the period in which Copernicus lived, problems in astronomy were viewed with

[3] N. R. F. Maier, An Aspect of Human Reasoning. *Brit. J. Psychol. (Gen. Sec.)*, 1933, **25**, 144–155.

the earth both as stationary and as the center of the universe. The system of Copernicus reversed both of these assumptions, giving the sun a fixed position and having the earth move in an orbit, as did other planets. This simple change in the formulation of the problem made it possible for Galileo to solve a number of problems and to make many fundamental experimental discoveries in astronomy.

Do not persist in a point of view if it fails to be productive. The mere fact that an obstacle is unusual does not give it merit. Obstacles that possess merit for problem solving can be overcome. This means that a problem solver must not continue to follow any given approach. If one location of the difficulty does not lead to the desired objective, it is necessary to approach the problem from a different direction, i.e., seek a different location of the problem. Change and variety become important activities in solving difficult problems.

Do not be misled by near successes. Persistence in a given approach is most likely to become obstinacy when one is partially successful or when one falls just short of the goal. In the example of the string problem, a person will persist in stretching his arms for the second string when this string is almost within reach, but he will readily give up this approach when his reach falls short of the string by a foot or more. When a person experiences a near success, he tends to make minor modifications or adjustments in an attempt to correct for the minor discrepancy. It is important for the conference leader to be aware of this trap so that near successes in group problem solving will not prevent the exploration of other possibilities.

Application of principles to group problem solving. The experiments which tested these principles demonstrated that college students improved their individual problem solving when the above principles were explained prior to their exposure to problems that were difficult in the sense that they demanded creativity. When a person is a conference leader, he can go even further because he can ask for the unusual, giving unusual ideas more time for exposition and protecting individuals with unpopular ideas from unfavorable group pressure. Brainstorming[4] is a method that depends upon these principles to a considerable degree.

The conference leader can also prevent excessive persistence by encouraging differences, or variety, in ways of looking at a problem. With different minds at his disposal, he can cause the direction of thinking to change. Each difficulty posed sets the minds to thinking along different lines, and these constitute *directions* in thinking.[5] Groups as well as individuals may persist in one direction, but for a skillful conference leader persistence in thinking need be no serious problem.

The possibility that near success may prevent the exploration of different alternatives also can be controlled by the leader. Frequently he is the worst offender since he has an important stake in a solution. This means that he must not only prevent others from falling into this trap but avoid it himself.

A leader can best practice these principles if he does not become too involved in the problem as such but continues to be concerned with the problem-solving process. His function is to stimulate the problem-solving behavior of others, rather than try to solve the problem himself.

THE LOCATION OF A PROBLEM IN THE SITUATION, IN THE INDIVIDUAL, AND IN THE GROUP

When faced with the same practical problem situation with a group of their subordinates, different supervisors may see the difficulty in a number of ways or give the problem quite varied locations. Some may see the difficulty as located in the work situation, others may see it as trouble with cer-

[4] A. F. Osborn, *Applied Imagination: Principles and Procedures of Creative Thinking.* Charles Scribner's Sons, New York, 1953.

[5] N. R. F. Maier, Reasoning in Humans: I. On Direction. *J. comp. Psychol.*, 1930, **10**, 115–143.

tain individuals, and still others may see it as a group problem. These three locations suggest quite different approaches.

If the problem is approached as being in the *situation,* the supervisor does not need to talk to his employees, but instead analyzes and alters the situation. For example, an inspection department may have a problem because inspectors are letting low-quality parts through. This condition might be seen as related to the nature of the work situation or the work layout. Solutions that might be considered as relevant from such an approach are illustrated in the list below:

Improving lighting

Introducing coffee bars

Putting more variety in the job

Improving the seats

Introducing job rotation

Training supervisors in human relations

Changing job so that inspectors work as members of teams rather than as individuals

It will be observed that these solutions are quite different and depend upon the aspect of the situation that would profit most from a change. In order to determine the aspect in need of improvement, various facts and production indices should be analyzed. The possibilities for changes in the situation are so very great that this is a fruitful area for study.

If the problem of poor inspection is seen as being due to certain *individuals,* an analysis of this location might lead to the consideration of solutions such as the following:

Training employees doing the poorest work

Disciplining poor workers in some way

Praising or rewarding good workers

Counseling poor workers to improve their emotional adjustment

Conducting appraisal interviews

Interviewing problem employees to learn their attitudes

Discharging the poorest inspectors

The opportunities for correcting a condition by changing the individual are limited by training possibilities, changing attitudes, and improvement through counseling. Discipline would be an attempt to train or motivate him, and discharge would be a way of changing an employee by *exchanging* him for another.

Finally, if the inspection problem is seen as having its location in the *group*, the problem becomes one that is connected with the group structure or social organization. An analysis of the problem situation from this approach or location might suggest the solutions given below.

Setting up a training program for the group as a whole

Discussing how superior inspectors may help or train others

Asking the group to participate in setting goals for both quality and quantity

Discussing the problems of how to improve inspection with the group

Asking the group how the work situation might be improved so as to make it more satisfying

Correcting a condition by locating the problem in the group assumes a group influence. When employees restrict production by agreement, when one group of workers will not eat at the same table with another group, when some employees are tardy because others regularly show up late, and when there is frequent complaint about fair treatment, we are posing problems that arise because employees are members of a group.

Since various supervisors may locate the same inspection problem quite differently, it is apparent that the degree of success in supervision may be associated with this initial judgment. In order to be assured of greater success, it is suggested that each of the three locations be thoroughly explored before one of them is selected. The possible locations of the *situation*—the *individual* and the *group*—exist whenever the problem concerns the behavior of people. It should also be pointed out that when a supervisor is emotionally involved in a problem situation, the most obvious thing for him to do is to locate the problem in some individual. This occurs because frustration makes people seek someone to blame. The least likely location of a problem under such circumstances is the situation. If a supervisor cannot blame certain individuals—in a group he can usually find some faults —he may blame everyone, but this often is avoided because general faultfinding appears unreasonable to others. The work situation is likely to be overlooked for several reasons: (1) the supervisor himself is part of it, (2) it is partly of his own making, and (3) its connection with behavior is less apparent than that of the persons who do the behaving.

PINPOINTING THE LOCATION OF A PROBLEM

Even after a person is aware of the fact that the problem may be located in the *situation*, in *individuals*, or in the *group*, the specific nature of the problem needs to be clarified. The three possible locations thus serve only to guide one in the search for a variety of general locations. Once the general locations are indicated, detailed locations must be sought.

To illustrate the skill involved in locating the problem, let us take a description of a situation confronting a supervisor [6] and explore some of its specific locations.

Jim Telfer is the supervisor in a general office of an insurance company. The group he supervises is made up of five girls who work at desks. A good deal of the work involves telephone contacts with company people who require information which various girls have in their files. Since all of the phones are on one line, the person who answers uses a buzzer signal, and in this way

[6] Case modified from N. R. F. Maier, A. R. Solem, and A. A. Maier, *Supervisory and Executive Development*. John Wiley & Sons, Inc., 1957.

the person requested, or the person who has the needed information, can take over the call. Mr. Telfer never answers the phone unless one of the girls informs him by buzzer that the call is for him. Ordinarily the girl with the least service answers the phone and then buzzes the girl who can handle the call.

A relief period of fifteen minutes both morning and afternoon is given to the girls, and this is regarded as adequate for the usual personal needs. Mr. Telfer has asked them to take their relief one at a time so as to keep coverage of the office. When the work is heavy, the girls frequently skip their relief.

Mr. Telfer's boss complained that Telfer was hard to reach by phone because the line was always busy. He said that he could reach other units which do the same type of work as Telfer's, and he expressed the opinion that Telfer's group was making too many personal calls. Telfer knows that the girls make outside calls rather freely and that they receive quite a number of personal calls because, on several occasions, he picked up his phone and found that the conversation had nothing to do with business. For example, twice during the past week he found Irene Wilson talking with her boyfriend. Telfer told his boss that he would do something about it and has decided to talk the problem over with the girls.

The girls' general performance ratings are as follows:

Betty Northrup—rated as slow but very conscientious

Mary Olsen—rated as very superior

Irene Wilson—rated as very productive but breaks rules

Mabel Zimmer—rated as average

Stella Browning—rated as progressing very rapidly

Some possible locations of the problem that one may extract from this description are the following:

1. Abuses of phone privileges by the group
2. Abuses of phone privileges by certain girls
3. Telfer's attitude toward personal calls
4. Attitude of Telfer's boss
5. Proper number of personal calls
6. Efficient use of telephone lines
7. Better answering service

Each of these locations specifies a somewhat different

objective, and it is for this reason that a wide range of different problem locations might be envisaged by persons finding themselves in Mr. Telfer's position. We have already found that even with the same objectives, different locations are possible; but when the objective is not specified, the range of possible locations increases even more.

Nevertheless, it will be seen that the locations in the *situation,* in the *individual,* and in the *group* are represented in the above list. Situational [7] locations are represented by problem locations numbers 3, 4, and 5; individual locations by number 2; and group locations by numbers 1, 6, and 7.

It will be observed that some of the problems in the list are more readily soluble than others. However, the desired objective should not be sacrificed in order to locate a problem that is easily soluble. The important thing is to spend considerable time exploring various locations before attempting to find or adopt a remedy. Since one of the main functions of a conference leader is to take problems to the group, it is important that he spend considerable time locating the problem before confronting his group with it. (In the next chapter we will consider the skills needed in stating a problem to the group.) To become skilled in locating problems, it is imperative that a conference leader confine himself to the problem itself and not confuse it with solutions that invariably suggest themselves. It is this tendency to confuse problems with solutions that frequently leads to conflict and failure to reach agreement in group discussion.

THE CONFUSION BETWEEN PROBLEMS, SOLUTIONS, AND CHOICES

Differentiating problems and solutions. A manager poses the following problem: How can I transfer a man who is popular in the group but disrupts the work of the others, without causing resentment? This statement of the problem

---

[7] Problems 3 and 4 are situational because the problem concerns the behavior of the girls, and for them the behavior of Telfer and his boss are part of the work situation.

appears insoluble and reminds one of the problem of having one's cake and eating it too. In one sense the above statement of the problem is a dilemma, but in another sense it confuses merely because it incorporates a solution into the statement of the problem. In essence, the manager is asking, How can I apply my solution to the problem and get the group to accept it or even endorse it?

In such cases, the effective procedure is to separate the solution from the problem. It is clear that an employee who has the support of the group is causing the manager some kind of trouble. Just what kind of trouble caused the manager to wish to transfer the employee? Is this employee an unofficial leader who is taking a position against the manager? Is there a personal clash between the manager and the employee? Is the employee uncooperative because he lacks ability or because he is superior in ability? Is the problem caused by the employee in question or by the group's tendency to support him?

In order to separate the solution from the problem, one may ask the manager, "Why do you wish to transfer this employee?" In the above instance, he replied that it was because the employee was the slowest worker on an assembly operation and so was causing a bottleneck.

The problem can now be stated as follows: How should one deal with an assembly operation in which the slow work of one man holds up the others? There are many possible solutions to this problem, and transfer is only one of them. Actually, the action of getting rid of the slowest worker merely creates another problem—a new slowest worker. How long can one eliminate the slow employees without threatening the security of the whole group? It is this threat that causes groups to organize and protect inferior workers.

Solutions to this new problem that suggest themselves are:

Fitting the size of each operation in the assembly to the ability of the man

Arranging for faster workers to help the slower ones

Having an extra man step in and help out men who get behind

Making up teams with men who have similar amounts of ability

Introducing machines so that the pace of the work depends more on the machine than on the man

The solution that is most appropriate will depend upon a number of factors. Most of those mentioned above will require the acceptance of the workers, which means that the appropriate solution for a particular group might best be obtained through group decision.

Other examples of statements of problems that include a suggestion of a solution or imply that a solution is either known or impossible are given below.

How can I get men to accept improvements that I suggest in their work?

How can I get my subordinates to take a more realistic approach to problems?

What is the best way to lay off the poorest workers when new methods reduce the number of men required on the job?

How can one give more training to employees without taking them off the job?

How much should I delegate when my subordinates do not accept responsibility?

Actually, each of these problems implies that the individual with the problem has trouble in getting his views accepted. The same problems could be stated more effectively in the following ways:

How can I get employees to adopt improved work methods?

What is the best way to get my subordinates to do an effective job of problem solving?

How should one introduce laborsaving devices?

What are the possibilities of training workers who can-not be taken off the job?

What is the best way to get subordinates to accept responsibility?

Although the above problems are stated as questions, it should be observed that they cannot be answered by "yes" or "no." Rather, they require exploration and lead to the evaluation of a wide range of possibilities. Often the best method for one circumstance may be quite inadequate for another.

Differentiating choices and problems. It is common for people to state problems in terms of questions that request a "yes" or "no" reply. This approach restricts the problem solver to a choice between two alternative solutions. His problem solving is restricted since he is asked only to agree or disagree with the idea expressed. In other cases, the questioner states two or more alternatives and asks which is better.

The following questions are examples of problems that request the problem solver either to give a "yes" or "no" answer or to select one from several alternative solutions which are furnished to him. In other words, these problems require that a choice or decision be made, not that a solution be discovered.

Should one discharge an employee who disrupts the work of others?

If a female employee accuses her supervisor of making unwelcome advances toward her, and if he denies everything, should the company discharge the supervisor, the employee, or both?

Should one hire an applicant who is superior in ability to the requirements of the job available even if he is willing to take it?

Should I work through my immediate boss or bypass him when he is in constant disagreement with his superior regarding my work?

Should one carry out an order if one knows it is wrong?

Before attempting to translate these choice situations into problems, it would be well to probe for more details about the situation in order to determine what the questioner has in mind. It is possible that he has a solution in mind and is seeking support for it, that he has a limited perspective, or that he has lost track of his major objective. Further elaboration and examples would fill in this background.

However, to illustrate the point at issue, the list below represents examples of reformulations that turn the choice situations into problems. Note also that these restatements increase the number of possible solutions from which an eventual choice may be made.

1. How should one deal with a situation in which one employee disrupts the work of the whole group? It is clear that the solution will depend upon whether the employee in question is liked or disliked, whether or not he has ability, the nature of "disrupts," etc. When these conditions are clarified, even more specific locations of the problem can be found.

2. How should the company handle a situation in which a female employee accuses her boss of unwelcome advances, which the accused denies? Obviously the record and adjustments of each party would have to be considered. In addition to discharge, one would have to consider transfers, the marital status of each, their values to the company, and the nature of the charges.

3. What should one do with an applicant who is superior to the job for which he is applying? The answer to this depends upon whether the superiority of the applicant will cause him to (a) do inferior work, (b) become dissatisfied, or (c) disrupt the group in which he will work. The questions of whether better placement is possible in the near future and the rareness of his superiority also need to be considered.

4. How should I handle a situation when my immediate superior is in frequent disagreement with his superior regarding the work I should do? The solution to this problem includes a consideration of possible communication failures, the relative ability of the two men, the status of the men in the organization, and the seriousness of the assignments. Does the person who raises the question want to by-

pass his immediate boss? What are his opportunities for remaining neutral?

5. What should one do if given an order which appears to be wrong? In adding the word "appears," the statement of the problem is broadened to include the possibility of an error in the employee's judgment. The rephrasing removes the yes-no choice and introduces the opportunity to explore the order further with the boss. This new possibility can lead to a consideration of how best to approach the boss when one believes him to be wrong.

In rephrasing statements of problems, it is best to think in terms of specific instances and to consider illustrations. Generalized statements not only fail to be communicated, but they sometimes show little relation to the actual problem. One person can assist another in locating a problem by requesting an illustration or by asking him to clarify his objective. If he has several objectives, he should be asked to pick out the most important one. The reader can improve his own comprehension of a problem and bring it into sharper focus by describing his problem to someone else and by attempting to state the objective he wishes to reach. If a listener is not available, he can try to put the problem in writing.

OBTAINING ASSISTANCE IN LOCATING THE PROBLEM

In many instances, a supervisor is aware of difficulty in the work situation but does not know the nature of the problem. If productivity is falling, if absenteeism is increasing, if cooperation seems lacking, or if there is a great deal of bickering between employees, he may know he has some kind of a problem, and his objective may be clear, but he does not know where the trouble lies. He may make attitude surveys and analyze various work indices to obtain some information, but often these procedures require time and money and still may not be adequate. Are there other approaches more accessible to him?

On the one hand, a supervisor might learn considerable

about the causes of the difficulty if he confronted his group with a general problem of how to improve job satisfaction. On the other hand, it might be more appropriate if he asked his group whether or not they had some problems they would like to raise for discussion. In this type of meeting, the supervisor's role is to help clarify problems posed and bring them into focus. He might do this by asking for details or illustrations. When he himself understands the problem, he should write a brief summarized statement of it (five to twenty words) on an easel. Any personal attacks directed at specific persons should be removed by phrasing the problem in an objective or impersonal manner. When he has completed his formulation, he should ask the person who posed the problem whether or not the statement accurately expresses the meaning intended. Corrections or modifications should be made until the statement is approved by the person who initiated it and is clear to others in the group. (This procedure is adapted from a discussion method called "posting problems," which is described in Chapter 7.)

In rephrasing or summarizing a problem, it is best for the discussion leader to use his own words. When he can state, in his words, exactly what the participant meant, there is good reason to believe that communication has been successful. Since one person can repeat another's words without understanding them, this process of rephrasing is important not only for communication purposes but also for creating an acceptant discussion climate—one in which the leader is trying to understand rather than stand in judgment of the participants. Soon all members of the group get into the spirit and do more of the kind of listening that makes for understanding.

When the problem is clearly understood, there should be some discussion to determine the extent to which others agree. If all agree, he can turn the discussion to the search for other possible problems. If, however, there is disagreement, then different views or locations might be explored. Group members might agree that the pace of the work should be changed but fail to agree on whether it should be slowed down or speeded up. The problem might then become one of finding a way to pace the work to suit different aptitudes. Disagreement over the food in the company restaurant, the job layout, fair job assignments, etc., might occur in any group, and discussion could be used to clarify whether or not the problem had several locations or whether the members disagreed on the location.

The process of discussing a problem has value not only in allowing persons to give vent to feelings, but also because the process of bringing problems into focus begins to suggest solutions. This tendency for solutions to suggest themselves is so strong that the conference leader will have to use his influence to keep the discussion on the topic of problems. It is important that the problems in a group are carefully explored before turning to the process of solving them.

In order to prevent these discussions from becoming time-consuming, it is suggested that a half hour per week be set aside for the discussion of problems or the solving of problems. If this time seems to be fruitful, a supervisor may wish to extend it.

Discussions of this kind may be held at any level in the organization. The president may have discussions with the officers reporting to him, the operating vice-president with department heads, department heads with superintendents, superintendents with general foremen, general foremen with foremen, and foremen with employees. Many problems discussed at one level might suggest problems that should be raised at another.

One of the greatest failures in subordinate-superior relationships is due to the fact that a subordinate does not discuss his problems with his superior. Although a superior may confidently believe that he knows the kinds of problems his subordinate faces, it is rare that this confidence is justified. This discrepancy in points of view was clearly demonstrated in a study of communication problems in middle management.[8]

[8] N. R. F. Maier, L. R. Hoffman, J. G. Hooven, and W. H. Read, Superior-Subordinate Communication. *A.M.A. Res. Rep.*, 1961.

It was further found [9] that upward communication was least effective when subordinates were ambitious. Apparently there is a reluctance to communicate problems upward for fear the superior may pass unfavorable judgment on a subordinate who has problems. Such failures in communication can become an effective block to the development of subordinates as well as to improved productivity.

THE AREA OF FREEDOM

Problems for group decision should be located in the leader's area of freedom. Problem solving is successful only when the solution reached is one which can be put into practice. If a person or group lacks the ability to put a solution into effect, the problem remains unsolved. It follows, therefore, that a supervisor should locate problems that fall within his jurisdiction for taking action. This region over which he has such control is his "area of freedom." Each level of supervision has an area of freedom, and its boundaries may be clear or vague, large or small. One of the problems in delegation is to clearly delineate the boundaries.

A first-line supervisor cannot make decisions regarding pay rates when these are covered by union contract; he cannot grant wash-up privileges to his group when the maintenance of uniform working conditions is the problem of his superior; he cannot hire a relative when the personnel department is vested with the responsibility for recruiting help; he cannot discharge an employee because of religious differences when this is in conflict with company policy; and he cannot permit a female employee to work ten consecutive hours when this conflicts with legislation. Thus the area of freedom is delimited by union contracts, higher management, staff or specialized departments, company policies and practices, and legislation. In other words, a supervisor must confine his decision making to matters over which he has the right to make decisions. Problems, therefore, must be so

[9] W. H. Read, Upward Communication in Industrial Hierarchies. *Human Relat.*, 1962, **15**, 3–15.

formulated that their solutions fall within the leader's authority to take action, and these are the problems that he may share with his immediate subordinates. When he does so, the group's decisions become his decisions, and he can be held responsible for them. Problems or decisions that fall within the authority of higher management can be discussed at lower levels, but in such cases the group's decision must be confined to a recommendation. Lower groups may have the freedom to make suggestions for higher levels to consider.

An example will illustrate how the proper location of a problem may place it within the scope of a supervisor's limited area of freedom. Let us suppose an office manager has money in his budget for decorating the lounge. If he presents the problem of how to decorate the lounge to his group, the group's decision might be one that exceeds the budget. He will therefore find himself in the situation of having to reject various decisions as too costly. However, if he locates the problem as being one of how to use the allocated sum of money to decorate the lounge, the decisions will fall within his authority. This latter location is more specific and as a consequence is more likely to keep the discussion in the area of freedom. A group readily accepts the limitations that the area of freedom imposes, and there is no reason why the boundaries should not be clarified for them.

Despite the attempt to confine a problem to the area of freedom, solutions will sometimes be recommended demanding that others take action. Suppose there is a problem of material handlers in keeping production lines supplied. Suggested solutions might include the following: get better trucks; reorganize storeroom; make each material handler responsible for specific supplies; change production layout; secure better cooperation from foremen on production lines; raise wages; give rest pauses; adopt signals to indicate when supplies are low, etc. This list of solutions includes some that involve higher management and lateral work units as well as the group. To attempt to delimit the problem by stating it in terms of "what we can do" not only would discourage the constructive suggestions that might be used as recommendations to higher management, but it might also cause the group to resent the implication that other units were not supposed to cooperate with them. When it is evident that the group feels obliged to involve others in the solution, it is desirable to include such suggestions in a list of possibilities. When the list is complete, the solutions can be sorted in terms of those that fall within the leader's authority and those that should be recommended for consideration by other units or higher management. The final decision about what the group wishes to do and what it wishes to recommend would be based on an evaluation of the various ideas discussed. In general, the group's final evaluation favors choosing ideas over which they themselves have control.

Problem solving in the area of freedom is most constructive. Ideas for improvement are frequently expressed in the form of actions that others should take. Workers tend to blame their superiors or higher management when things go wrong, and higher management tends to blame the attitude of workers for production difficulties. Thus the problem solver tends to overlook himself as an object of change. This tendency to formulate solutions that others should execute is unproductive because it requires action from an outsider, and the problem solver finds himself rather helpless while he waits for other persons to make the changes he recommends. Problem solving is most effective when it is in terms of "what we can do to improve the situation." When problems are located in the area of freedom, this constructive emphasis is present; hence problem solving tends to be upgraded.

Furthermore, groups are best informed on matters that concern their own activity. Thus the solutions recommended tend to be based upon factual considerations, and this knowledge operates to improve the quality of decisions. However, this does not mean that the group that takes the problem under consideration is morally obliged to make the improvements. Justice would demand that the persons at fault should change. However, at this point we are not considering the matter of justice; rather, our concern is with how to improve matters and make the best of a given situation. The questions of justice and how best to improve a situation are independent objectives and should not be confused.

The tendency to blame others is a backward-looking approach. The past is beyond control and cannot be altered. Only the present and the future are subject to change, and hence only they can be controlled through decisions. The problem-solving approach, therefore, must incorporate an attitude that accepts the past and takes up the problem of what to do to reach present objectives.

This problem-solving attitude is not present during frustration. Frustrated persons are most inclined to blame others. Solutions designed to fix the blame are in conflict with a problem-solving attitude because they represent attempts to correct the past rather than to control the future.

Since it is human to be subject to frustration and hence to become handicapped in problem solving, it follows that group decisions made by persons who are angry or on the defensive will lack quality. True problem solving can only begin after this adverse condition has been corrected. This matter will be discussed further in Chapter 5.

CHAPTER FOUR

Presenting the problem for group discussion

INVOLVING THE GROUP IN A PROBLEM

If it is assumed that the discussion leader has located the problem he wishes to introduce to his group, his next step is to consider the best way to present it to them. Even though the analysis of the situation may have led to a precise location of the problem, it does not follow that all formulations of it will be equally effective in initiating problem-solving behavior in the group. Success or failure of a group meeting can hinge upon this brief phase of a meeting. Although it is possible to recover from a poor presentation, it takes considerable skill to prevent a bad start from becoming worse.

A statement of a problem that places blame on a group will stimulate defensiveness, and this behavior is in conflict with problem solving. Some statements of problems are threatening, and the group's response is then one of hostility rather than an interest in the problem. Thus, statements that produce emotional reactions rather than an intellectual interest in problems hinder rather than facilitate problem solving.

Frequently, problems are stated in such vague or general terms that the participants do not know what the leader is driving at. This occurs when the leader tries (1) to avoid hurting someone's feelings or (2) to achieve several objectives at the same time.

The first of these conditions is likely to occur when a leader is concerned with good human relations. He hesitates to criticize and yet feels that something must be done to improve matters. As a consequence, he approaches the problem in a roundabout manner. His vague and extensive introduction to the problem serves to confuse the issue, and it may create anxiety.

The second condition is most probable when the leader has a solution in mind. Any solution, when carefully examined, will be seen to accomplish a number of objectives. For example, a particular route from the hotel to the city hall may take one past the park, the federal bank, and the community theater. If we now state the problem in terms of how to get to the park, the federal bank, the city hall, and the community theater in the most economical manner, one would be limiting the route to approximately the one the leader used as a guide in stating the problem. However, does he wish to accomplish all of these objectives, or is he trying to ensure that his particular solution (route) is discovered? If he is trying to have the group arrive at the solution he has in mind, then we would classify his approach as manipulative and failing to qualify as a group decision approach.

Manipulating versus helping. Manipulating and helping should be clearly distinguished in group processes. Any procedure a leader uses to steer the thinking of a group into his way of thinking, without openly revealing his personal preference, may be regarded as manipulative. If the leader's objective is to reach the best possible solution (not his own), then he can openly state this objective, since the best solution can also be an objective of the group. Anything the leader does to reach this group objective ceases to be a personal gain and is a gain for all concerned. When a leader's performance causes the group to work and think efficiently, he is helping or facilitating the group process. The question at issue here is not merely a moral one but one of efficiency. It is found that a group solution frequently is superior to the one the leader had hoped to achieve. This fact comes as a surprise to most leaders. Solutions inferior to what the leader had in mind tend to be rare and often are a rebellion against the leader's attempt to manipulate. It is always gratifying when what is best from the ethical point of view is also the most efficient.

Both manipulating and helping people are forms of influence. Some forms of influence are socially acceptable; others approach dishonesty and deception. To regard all forms of influence as manipulation reduces most social interaction to manipulation. For our purposes we will distinguish between actions that aid or upgrade a group's product and trickery that causes others to support one's own position.

Guiding principles. Six principles in stating a problem to a group may be used as guides for aiding the problem-solving process and avoiding emotional responses and confusion. Briefly stated these principles are as follows: [1]

1. Problems should be stated in situational rather than in behavioral terms.

2. A problem statement should encourage freedom of thought. To imply a solution or to suggest alternatives restricts freedom.

3. A mutual interest should be apparent in the statement of the problem.

4. Only one objective should be clearly specified.

[1] Modified from N. R. F. Maier, A. R. Solem, and A. A. Maier, *Supervisory and Executive Development.* John Wiley & Sons, Inc., New York, 1957.

5. The statement of the problem should be brief.

6. Essential information should be shared.

Although it is desirable to utilize all of these principles, the reader should be encouraged if he can incorporate the first two principles into his initial attempts with statements of problems. Since it is not uncommon for discussion leaders to violate all of these principles, almost any use of them represents a gain. In order to accomplish benefits in conference outcomes, therefore, it is unnecessary to do a perfect job.

However, this skill area is important enough to warrant careful preparation preceding a conference. It is especially critical because the statement of the problem sets the mood of the meeting. A poorly stated problem creates a good deal of misunderstanding, and even when this is discovered, it takes considerable time and patience to clear away these irrelevant obstacles. Problem solving is sufficiently difficult when only the necessary obstacles need to be dealt with.

USING SITUATIONAL RATHER THAN BEHAVIORAL STATEMENTS OF PROBLEMS (PRINCIPLE 1)

Changing situations may be easier than changing people. In formulating problems involving people in a work situation, one may either place emphasis upon the inadequacy of behavior displayed or refer to a deficiency in the situation. For example, a problem regarding violations of a safety regulation might focus on the *violations* or on the *regulation*. The central part of the problem in the first instance is *behavior* and in the second, the *situation*.

When a supervisor states a problem to a group in behavioral terms, it means that he is not satisfied with the performance of his employees; it represents disapproval not only of their behavior but of them. Thus, with a single stroke he sets himself apart from the group, so that mutual goals are no longer in effect. This action tends to cause the subordinates to band together so that differences among them, which might have led to improvements, now are set aside to defend themselves against their common opponent—the supervisor.

Statements of problems that make reference to tardiness, safety violations, slow work, lack of responsibility, poor co-operation, low standards, and inability to make decisions, refer to behavior and cause group members to respond defensively or even with hostility. Such responses may interfere with problem solving and at best are nonconstructive. Defensive responses may take the form of asking the leader embarrassing questions or of blaming someone else. The following are examples of unconstructive responses to a statement of a problem.

> Are we worse than others?
> What's the evidence?
> What do you intend to do about it?
> I'm doing the best I can.
> Give us better facilities.
> It's not our fault.
> What do you expect for the wages you pay?

Although these statements may be couched in polite manners or remain unexpressed, they are the overt responses made by members of a group when they are unafraid. When fear is present, the response may be one of silence, and this is one of the most difficult kinds of defensive behaviors with which a conference leader must deal.

In contrast, statements of problems made in situational terms are impersonal. People generally are willing to contribute ideas that will lead to improvements or that will correct situations. Thus problems stated in situational terms stimulate thought and arouse interest. A statement of a problem in situational terms can be a challenge because it does not threaten or degrade. Instead it is a request for help from the group and therefore is an act of sharing something with the group rather than standing in judgment of them.

Statements of problems that refer to (1) setting goals for attendance, production, quality, or safety; (2) improving the work situation to make it safer, more efficient, or easier; and (3) achieving fairness in work assignments, work schedules, or the allocation of new equipment serve to place the problem in situational terms and avoid the implication that the group is supposed to change. Altering situations is easier than changing people. However, people will welcome changes in their behavior if it is their own idea. It follows, therefore, that a discussion to change the situation may lead to suggestions for behavior modification. Resistance to change is primarily a form of defense, and a group's defense is greatest when it has been criticized or attacked from the outside.

Problems that are located in the behavior of the group or of certain individuals are most difficult to formulate in situational terms. It follows, therefore, that problems associated with disciplinary action would be most difficult to present in situational terms, while those having to do with purely objective matters would be least likely to cause difficulty with this principle.

Corresponding situational and behavioral statements. In Chapter 3 (page 61), seven locations of the "telephone abuse" problem were indicated. As an exercise in developing skill in stating a problem let us examine these locations and see how each may be stated in either situational or behavioral terms. Although there may be more appropriate statements, these examples will serve to demonstrate how the presentation of a problem can vary even though the location remains the same.

Location—group abuses of telephone privileges. Let us take the location "abuses of the phone privileges by the group." A behavioral statement might be: How can we best deal with the matter of unnecessary use of the company phone for personal purposes? The situational statement of this location might be: What would be a fair goal to set for personal calls? Note that the word "abuses" does not appear in either statement. "Abuses" refers to an outsider's unfavorable judgment of an act. However, even by substituting the more descriptive term "unnecessary" in the behavioral statement the accusation that the group should change is implied. In contrast, "setting a goal" is a target to aim for and therefore introduces a factor outside the individual.

Location—individual abuses of telephone privileges. The location "abuses by certain individuals" may not be a problem to present to the group and perhaps should be handled through interviews. Nevertheless individual problems can often be presented to the group, and hence this approach should be considered. The behavior approach to this problem might be: Some of us use the phone for personal purposes more than others. To what extent and how should we control this? The situational statement is a difficult one to formulate. One example might be: Should we keep records of personal calls by the individual or by the unit? This statement of a problem might be unsatisfactory if the group did not feel that abuses existed, but they might welcome such a statement if they felt that certain individuals were taking advantage of the situation. In this case the behavioral statement might cause hard feelings in the group, whereas the situational one would be less likely to isolate an individual.

Location—Mr. Telfer's attitude. The location that refers to Mr. Telfer's attitude is easier to state in situational than in behavioral terms since his behavior is part of the work situation. Nevertheless an examination of the two types of statements is of interest for comparison. The behavioral statement Mr. Telfer might use is: I feel somewhat disturbed when I find you using the phone for personal purposes. What are you willing to do to adjust to this attitude of mine? A situational statement might be: What would be a fair attitude for me to take regarding personal calls during working hours?

Location—the attitude of Telfer's superior. Telfer's boss is also part of the work situation. Since he asked Mr. Telfer to do something about the "abuses," he, in a sense, created the problem. A behavioral statement of this problem to the group might be: My boss has complained about the use of phones for personal purposes. What can we do to make ourselves less subject to his criticism? The situational approach might be: My boss has difficulty in reaching this office. Is there any way in which we can plan our work so as to make this unit more available to him?

Location—adequate telephone service. The location having to do with the proper number of lines is clearly in the work situation. Asking: How many lines do we need to satisfy our needs or to render the kind of service we should give? suggests increasing the number of lines. In this instance it is difficult to state a good problem in either situational or behavioral terms. As a matter of fact, when the problem is thus located, it probably falls in the *area of freedom* of a higher level of management. The problem would then be limited to what to recommend.

Location—efficient use of phones. Locating the problem as one of making the most efficient use of present lines places the problem clearly within the area of freedom of the supervisor. Perhaps, in some instances, it would be desirable to increase the number of lines, but such a possibility is excluded by this location of the problem. If this location of the problem were to be stated in behavioral terms it might be put as follows: How can we use our present lines more efficiently? Note that this statement arouses only a limited amount of defensiveness since it avoids the hint of abuses and instead points in the direction of service. Nevertheless a situational statement such as: How can the job be organized to get the most service out of our single line? is a distinct improvement.

Location—better service. Finally, the location of the problem in the area of better answering service quite obviously stresses the situation, but the location is rather a general one. Instead of dealing with the time spent on the telephone (either for personal or business reasons), the discussion it arouses might include ways of responding, how to be more pleasant, how to handle unreasonable requests, etc.

A general location of a problem may fail to solve the specific problem the supervisor has in mind, and it therefore behooves him to be discreet in his selection of a location.

The possibility should not be overlooked, however, that sometimes when the group solves the larger problem more may be accomplished than when they solve the specific problem the supervisor may initially have had in mind. Perhaps an improvement in service would accomplish more than the elimination of personal calls. Perhaps an awareness of responsibility for service would cause a reduction or better timing of personal calls without the latter problem ever being mentioned.

Recognizing that the answering service is a more general location, how can it be stated? The behavioral situation might be: How can we do a better job in giving service to the persons requesting information? while a situational statement might be: What kind of a service index might we establish for our unit? Again it seems apparent that the behavioral statement is preferable.

Selection of a statement that the leader can accept. The fourteen statements of the problem discussed above are sufficiently different to cause the initial part of the discussion at least to vary in effectiveness. Under skilled leadership a poor beginning can be salvaged, but this means that some new problems must also be solved. Every discussion may begin with a problem, but if misunderstandings occur, these become new problems that serve as distractions. Defensive behavior is an example of such a distraction that may enter into a problem-solving discussion. When group members become too concerned with protecting themselves to solve the problem presented, the discussion leader either may in turn become defensive or he may lose his confidence in the group's ability. There is a danger, therefore, that a poor start in a discussion may cause the interaction to go from bad to worse rather than lead to a correction of the misunderstanding.

In general it will be apparent that the behavioral statements are more likely to arouse defensive behavior than the situational statements. This differentiation then becomes the first step in selecting a statement of a problem even though the best of the behavioral statements sometimes may be better than poor situational ones.

The seven behavioral statements are by no means of equal value. It might be found that certain locations of the problem are difficult to state in behavioral terms, while other locations are inconsistent with the views of the discussion leader. In preparing himself for the discussion, the leader may wish to develop several behavioral statements so that he has a greater opportunity for selection. He must then examine the alternatives from the point of view of selecting one which is most likely to lead to a solution to the problem that concerns him. If service is improved without a reduction in personal calls, has the supervisor's problem been solved? This is a decision that only he can make.

It is apparent, therefore, that the selection of the statement to be used will be a function of the viewpoint of the supervisor. An examination of statements of the problem in various locations will aid him in making a selection and bring his primary problem into focus. He may discover either that he has a solution in mind (reducing personal calls) and has been attempting to state a solution rather than a problem or that he has two problems from which a selection should be made. It is important that he find a statement that he can accept; otherwise he will find himself in the position of attempting to influence the discussion. Anything he does to approve or disapprove ideas or opinions expressed will be taken as an attempt to influence the outcome. This unfavorable group reaction merely emphasizes the fact that a discussion leader's tendency to evaluate ideas conflicts with his skill in accepting and understanding contributions from the group. Thus, if he selects a problem that he can emotionally approve, his skill in handling a discussion will be greater because he will be a more acceptant and patient leader.

THE STATEMENT OF A PROBLEM SHOULD ENCOURAGE FREEDOM OF THOUGHT (PRINCIPLE 2)

When a person has spent a good deal of time thinking about a problem, his thoughts tend to move in a particular direction, and invariably certain solutions suggest themselves. It is difficult, therefore, not to hint at these solutions when presenting the problem to a group, in the hope that this will give them the benefit of his thinking. However, this practice interferes with free thinking, and the ideas expressed are inclined to be reactions to the suggestions made by the leader.

One type of group response to such suggestions is to accept them. A conference leader who offers his own ideas for solving a problem may find that he does all of the thinking for the group and that they assume little or no responsibility. This often occurs in middle management where subordinates fear that their ideas will meet with unfavorable reactions from their superiors. A conference leader who likes to reveal his own ideas and who regards ideas differing from his own as a threat tends to develop yes-men. His subordinates learn not to place him on the defensive and instead praise his ideas.

The other type of reaction, when a superior suggests a solution, is to criticize it. If this is the only solution suggested, then the process of evaluation is confined to accepting or rejecting the solution. A common first reaction to an idea (particularly if it is new) is a negative one—people look for its possible weaknesses. Thus a conference leader who merely hints at a possible remedy may find that all members of a group oppose it, and invariably this places him on the defensive.

Since neither of the alternatives is a happy one, the best preventive is to avoid suggesting a solution and to leave the problem situation as free as possible. There are many ways to reach an objective, and the starting point is richest in these possibilities. Figure 4 illustrates this point diagrammatically.

From this analysis it follows that in stating a problem it is well for the conference leader to back away from the direction his thinking has taken him and to ask himself what there is about the problem that concerns him. Does he want to reduce accidents or violations of safety practices; increase production or get more work out of certain individuals; increase job interest or reduce absenteeism; increase responsibility or decrease irresponsibility? Note that each of these pairs of alternatives overlaps in their objectives, but the second member of each pair is more restrictive and represents a step toward a particular kind of solution which the first alternative suggests. It is apparent that the first

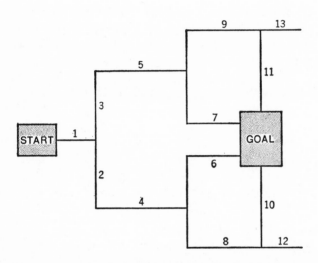

Fig. 4. Solution possibilities in relation to the goal. The above diagram shows four solutions to a problem, represented by routes leading from the starting point to the goal. Note that if one travels route 1-3-5-9, the only opportunity for reaching the goal is to choose path 11 rather than path 13. If a person retreats to path 5 he can reach the goal by traveling by paths 7 or 9. However, if a person retreats to the starting point, four solutions become possible. These solutions become quite different as illustrated by the fact that the number of common paths change (the change from odd-numbered to even-numbered paths).

The reader will recognize that complex problems are often solved not by persisting in pursuing a path, but by making an entirely new start. Solution possibilities are richest if one returns to the starting point of the problem. However, this is difficult to do because once one experiences progress along the path toward a goal, it is difficult to give up the gains and start over. Nevertheless, it is apparent that the best solution can be found only with a thorough exploration of many and different possibilities. (*Modified from N. R. F. Maier, The Appraisal Interview, 1958, New York, John Wiley & Sons, Inc., p.* 196.)

member of each pair also encourages the greater freedom for thought.

The effect of freedom of action on problem solving was demonstrated by some experimental work of Epstein.[2] He gave the same management problem to groups of students under the following conditions:

1. Clear authority   with   large area of freedom
2. Clear authority   with   small area of freedom
3. Vague authority   with   large area of freedom
4. Vague authority   with   small area of freedom

It was found that the quality of solutions, measured in terms of cost and workability, was greatest for condition 1 and worst for condition 4, while conditions 2 and 3 were about equal and intermediate between conditions 1 and 4.

It appeared that when the authority was vague, people played safe and restricted their thinking, so that vague authority had an effect similar to limited authority. When delegation was *clear* and freedom *large* (Solve the problem in the way that seems best, and I'll back you up), more ideas were considered, and less money was needed to solve the problem. However, when delegation was *vague* and *limited* (I'll accept the solution if it's a good one and doesn't cost too much), few ideas were engendered, and the thinking tended to be restricted and unimaginative.

A large and clear-cut area of freedom stimulates problem solvers to explore a greater variety of directions, and even though some of the ideas suggested are impractical, these can be eliminated later on when a selection is made from the various ideas presented. The important thing is to stimulate exploration rather than impose limitations during the initial phases of the problem-solving discussion.

[2] S. Epstein, An Experimental Study of Some of the Effects of Variations in the Clarity and Extent of a Supervisor's Area of Freedom upon His Supervisory Behavior. Doctoral Dissertation, University of Michigan, Ann Arbor, Mich., 1956.

THE STATEMENT OF A PROBLEM SHOULD
INCORPORATE MUTUAL INTERESTS (PRINCIPLE 3)

Company goals and personal goals. The effectiveness of a problem-solving discussion is influenced by the amount of interest the problem arouses. For example, the elimination of personal calls made on company telephones is not usually of interest to a group. On some occasions certain individuals in the group may feel that others are taking advantage of a situation, and they would like to correct it, but this would be a personal rather than a group interest. Finding an interest in the group that is consistent not only with that of the supervisor but with that of the company is essential to cooperation.

It is apparent that problems that do not fall within the comprehension of the group involved are not of interest to them. Only higher levels of management would be interested in problems such as (1) where to raise capital, (2) matters of overall company policy, (3) which markets to emphasize, (4) what price to charge for a product, etc. Note that all of these problems fall outside the area of freedom of lower levels of management and rank-and-file employees and for this reason are not appropriate problems for group decision at those levels. It is fortunate that problems that fail to fall in the area of freedom of the immediate supervisor are least likely to have strong interest value.

In contrast, problems such as (1) who gets a particular office or desk, (2) desirable vacation schedules, (3) fair distribution of work load, (4) whom to transfer to other locations, etc., are understood by the subordinates of lower levels of management and are of interest to them. The solutions to these problems are usually in the immediate superior's area of freedom, and, if not, the possibility of placing them in his area of freedom should be seriously considered by higher management. Increased delegation would permit more flexibility in problem solving at lower levels.

Problems that concern the employees' immediate surroundings invariably are of interest to them. It is this work environment that contains many of the incentives that satisfy men's personal needs. Such factors as status, fairness, recognition, group acceptance, experience of progress, and experience of success or failure come under this heading. These needs may or may not conflict with company objectives. In so far as they harmonize, a mutual interest can be established. Satisfactory statements of problems that harmonize personal and company objectives are one aspect of the operation of the principle of stating problems in terms of mutual interest.

The other aspect of mutual interest is to state problems in such a manner that they will appeal to the interests of all participants. The personal needs and interests of various members of a group may be in conflict. For example, questions like, Who gets a desired promotion? Whose budget should be cut? Which job should be eliminated? arouse personal interests which are in conflict with each other. Posing these problems in terms of fairness makes for group interest.

Comparison of statements varying in interest value. Examples of various statements of basically the same problem will clarify some of the skill points in the application of the principle of stating problems in terms of mutual interest. Returning to our problem of personal telephone calls let us select the location "efficient use of present lines." In presenting this problem in situational terms, the statement used in our illustration was: How can the job be organized to get the most service out of our single line? This statement may be given against three quite different backgrounds with respect to mutual interest.

For example, one might preface the statement of the problem by pointing out that the company wishes to cut costs without sacrificing service. This approach clearly lessens the interest of the group because it requires that employees be interested in the company objective.

A second approach might be something like the following: "Some of you are more efficient than others in handling the phones. This suggests that we are not getting the most out of our present facilities." Following this explanation the problem might be stated. Note how this preface to the statement of the problem tends to place the interests of the group in conflict with each other.

Finally, the problem might be stated against a background such as: Let us take a look at the problems we have in covering our jobs. This approach arouses mutual interest because most groups would like to solve their problems and the company can reasonably have the same interest. Posing a problem in such a manner that there is no apparent or obvious solution also arouses interest since it serves as a challenge. The general interest people have in working with puzzles is an example of the type of motivation that thought-provoking questions arouse.

Lack of interest often indicates the existence of some fear. Improving production can be an interesting problem if the fear that this could lead to layoffs, rate cuts, or unreasonable work pressures does not exist. Keeping records or measuring production would have the same value as keeping score in a game, if the fear of being penalized for a poor record were not present. Competition has interest value if it does not lead to unpleasantness. Golf clubs often use handicap methods of keeping scores in order to give everyone a better chance of winning. Competing under these conditions increases the interest of the game, both for persons of high and low ability, and losing is neither a disgrace nor a threat.

To suppose that people have only selfish motives is to overlook the many sources of satisfaction that work can offer if negative factors are removed. Thus, statements of problems in terms of goals for production, quality, tardiness, accidents, absenteeism, etc., can have interest value providing the group feels that this will not lead to the loss of certain other important goals such as comfort, security, freedom, etc. Furthermore, group participation offers superior performers an opportunity to gain prestige in a group since they can contribute to the group's performance. In most supervisory conditions the superior performer is a threat to the less gifted and so becomes an undesirable group member. Thus superior persons are motivated by group pressure to restrict their productivity.[3]

An illustration of how superior performers are motivated to help the less gifted was demonstrated experimentally by Hoffman and Maier.[4] College students had worked together in groups of four in a laboratory course over a period of a semester. At the end of the period each group was given nineteen points to divide, with the understanding that these points would be added to their individual scores and raise their grades in the course. If, however, the group failed to agree on a satisfactory distribution of points, each person would automatically receive four points. Thus no one had to take fewer than four points. The findings of special interest for the present discussion are as follows:

1. No group failed to reach unanimous agreement.

2. The distribution of points per individual ranged from zero to nineteen.

3. Persons most satisfied were the ones receiving the fewest points, followed by those receiving the most. Lowest satisfaction occurred when participants received approximately equal numbers of points.

4. The guiding principle in the distribution of points was that of helping the neediest. Students with poor grades were invariably being helped by students with above-average grades.

A teacher could not assign points in this fashion without having the superior students complain; similarly, a foreman could not ask a good worker to help out a weak one. However, the superior worker might be glad to help his less-gifted partner if this were his decision to make.

In setting goals it is desirable to strive for specific and

[3] N. R. F. Maier, *Psychology in Industry.* Houghton Mifflin Company, Boston, 1955.

[4] L. R. Hoffman and N. R. F. Maier, The Use of Group Decision to Resolve a Problem of Fairness. *Personnel Psychol.,* 1959, **12**, 545–559.

measurable targets. Experiences of success and failure are dependent upon the relationship between what a person expects to accomplish and his actual accomplishment.[5] People exert themselves to reach the scores they set for themselves because such scores are fair. Reaching such a goal promotes the experience of success and hence gives the group the opportunity to experience job satisfaction. Since setting specific and measurable objectives also is of interest to management, setting goals raises problems of mutual interest.

Mutual interests in higher management. Problems in middle management are less likely to be thought of as having conflicting interests than those involving nonmanagement employees. It is generally assumed that everyone in management is motivated by company goals, but it is possible that the extent of this mutual interest has been exaggerated. Sales and production executives are frequently in conflict with each other, each believing that the importance of his department is underestimated by the other. As a consequence each feels that company objectives should be more consistent with the objectives of his department.

A discussion of budget cuts would soon reveal that the various departments did not agree on where the major cuts should be made. The various departmental objectives would thus be in conflict, and hence all could not be in harmony with the company objective. The formulation of problems in terms of mutual interests would tend to resolve some of these conflicts.

THE STATEMENT OF A PROBLEM SHOULD SPECIFY ONE OBJECTIVE (PRINCIPLE 4)

The solution of a problem may accomplish a variety of objectives. In achieving these values a number of undesirable things also may be accomplished and certain risks may be taken as well. In order to evaluate a particular solution it must be examined, therefore, from the point of view of

[5] F. Hoppe, Erfolg und Misserfolg. *Psychol. Forsch.*, 1930, **14**, 1–62.

what it gains and what it loses. The initial purpose of a solution is to achieve a particular objective while the incidental gains and losses may be regarded as positive and negative by-products. If several solutions achieve the same initial objective, they may then be compared in terms of these by-products.

In order not to confuse by-products with the original objective, it is essential that the statement of a problem specify this objective as the desired goal. Only solutions that achieve this objective can be considered to be solutions to the problem under consideration. For example, an executive appraisal program may be adopted as a method for developing subordinates. This program requires all superiors to evaluate their subordinates, after which each is interviewed to discuss a program of improvement. One of the hoped-for positive by-products of this plan is that it lets employees know where they stand, while one of the too frequent negative by-products is that it causes subordinates to become reluctant to discuss their problems with their superior since they fear that he will judge them unfavorably. If the original objective is to develop subordinates, this purpose might be accomplished without the superior making an appraisal, and if the appraisal were omitted, the by-products would change. In other words, an employee might be developed if a superior (1) involved him in some of the decision making, (2) increased his responsibility, (3) improved upward communication, (4) placed him in an executive development program, or (5) just discussed job problems with him without mentioning an appraisal.

Another illustration is the wide use of suggestion plans. Many companies have adopted an employee suggestion plan, and both positive and negative results are claimed by adherents and opponents. But what was the initial objective of this program? Was it to get ideas from employees or to stimulate employee interest in company problems? Alternate solutions to these two objectives would differ greatly. It would seem that many companies have adopted a suggestion plan more because they have imitated other companies than because they had a clear-cut objective to start with. For the purpose of problem solving it is desirable to distinguish between solutions which are accepted because of the total negative and positive accomplishments and solutions which are developed to solve a particular problem.

In order to evaluate solutions of the latter type it is essential to know the initial objective so that they can be compared with reference to the efficiency with which this objective is achieved and also with reference to both positive and negative by-products. The negative by-products include not only the costs of implementing the solution but also the new problems that each solution may create.

If this analysis is accepted, it follows that problem solving should begin by having the major objective clearly stated so that all solutions under consideration can be compared with the same standard in mind. This means that the conference leader should focus on this objective and for the time being forget about the by-products that certain solutions introduce. If he fails to do this, he will find himself in the position of trying to *sell* a particular solution, and this activity is in conflict with having subordinates share in the solving of a problem.

THE STATEMENT OF A PROBLEM SHOULD BE BRIEF (PRINCIPLE 5)

Generally speaking, conference leaders spend too much time introducing a problem before they invite discussion. There seems to be a reluctance to share a problem without attempting to exclude unsatisfactory solutions. Long introductions tend to depress discussion and to convey the impression that the leader is manipulating the thinking or selling his point of view. The evaluative process which often concerns him should come later in the discussion and should not prevent the exploration of various ideas.

Long introductions also permit more misunderstanding

regarding what the problem actually is. If a problem is clearly in focus in the superior's mind, it should not require a long introduction since immediate subordinates are sufficiently close to the situation to understand the issues involved.

Frequently a conference leader states a problem and gets no immediate response. He then feels compelled to make further statements. In restating the problem the emphasis may be changed, or a different problem may be suggested. A new source of confusion is introduced because the subordinates are required to listen and to think of ideas at the same time. If the conference leader is willing to wait for responses after the initial statement of a problem, he will find that participation greatly improves. The first pause is difficult to wait out, but this pause allows thinking and puts responsibility for participating on group members. If his statement is unclear, participants will ask questions. The leader's response to these questions should be such as to clarify the problem, not to offer suggestions. If group members ask the leader to express his views on the matter, he should avoid supplying his views and state that he wants the benefit of the group's thinking. Questions are frequently used to test the conference leader's sincerity, and he should not fall into the trap of selling his own ideas on how the problem should be solved.

If every conference leader could pause twice as long as he is inclined to do after stating a problem, he would find that the resulting participation he obtains will materially improve. Thus the first skill in getting reactions to a statement of a problem is the ability to pause and wait for the group to respond. It only takes one response to break the silence. Pausing is a difficult skill, and if a leader remembers that the pause not only is difficult for him, but also for the group to withstand, his task is made easier. A pause puts pressure on everyone, and it should be used for increasing participation and thinking.

SHARING ESSENTIAL INFORMATION
(PRINCIPLE 6)

Closely associated with the statement of a problem is the sharing of information. Facts in a leader's possession give him an advantage, and he should share his knowledge as well as furnish situational details. If new equipment is not available, if decisions have to be made within a certain budget, if a higher level of management has set certain limits on the area of freedom—these are forms of information that influence the choice of a decision. A proper presentation of these facts can place the problem within the group's authority to act.

However, the presentation of certain facts should not be confused with attempts to influence the decision. The fact that costs have to be cut—or how much they should be cut —does not prevent problem solving on how they should be cut. The important thing is to supply information without interpreting it or suggesting how the information is to be used.

Persons in possession of knowledge often feel compelled to suggest solutions because they rightfully feel that they have an advantage. In sharing this knowledge with a group of subordinates, however, one increases their problem-solving competence. As a matter of fact, various subordinates also may have personal knowledge about the job, even though each may possess less complete knowledge than the superior. It is in the pooling of information and experiences that much is to be gained in group problem solving.

The process of supplying and posting information will vary greatly with the problem. In some instances no information need be supplied at the outset. Usually more background facts are supplied by a conference leader than is necessary. When this is done, it may (1) exceed the amount of information that can be digested at the outset, (2) give the impression of attempting to influence the acceptance of a preconceived solution, or (3) make subordinates feel that the superior is talking down to them. If discussion is to be full and unrestrained, the objective should be to get into group interaction as quickly as possible. If a problem and its relevant facts cannot be supplied within the first five minutes, serious thought should be given to attempting a revised approach. *It should be remembered that additional information and facts can be supplied after the discussion has begun.*

Facts and the interpretation of facts should be clearly distinguished. For example, accident figures may be supplied without using such expressions as "too many," "something has to be done," "some locations seem to be doing better than others," etc. Facts by themselves are neither good nor bad—it is in their interpretation that such values are introduced. Because the same facts usually permit a variety of interpretations, they frequently become the center of disagreement. Facts in themselves are seldom threatening, and they are of mutual interest when they become the subject for problem solving. Although facts delimit the conditions for problem solving, these restrictions are generally acceptable and stand in contrast to restrictions created by an authority, which are generally resented. Usually, imposed restrictions are based upon interpretations of facts rather than the facts themselves. It is not uncommon for leaders to make up facts to reject the solution that threaten one they have in mind.

SUMMARY AND CONCLUSIONS

Before a superior presents a problem to his subordinates, it is important that he examine the limits of his right to take action. If he is unsure of his delegated authority, he may wish to check with his own superior. Remembering that vague delegation (see page 86) makes a discussion leader overcautious, it is well for him to have a clear picture of his area of freedom.

A leader can supply information to communicate that there are limits to his authority. This kind of limitation does not depress problem solving. Reasonable obstacles act as hurdles and can be challenging to the group unless they are seen as arbitrary—which means they are seen as someone else's way of controlling the outcome.

Once the area of freedom has been examined, the next step is to see that the problem statement does not suggest a solution. In the event that there is difficulty in separating the problem from a desired solution, the superior might ask himself why he thinks he has a problem. Why reduce personal telephone calls, tardiness, or absenteeism? If there is a desire to reduce them, there must be a reason. This approach often brings several problems into focus: need for discipline, preventing widespread abuses, improved production, better service, etc. From these, one must be selected, and it should be one clear-cut objective.

The principles of stating the problem in situational terms and in such a manner that a mutual interest is aroused now can be applied. A variety of statements should be examined so that an effective one can be selected. Once a selection has been made, the question of an efficient and brief presentation should be considered. The initial introduction need not be a complete coverage of relevant background. Further elaboration of facts, areas of freedom, company policy, etc., may be introduced as the need arises.

CHAPTER FIVE

Conducting the discussion

TWO BASIC TYPES OF DISCUSSION

All discussions may be analyzed in terms of the extent to which emotions or feelings determine the behavior and the extent to which intellectual considerations are the determiners. These are the two dimensions of a human being's thought processes—the feeling content and the intellectual content. The logic of feeling and the logic of the mind are distinctly different; for this reason attempts to influence feeling by intellectual considerations are ineffective, while attempts to solve intellectual problems by wishful and emotional thinking likewise lead to failures.

The basic difference in these two classes of behavior was demonstrated in a series of studies on frustration.[1] A

[1] N. R. F. Maier, *Frustration: The Study of Behavior without a Goal.* McGraw-Hill Book Company, Inc., New York, 1949. Reissued by The University of Michigan Press, Ann Arbor, Mich., 1961.

problem situation may give rise to problem-solving behavior, which is characterized by the exploration of ways to overcome an obstacle and reach a goal, or it can give rise to behavior which is characterized by hostility (aggression), childishness (regression), and stubbornness (fixation). Which of these two types of behavior occurs depends upon how easily an individual is frustrated and upon the difficulty of the problem. This means that a given individual when placed in a problem situation may initially approach it by trying to overcome obstacles, but with repeated failures and with an inability to escape from the situation, he may become frustrated. If this occurs, he may become angry and abusive, blame others for his failures, or become rigid and repeat the same activities that have failed to solve the problem. These nonconstructive activities are in sharp contrast to problem-solving activity in which various ideas are considered and evaluated in terms of how effectively they deal with the objective facts in the situation.

A problem-solving approach is one in which the person deals with realistic and factual matters, and the concern is with what can be done to correct a fault or overcome a difficulty. However, when a problem situation arouses hostility, causes the person to blame others, feel sorry for himself, or to engage in emotional behavior unrelated to correcting the situation, it is evident that the problem has produced a state of frustration and that this condition has replaced the problem-solving activity. Since problem-solving behavior and frustrated behavior are in sharp contrast with each other, it is not too difficult to detect which of the conditions is dominating the individual or the group.

The first step in conducting a discussion is to determine the state of mind of the conferees. Because the methods for dealing with feelings and intellectual behavior are so different, a successful conference leader must make this diagnosis of his group his first skill in developing proficiency in discussion leadership.

Since problem solving cannot proceed effectually until the emotional aspects have been dealt with, it is wise to play safe and explore and respect the attitudes that may be present in the group. This means that the discussion leader should obtain a broad sample of reactions and recognize that a logical statement or argument might be a person's rationalization for the feelings and attitudes that really determine whether he is for or against something. Generally speaking, feelings and attitudes are not acceptable to others and are regarded as signs of immaturity or indications of emotional bias. Since childhood, people are trained to hide unfriendly feelings so they learn to justify them intellectually. When a child tells his mother that he hates his father, he is told that this is bad and soon finds himself confronted with a lecture proving that the father is someone to love. The child learns either to keep such feelings to himself or to develop a counterargument designed to prove that the father is evil. He may even manufacture facts to support his position. Thus our whole training background leads us to suppress certain feelings or to couch them in some acceptable intellectual framework.

As long as the true nature of a person's viewpoint is unknown, problem-solving activity cannot proceed, since the feelings and views remain unchanged because they are isolated by protective walls. This means that feelings and attitudes must be dealt with for what they are. Criticism suppresses them and builds up tensions; acceptance and understanding encourage their expression and reduce tensions.

DETERMINING THE APPROPRIATE TYPE OF DISCUSSION

In order to familiarize the reader with the problem of diagnosing a group's state of mind, it is best to proceed with a case study. The case of the Change of Work Procedure, which was discussed in Chapter 2, serves this purpose. This case study has been role-played many times and serves as a rich supply of typical reactions in a group discussion.

It will be recalled that the discussion dealt with the

problem of getting workers to accept a change in work methods. The situation involved a foreman and a three-man team of workers who assembled fuel pumps. In order to have a little variety in their work, the men had adopted a system of rotating their job positions hourly so that each man performed each of the three operations in turn.

The foreman was given some private information supplied by the time-study man. This information revealed that each man performed best at one of the positions, and this suggested that a saving would occur if each man remained in a fixed position. Since the men worked on a team piece-rate basis, they, as well as the company, would profit from increased production.

The three workers' roles were so structured that they experience boredom, resent time study, and fear speed-up tactics. Thus their frame of reference tends to conflict with that of the foreman.

As in all attempts to introduce change, the workers in this case resist the foreman's suggestion of abandoning the old work pattern and adopting the new. This resistance reveals itself in three ways: hostility, fear, and situational obstacles.

1. Hostility toward time study and the time-study man, Jim Clark, is expressed by accusing Clark of spying on them, questioning the accuracy of time-study methods, blaming the company for speed-up tactics, pointing out that the work sample is poor since they change their work pace from time to time, saying the company is trying to expose someone and break up the group, etc. The manner of expression and the use of uncomplimentary adjectives clearly reveal the presence of emotion.

2. Fear of the consequences of the change are apparent from statements about the company attempting to cut rates, reduce the number of workers, and get more work out of the men by trickery. The fact that the men refer to the technological unemployment of many years ago, make accusations that are inconsistent with their own work experience in the company, and question the foreman's good faith reveals un-

reasonableness and suspicion. Distrust and suspicion are matters of feeling, and when they are more extreme than the
situation warrants, it is apparent that feelings rather than
facts are influencing the resistance.

3. Monotony and boredom may be the first expression of
resistance, and it will be noted that this reaction may be a
logical consequence of the new method of work. This type of
argument makes reference to the situation and has a foundation in fact. Because it is a factual argument, it is the safest
one for the workers to put forward. However, even in this
instance, the feelings may reveal themselves by the way the
boredom is exaggerated.

These same types of reactions, as well as others, are
obtained in real life situations when attempts are made by
management to introduce change, and they occur in connection with this case when it is role-played. It is evident that
only a small part of the above reactions would be sufficient to
permit a discussion leader to conclude that the group was not
ready to willingly accept a change in work methods. His cue
would be the presence of feelings of hostility and fear, not
the soundness of the arguments raised against change. As
long as such feelings are present, the group is not ready to
respect facts or to cooperate in solving a work problem.

PROCEDURE FOR DEALING WITH FEELINGS IN A DISCUSSION

The procedures for dealing with feelings are primarily
those that are effective in counseling situations. An emotionally disturbed person has many pent-up feelings which
stand in the way of problem solving. Hence one of the basic
principles for dealing with feelings is to help the person to
express them in harmless ways. Ordinarily, the expression of
childish or hostile behavior gets a person into trouble. Other
people react to such behavior by striking back or by rejecting
the person and in this way aggravate the already disturbed
condition. Harmless channels for expressing such feeling prevent this reaction.

The second way in which a person can be helped is to give him whatever assurance or security one is able to offer. Assurance must not be confused with pitying or agreeing with a person.

Let us now examine in detail the methods for giving assurance and for assisting others to outwardly express their feelings. These two kinds of assistance are independent of each other and may be offered at any stage of the discussion, depending on the need.

Giving assurance. When management wishes to introduce change, it is common for subordinates to feel threatened. Under the existing work condition each person knows pretty well how he stands in relation to other members of his group. He knows roughly how his skills compare with others, the extent of his influence, the degree to which his associates and his superiors accept him, the demands that are made upon him, and the ways in which he may improve. A job change disturbs this state of affairs. Will his relative skills be altered, will he have to work with different associates, will he be expected to do more, will he be placed in an unfavorable position promotion-wise or socially, and can he learn the new methods as readily as others? These and other questions arise.

If management initiates the change, it is apparent to workers that the change is intended to benefit management. A gain for management may represent a loss for the workers. It is possible that everyone can profit from a change, but this mutual gain is questioned, particularly when there is a lack of trust between labor and management. Loyal employees, therefore, are threatened less by a change than are employees who lack faith in management.

Assurance in the Change of Work Procedure case might take the form of guaranteeing the men that there will be no layoffs and reduction in the piece rate. A foreman who has been given the authority to make such guarantees will have a much easier time than one who lacks either the authority or the confidence in management's motives to speak for management.

In giving assurance, a leader should not make idle promises that all will go well, that there is nothing to fear. Assurance must be realistic to be sincere. If a discussion leader entertains the possibility that the company may have overlooked something, indicates that all sides of a question are to be explored, and clarifies the purpose of the change, he helps reduce the threat of a change. The mere willingness to explore objections and to entertain alternate ideas increases a group's security.

The importance of a company's willingness to consider the possibility that a mistake had been made rather than to become defensive may be illustrated by an incident that occurred in Cleveland, Ohio. The company in question had built a modern plant in which working conditions were unquestionably improved. Since the move also involved a change in the flow of work, new standards had to be worked out by the time-study department. This restudy was agreed to by the union.

After the move, production on these lines was extremely disappointing. The initial failure to reach standard was attributed to adjustments to the move, but when it remained in the vicinity of 50 per cent of standard for a month, it was viewed as a serious problem. Since the company needed the output, it continued to add new employees until it became too crowded to work. The best that was accomplished was 57 per cent of standard.

Naturally tension began to rise. Pressure was put on foremen, and the union committee complained to the personnel director. Finally a meeting was held which was attended by four superintendents, the personnel director, the time-study director, and the works manager, as well as the author, who was in the position of a consultant. There was little agreement on the cause of the difficulty, and, as might be expected in a tense situation that had lasted for two months, everyone had already done something that was open to criticism. After various conflicting views had been aired for a period of more than an hour, the consultant asked whether there was a possibility that an error had been made in the time study, as charged by the union. The reply from the time-study director was to the effect that there was the possibility of a small error, perhaps 10 per cent, but that this applied to only half of the work group involved. The consultant's response was "Good—now would you be willing to check the error in the time study?" This he agreed to also. Next the consultant asked, "Would you be willing to make the correction if you found an error, even if it were a small unimportant one?" This corrective procedure was agreed to by all attending, but none felt that the problem would be solved since most of the participants believed that the main trouble was due to the conflict between foremen and workers.

Nevertheless the time-study department rechecked the work and found a 9 per cent error that applied to half of the workers in the department. When this error was admitted by the company and corrected, it resulted in an immediate improvement. The weekly production of the work group where the error applied rose from 54 to 88 per cent of standard (an improvement of 34 percentage points), and the production of the group for which the error did not apply rose from 58 to 83 per cent (an improvement of 25 percentage points). It appears that there was an improvement of 25 percentage points for the willingness to correct the error and a change of 9 percentage points for the removal of the error.

From this analysis it would appear that it might be worth while to consider making corrective changes under such conditions even when no error actually has been made. Failure to give ground and stand on facts constitutes threat, whereas willingness to consider the possibilities of finding a more agreeable solution reduces tension and makes all concerned more willing to face realities.

The best way to give assurance is to let employees know that they need not accept a change. Insisting on a change is most threatening. Sincerely presenting a suggested change as a choice reduces the threat, while supplying information that raises the *possibility* that some kind of change *might* lead to an improvement is least threatening, particularly if there is an opportunity to consider a variety of possible changes.

To illustrate this approach, let us consider further the Change of Work Procedure case study. The facts given to the foreman indicated that each worker has a different degree of skill in the three positions. This information suggests the possibility that there is room for improving the work pattern. Informing workers that time study indicated that each man should work only on his best position is likely to be resisted. It specifies how the information is to be used, and if the new method is disliked, the facts on which the method is based will also be disliked. With this approach, interest in the facts supplied is at a minimum, and they may even be questioned. However, if the men are told that the time-study data do not have to be used, they are more inclined to want to see the evidence. Removal of the threat, therefore, makes for greater interest in objective facts. In this instance, the foreman has the greatest degree of success if he tells the men that the time-study department lacks the authority to impose the change and that a different method will be introduced only if the men are willing to accept it. This leaves the men free to consider acceptable ways to utilize the new information.

If the leader suggests trial periods or the possibility of experimenting with different work methods, he also reduces the threat of change. In contrast, if he shows a strong desire to get the men to accept a particular change, he increases the threat of the new method.

It is possible to generalize this permissive approach by saying that threat increases as the leader insists on change and decreases as he sincerely makes change a free choice. It becomes clear that a foreman who is assigned the task of *selling* a change to his men is handicapped. A foreman with some more freedom of choice is in a better position to get an improvement considered, and even if he cannot get the whole change accepted, he might obtain a compromise or a willingness to try out several possible methods. It will be recalled that a number of alternate solutions were available. Foremen who have larger areas of freedom, therefore, have an easier task and can accomplish more than foremen whose decision-making freedom is unduly restricted.

Sometimes the foreman is bypassed and changes are introduced arbitrarily from above. The reason for this action is primarily a lack of faith in the foreman's ability to sell the change. Enforced changes, of course, are the most threatening to workers, and even when they do not lead to work stoppages, the result is a minimum acceptance of change. In failing to delegate sufficient problem-solving freedom to subordinates, higher management decreases the opportunities for gaining the acceptance of decisions at lower echelons.

Releasing expression of feeling in harmless channels. When a superior evaluates his subordinates, disagrees with their ideas, or appears surprised by their opinions, he unwittingly encourages them to be cautious of what they say, to suppress their feelings, or to be prepared to supply intellectual support for any ideas or thoughts they express. The origins of certain feelings often are unknown, and even when the reason is known, it is likely to be due to an experience that cannot be intellectually defended. A critical attitude on the part of a superior, therefore, tends to discourage subordinates from freely expressing their true feelings. When frustrations are expressed because the person is unable to restrain himself, harmful consequences often occur because other people strike back. Thus unrestrained expression, instead of bringing relief, leads to further frustration and an increase in the very condition that caused the outburst. The expression of feeling, in such instances, backfires and aggravates the condition that caused it. The opportunity to freely express frustration-induced behavior has a therapeutic value when it is accepted by the listener. This simple process of gaining relief through expression is known as "catharsis." The exact reason for the reduction in tensions and in the state of frustration is not fully understood, but the value achieved is generally recognized. Actually the therapeutic value of catharsis is hard to explain when one follows the usual line of logic or reason.

It appears that feelings are misunderstood largely because they have been approached from an intellectual point of view. This is not surprising since man's intellect dominates his scholarly pursuits. If, however, the logic of feeling is different from the logic of the mind, it follows that what is plausible intellectually may not alter feelings. People cannot make themselves happy by proving with facts that they ought to be happy. A shot of gin may serve the purpose better because it influences the internal organs that contribute to feelings.

For many years therapists have been perplexed by some of the conditions that give emotional relief. They ask such intellectual questions as: Why should a child feel less hostile toward his mother if, in a play therapy situation, he can stick pins into a doll that he calls "mother"? He also feels better toward his mother if he can tear up rags in such a free situation. The explanation seems to be simply that pent-up aggression needs release, and the release need not be directed toward the source of frustration. Children who feel rejected at home are inclined to fight in school, engage in vandalism, and feel hostile toward everything in general. Since these expressions of feeling are not generally acceptable, they tend to be withheld and so they lead to further anxiety and eventual eruption. The simple rule for helping this condition, therefore, is to furnish acceptable opportunities for diverting the expression of hostile and immature behavior into harmless channels. The reader may have experienced the benefit of writing a hostile letter. If he does not mail the letter, he has the benefit of expression without having to suffer any consequences. Frequently the mere writing of the letter removes the desire to mail it. Expression is a form of relief, and it differs from satisfaction which is only reached when the act leads to some accomplishment.

Another reason why expression of feelings restores a more constructive outlook is that the act of expression puts the feeling outside the person where it can be viewed more objectively. A person might say, "That time-study man is out to get us," but once this is said, the statement may be seen as too extreme and be followed with the statement, "But I suppose he's got a job to do." Unexpressed feelings also are vague and when verbalized, they may become clarified. The mere expression of feeling therefore has at least three possible benefits: relief, objectivity, and clarification.

A conference leader is in a good position not only to permit, but to actually encourage the verbal release of hostility, and if he realizes that bitter feelings are modified thereby, his own feelings on the matter are less inclined to be aroused. The essential skill points that a leader may use in facilitating the processes of releasing the expression of feelings may be classified according to the five guiding principles discussed on the following pages.

Sensitivity to guarded expressions of resentment—don't be blinded by concentrating on a line of thought on which you are embarking. Frequently members of a group make a comment loaded with feeling that is ignored by the leader. This often occurs at the beginning of a meeting and may go unnoticed by the leader because he is busy presenting the problem. For example, in the Change of Work Procedure case the foreman may begin by saying, "Jim Clark, the time-study man, has been around making some measures. Some of you men have seen him. Well, he—" At this point Jack may make a comment such as, "I'll say," while the foreman continues to explain the functions of time study. In letting such a loaded expression pass unnoticed, the foreman is implying that he is siding with the time-study man and that the remark is out of order. Later when he asks for opinions about the matter, he may find his question is met with silence and will wonder why he gets so little participation.

This side remark indicates the presence of feelings, and the best time to explore these feelings is when they appear spontaneously. The beginning and the close of every conference frequently offer opportunities to capitalize on such "uncalled for" expressions of feelings.

Introducing long pauses forces expression and the taking of an active part; dominating the talking encourages the group to take a passive role. When a conference leader puts a question to the group, he tends to forget that he has stimulated some thought. As a consequence, the failure to receive an immediate response causes him to state the question differently. Soon he has stated the question in so many ways that participants can't keep up with the changing scene. In the absence of contributions, the leader may become discouraged and supply all the answers. A well-stated question does not have to be repeated, modified, or elaborated. What participants need is an opportunity to think and plan what to say. This means that the first response from a group often comes after a long painful pause. The conference leader who can tolerate a long pause will find that once he gets a response from one person and handles it properly, other members will participate more spontaneously.

Accepting expression of feeling—not rejecting, disagreeing, or arguing. Accepting does not mean agreeing—rather it means that one receives another's feelings or ideas as worthy of attention. The principle of acceptance not only applies to thoughts expressed, but to the individuals as well. The conference leader accepts the participants when he regards them as worthwhile members of the group and important to the success of a venture. In other words, a conference leader shows skill in acceptance when he demonstrates respect for the dignity of his group members as well as for the importance of their feelings and thoughts. Part of the process of acceptance, therefore, is a favorable attitude toward subordinates or participants in a group. The skill requirement is primarily one of inhibiting the thoughts that occur to him. In order to release further expression and full participation, the leader must not interrupt the thought processes of a contributor by commenting on what he is saying.

Instead, remarks such as "I see," "Mmhm," "Yes," and such behaviors as nodding the head, paying attention, and other postures related to listening are acts of acceptance and do not involve interruptions. All of these behaviors add up to *active listening.*

Understanding a participant's thoughts and feelings— not evaluating or acting as a judge. People do not show themselves as they are in front of a judge—rather they try to appear the way they think the judge would have them be if he were to pass favorable judgment. Understanding rather than evaluating is especially difficult because it means that the supervisor, in the role of a conference leader, must avoid an activity which he may feel is essential to his position as a supervisor. However, once it is realized that most of the disagreements and failures to communicate are due to misunderstandings rather than to "bad people," the suppression of the act of passing judgment is not so disturbing.

The reader may recall that frequently his own contributions have been made to appear in a different light than he intended and that often people have given answers to his questions that were not satisfactorily related to what he wished to learn. Small differences in ideas grow into large differences because human beings are inclined to jump to conclusions. Even no difference in views can become a perceived difference because of one person's failure to express himself well or another's failure to listen well.

Semantic problems are only part of the communication failure. An equally large source of difficulty arises from the fact that the speaker talks from a particular background of experience while the listener receives what is said against a different background of experience or even a different mental set.

To illustrate this type of misunderstanding, let us consider the following description of a situation: A man had a window in his garage that was 12 inches high and 12 inches wide. It was too small, so he sawed around it and made the window twice as large. He then measured the window and found it to be 12 inches high and 12 inches wide. If this description doesn't make sense, read it again before passing judgment to see that you have not overlooked something. If a rereading does not clear up matters, you may suspect that there has been a misprint.

However, you are now assured that the description makes sense to the author. Before you judge him as irrational, consider the possibility that you have misunderstood this simple communication.

Perhaps more information about background considerations will help. You have probably visualized the garage window with the base parallel to the ground, the usual way a window is set. This is the background against which you are reading the description. However, the writer wrote the description of the window against a background in which the window has the four angles pointing up, down, right, and left, respectively. Against this background the height and width of the window are diagonals. The way the window is doubled in size by sawing around it is shown in Figure 5.

This type of misunderstanding is not due to a language difficulty, and it is one of the most frequent sources of failure to communicate. One might generalize from this illustration that before one concludes that the person whose statements appear irrational is an irrational person, it may be well to explore the backgrounds from which his statement is made and the background against which it is received.

Some specific skill pointers to assist understanding. In order to better avoid jumping to a false conclusion, certain skills may be helpful. The sequence in which these are listed below is irrelevant, and the combination to be used will have to be adapted to the circumstances. Briefly, these skill points are as follows:

1. Hear a person out, with an attitude of withholding judgment and with a desire to understand.

2. Ask other members of the group if they understand. This will give others the opportunity to elaborate or to ask questions.

3. Question the person who expresses an unusual idea to get him to say more. These questions should not be in the form of a cross-examination so as to expose a lack of knowledge but should be given in a way that will elicit elaboration.

Questions such as the following: "How do you mean that?" "Can you enlarge on that?" "Is that the way other people feel too?" tend to encourage further information which may reveal the background.

4. A comment such as "I'm not sure that I understand" indicates a wish to understand as well as lets the person know that he may use up discussion time. More misunderstandings will occur if the contributor feels that there is not much opportunity to participate.

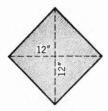 

Before enlargement   After enlargement

Fɪɢ. 5. Windows 12 inches high and 12 inches wide. The claim that a window 12 inches high and 12 inches wide can be doubled in size and still leave it 12 inches high and 12 inches wide seems preposterous at first. However, the window on the left can be enlarged and made into the one on the right. The claim seemed preposterous only because the reader visualized the initial window to be like the one on the right.

5. A request for an illustration is extremely helpful. Comments are frequently of a general nature while an illustration is a specific instance and permits more ready communication. Often one finds an illustration to be quite unrelated to what the contributor said at the outset. In the Change of Work Procedure case, Steve once said, "If we listened to the time-study man, we'd all wind up in the poorhouse." The foreman asked, "How would that work, Steve? Can you give me an illustration?" Steve replied, "Sure, my grandfather was laid off after an efficiency expert changed things around, and he never got another steady job."

Reflecting feelings—not asking questions. Restating another person's thoughts in different words is a very helpful way for the leader to test his understanding of a participant's

remark. If the discussion leader can restate in his own words
what a group member has said, he must understand the contribution. This skill thus becomes a way of checking communication. If a group member finds the restatement inadequate, he can correct the leader and explain in greater detail
what he means. Steve's last comment (see above) might be
restated as, "You feel that if we increase our production on
this job some of us might be laid off." Steve might thus be
encouraged to continue and elaborate further, thus sharing
more of his feelings.

It is important not to put these rephrased statements in
the form of questions. This same restatement expressed as a
question would indicate doubt or disapproval. Questions can
be threatening, and when they approach a cross-examination,
they cause answers to become brief and guarded.

Questions take on a number of forms. Such questions as
"How do you mean that?" "Can you explain that further?"
encourage expression and demonstrate a desire to understand. These questions neither indicate that the leader is
appraising nor direct the discussion along lines that the
leader wishes. This is the meaning of the nondirective approach to interpersonal relations. When persons have feelings to express, it is important that they themselves determine what they will contribute. Questions designed to reveal
facts or evidence direct the discussion to specific areas so
that a leader who uses such questions is using a directive approach. The directive approach is not conducive to finding
out how participants feel.

The technique of restating an emotionally loaded viewpoint is called "reflecting feelings." [2] Emphasis in this type of
response is on the feeling aspect of the contribution, and this
is the part that is most often misunderstood. A leader often
says, "I know just how you feel," but does he? A restatement
of a contribution tends to convey the desire as well as the
ability to understand feelings.

In the type of discussion that arises in the case regarding

[2] Carl Rogers, *Counseling and Psychotherapy.* Houghton Mifflin
Company, Boston, 1942, p. 450.

the Change in Work Procedure, the foreman often judges the
men to be unreasonable because they make charges and accusations that are quite unfounded. This judgment indicates
that he does not appreciate the difference in background
that his rank or authority in a work situation might create.
To be on the receiving end of a change is quite different from
being on the giving end.

*Involving all participants in the discussion—not getting
into a prolonged two-way exchange with one participant.* A
conference differs from an interview in that the leader must
relate himself to the group rather than to an individual. Although the leader will want to understand each individual,
he has the responsibility of keeping the other members of
the group involved. Some of the ways to spread the discussion are as follows:

1. Introducing pauses that are long enough to give
others an opportunity to participate.

2. Asking the group as a whole how they feel about an
idea expressed, thereby placing responsibility for contributing on the group.

3. Checking for agreement and other points of view re-
leases comment from others. For example, Steve (Change of
Work Procedure case) may express the view that the group
will eventually be broken up. The foreman might ask, "Do
the rest of you feel that the changes will break up the group?"
If the others nod, he might add, "Well, let's talk about how
that might work out (*this spreads discussion*) because this
certainly wasn't intended (*assurance*)."

4. Creating opportunities to indicate agreement or disagreement involves other participants without requiring
much discussion time. When agreement or disagreement is
registered in response to a question, other participants have
an opportunity to release expression and to participate with
a mere nod or shake of the head. Frequently the benefits of
releasing pent-up feelings are facilitated in a group situation
because other members benefit from the verbalization by
nodding whenever they are in agreement with the speaker.

It is common practice for discussion leaders to call on

certain members in order to spread the discussion. Generally speaking this is not a good procedure for the following reasons:

1. It may threaten the individual.

2. The person called on may have nothing worthwhile to contribute at the time.

3. Others may wonder why the individual was selected for special treatment.

4. It suggests that spontaneous responses are not in order.

5. It causes individuals to be ready with a response rather than to think about the problem under discussion.

PROCEDURE FOR AIDING PROBLEM SOLVING

Once a group has had the opportunity to express its feelings freely, including those it recognizes as exaggerated, it is readier to face the situation in an objective and constructive manner. The leader may then summarize a situational problem as it seems to emerge from the discussion. For example, the discussion in the Change of Work Procedure case might have centered around the boredom that would occur if each man worked in a fixed position. As a result, boredom might emerge as the basic objection to change. The situation then might be summarized as follows: "It seems then that a basic problem arises because the job might become too repetitious." If the fears and hostility have been ventilated, this statement of the problem would probably be accepted and would be met with nods. Since the problem is expressed in situational terms (repetitious in place of boring), the subject for discussion now becomes the job. The following principles are found to be an aid to discussions having to do with solving situational problems.

Broadening the problem-solving horizon. Once a problem is posed, the discussion may proceed with little assistance from the leader. If the group approaches the situation in a constructive manner, there is no need for the supervisor to do anything except to carefully follow the discussion so that he will be in a position to summarize the various ideas expressed. A summary permits all ideas to exert an influence, not just the last one. When a discussion spreads and loses its unity and nothing new is introduced, a summary is helpful in making further progress.

Often the discussion may lose momentum because only a few alternatives suggest themselves. The conference leader may initiate new directions in thinking (see Chapter 3) without either implying or suggesting solutions, by applying either one or both of the principles discussed below.

Turning a choice situation into a problem: Some discussions become restricted to a consideration of two or three obvious alternatives. In the Change of Work Procedure case the obvious alternatives are whether to (1) continue the old rotation method or (2) adopt the new method of each man working on his best position, as suggested by the time-study results. This simple choice situation can be turned into a problem situation by asking whether some additional alternatives can be created. This type of question directs thinking away from making a choice and into explorations for new possibilities. Creative solutions are the least obvious and hence are the most rare. For this reason opportunities for helping them develop should be introduced.

Finding ways to overcome obstacles in the path of a goal characterizes the problem-solving process, whereas selecting an alternative is choice behavior. Both are involved in decision making, but if choice behavior occurs too soon, new and unusual alternatives are not apt to be included. Figure 6 illustrates the difference between discovering solutions and making a choice between alternatives. The leader can initiate either type of group activity and thereby obtain the maximum value from each.

Turning a problem situation into a choice situation: When solutions are lacking and there are no alternatives to choose from, solutions must be created. However, there then exists a tendency to accept the first workable solution that is obtained. This means that the discovery of a solution tends to terminate the problem-solving activity. However, it

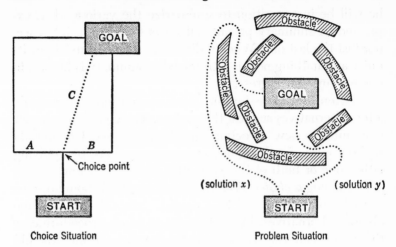

Choice Situation   Problem Situation

Fig. 6. Distinction between choice situations and problem situations. The diagram on the left represents a choice situation. Alternatives A and B are presented at the choice point. This situation requires a person to choose the best way to reach the goal. Behavior is blocked until a choice is made. The diagram on the right represents a problem situation. A goal is present but various obstacles lie in its path. This situation requires a person to find a way to reach the goal. Behavior is blocked until a route to the goal is invented or discovered. Such solutions or routes are shown as dotted lines. Note that the goal can be reached by getting around any of the several obstacles in the path. This illustrates that approaches to solutions should be directed toward overcoming different obstacles.

Choice situations can be turned into problems if a person tries to develop some additional alternatives. If a person created a new alternative such as C (represented by a dotted line in the diagram on the left), it might be possible to upgrade the decision. The natural tendency is for people to select from the available alternatives rather than create new ones.

Problem situations can be turned into choice situations by developing more than one solution to a problem (solutions *x* and *y* in diagram on the right). This allows a selection of the best from the solutions obtained. However, the natural tendency is to act on the first solution that is obtained.

Decisions are improved when both problem solving and choice behavior are combined. (*Modified from N. R. F. Maier, The Appraisal Interview. John Wiley & Sons, Inc., New York, 1958, pp. 190–191.*)

is possible that the first solution found may not be as good as some other possibilities. Most problems permit several solutions, and if the search ends before a number of alternatives are found, some superior solutions may be overlooked. If problem solving is continued, however, additional satisfactory solutions may be found.

When several solutions to a problem are obtained, a choice situation is created, since the group must then choose from among the alternatives. This means that a discussion leader can broaden the horizon for problem solving by turning a problem-solving situation into a choice situation, as well as the reverse.

Maier and Hoffman [3] found that group solutions were of higher quality when groups were instructed to find a second solution after they presumably had solved the problem by submitting their (first) solution. In this experiment, the Change of Work Procedure case was used. High-quality solutions (integrative type) were obtained by 11.1 per cent of the groups on their first solution, while 42.6 per cent of the same groups obtained this type as their second solution. The frequency with which each type of solution occurred under the two conditions is shown in Table 12.

TABLE 12. *Quality of First and Second Solution*

Solution	Number of groups	Per cent of old type solution	Per cent of new type solution	Per cent of integrative solutions
First	54	24.1	64.8	11.1
Second	54	25.9	31.5	42.6

It will be seen that while the number of integrative solutions increased for second solutions, the number of new type solutions (the kind suggested by time study) declined, indicating that the trend in thinking was away from choosing

[3] N. R. F. Maier and L. R. Hoffman, Quality of First and Second Solutions in Group Problem Solving. *J. appl. Psychol.*, 1960, **44**, 278–283.

between obvious alternatives and toward more consideration of new possibilities.

It should be pointed out that it was not necessary to change from one type of solution to another in order to find a second solution. There are several variations within each type of solution. As a matter of fact, groups developing an integrative type solution as their first solution tended to do so on their second.

The experiment demonstrates both the value of turning choice situations into problems and of turning problem situations into choices. The fact that integrative solutions were less frequent in the first set of solutions than in the second demonstrates that decisions tend to be made on the basis of the more obvious choices. Only after groups were asked to obtain another solution did the less obvious (integrative) solutions appear with important frequency.

The procedure of requiring groups to find a second solution caused them to return to the problem where they may have found the remaining obvious alternative unattractive. This required them to do one of three things: (1) modify their previous solution, (2) improve the undesirable alternative, or (3) innovate in some other way. The assignment of obtaining a second solution, therefore, tends to initiate activity in the area of *developing* alternatives rather than *choosing* between obvious alternatives.

The principle of turning problems into choices was effectively utilized in this experiment because the existence of two or more satisfactory solutions created the opportunity of choosing from among them. A choice between two acceptable solutions not only permits a further increase in the degree of acceptance but in the quality as well.

The value of having two or more solutions from which to choose is desirable regardless of whether the second tends to be superior to the first. The fact that the second solution tends to be superior to the first suggests that certain undesirable factors operated to a greater degree during the first than the second period of problem solving. Part of this advantage favoring the second period of problem solving has already been mentioned—the most attractive of the obvious alternatives may have been chosen so that no acceptable obvious alternative remained. The group therefore had to innovate. There are two additional advantages: (1) The leader may have successfully exerted his domination during the first period and hence was readier to entertain ideas from subordinates during the second. (2) The majority viewpoint may have dominated the thinking in the first period, thus allowing the minority member somewhat more influence in the second period. Both the leader's influence and majority pressure make for conformity.[4] It follows, therefore, that if a discussion leader can counteract these two unfavorable influences, which usually are present, he will broaden the horizon for problem solving.

Asking exploratory but not judgmental questions: Questioning a group member may be threatening when the question is viewed as an attempt to obtain facts that the person does not wish to divulge. An individual suspected of contributing to an accident protects himself when asked, "What were you doing at the time the incident occurred?" Behind such a question is a desire to evaluate or to "catch" the person questioned so that he may be judged unfavorably. Questions of this type, therefore, may be threatening and place group members in a defensive position. Hence they hinder rather than assist the problem-solving process. When the respondents give brief answers and supply no further information, the leader may conclude that his questioning has not been permissive and that he has failed to obtain the exploratory thinking he intended to initiate.

Exploratory questions tend to raise problems that require further exposition or thought. For example, a superintendent raised a problem with nine foremen on how to get a temporary increase of 25 per cent in production. Hiring temporary employees had been dismissed as being objectionable to the workers, so the group of foremen confined their thinking to considering overtime as the best way to handle

[4] N. R. F. Maier and J. J. Hayes, *Creative Management.* John Wiley & Sons, Inc., New York, 1962.

the matter. In estimating the cost of overtime the group took into account time-and-one-half pay rates but assumed that two hours of overtime (25 per cent) would yield an additional 25 per cent in production. In this connection the superintendent asked, "Can we assume that the production rate will hold up in the longer workweek?" This question caused the exploration of fatigue and motivation and the possibility of Saturday work. After some discussion, the group of foremen felt the problems should be put to the men. It was agreed that if the men thought they could produce 25 per cent more for the period in question, the company would go along with the plan. This idea of involving the workers in the decision led to a consideration of their preferences. The superintendent then asked, "Well, is this something we should put to the men?" This question turned the discussion toward a consideration of the value of asking the men for their opinions. Soon it was agreed that the men should be involved. The superintendent next raised the matter of how this should be done.

Before long each foreman agreed to raise the following problem with his men: Do you think that you could produce 25 per cent more by working overtime ten hours per week (time-and-one-half pay was assumed)? In all of the nine crews a nine-hour day was selected, with a five-hour day for Saturday. Needless to say the crews met the goal.

Good questions raise problems regarding facts and are directed toward a consideration of the situation. The following are examples of exploratory questions:

How will we adapt that plan to cold weather conditions?

What would happen if the power failed?

Do you think we should decide the matter for other groups as well as our own?

Would that change do away with the bottleneck or just reduce it?

Is there an entirely different approach to the problem?

What effect would this plan have on the group's morale?

In our example of the Change of Work Procedure case, the men may be reacting to the new work method as a source of boredom, while assuming that the old method lacked this fault. If the emotional stage seems to have passed, the foreman might ask, "Now are there any ways of handling boredom other than what we are now doing?" This question tends to take the thinking out of the rut, where the thinking had linked the old method and the absence of boredom with each other. Once the matter of boredom is dealt with as a separate problem, the group can think of rest pauses, music, rotating two positions rather than three positions, two men rather than three men rotating, experimenting with methods, etc.

It is customary for individuals as well as groups to think in obvious, habitual, or customary ways. Innovation results from disagreements,[5] and the leader can do much to encourage it and to request it, by asking such questions as the following:

Can any of you think of a different approach?

How can we capitalize on these good features and avoid the bad ones?

Can anyone think of how this idea might be improved?

What would be the direct opposite of that plan?

Stimulating and collecting ideas or solutions

Delaying the process of reaching a solution: Participants as well as discussion leaders focus on the objective of arriving at a solution and fail to give due consideration to an exploration of the problem. There is, therefore, a strong tendency to spend a great deal of time debating the merits of the first or the most obvious ideas. Procedures that delay the evaluation and selection of solutions and instead require that more time be spent discussing the problem tend to improve the quality of decisions.

[5] N. R. F. Maier, *The Appraisal Interview.* John Wiley & Sons, Inc., New York, 1958. L. R. Hoffman, Conditions for Creative Problem Solving. *J. Psychol.*, 1961, **52**, 429–444.

An experimental test of the value of delaying solutions was made with the Change of Work Procedure case.[6] One set of foremen received the standard instructions (control groups) while the others (experimental groups) were asked to use the following three steps in discussing the problem:

Step 1: Present the problem and then conduct a brief general discussion to obtain an expression of everyone's views on the problem

Step 2: After an initial airing of viewpoints, conduct a discussion for the purpose of exploring the important factors in the problem and develop a written list of these factors

Step 3: After all important factors have been listed, use the list as a basis for group discussion in deciding on the solution

The results of this experiment are shown in Table 13. It

TABLE 13. *Quality of Delayed Solutions*

Leaders	Number of groups	Per cent of old type solution	Per cent of new type solution	Per cent of integrative solutions
Without instructions ..	96	22.0	66.0	12.0
With instructions	50	20.8	37.5	41.7

will be noted that the instructed groups had more than three times as many integrative solutions (41.7 per cent) as the un-instructed groups (12.0 per cent). The results are very similar to those of Table 12, which represents second solutions to this same problem. Delaying the reaching of a solution therefore tends to prevent the acceptance of initial ideas and permits the more innovative ideas to have a greater influence. It also encourages the spending of more time exploring the problem so that the solution becomes a better fit to the real problem.

[6] N. R. F. Maier and A. R. Solem, Improving Solutions by Turning Choice Situations into Problems. *Personnel Psychol.*, 1962, **15**, 151–157.

Separating idea getting from idea evaluation: An important principle of problem solving is the separation of the process of *idea getting* from the process of *idea evaluation.*[7] Evaluation stifles *unusual* ideas because these are difficult to protect from criticism. The very fact that such ideas are unusual means that they are new and lack the support of commonsense experience. Unusual and original ideas are likely to be held or shared by a minority and hence tend to come under the criticism of the majority.

In the previous section, disagreement was regarded as a stimulant for getting different ideas, but unless it is properly guided, it may take the form of criticizing divergent viewpoints and thus become a form of evaluation. Disagreement with solutions offered should be turned into a process of offering alternative ideas. The leader's objective should be to make constructive use of disagreements and to delay the evaluation of contributions that are offered.

A simple way to separate the two processes is to make the collection of ideas a different stage of the discussion than the evaluation and selection stage. Thus the listing of ideas may be made the initial stage of the meeting, with the understanding that this part of the discussion is preliminary to the evaluation of ideas and the reaching of a final decision.

An easel or a blackboard is a valuable conference tool because it permits the leader to accept a contribution by making it public property for all to see and use as a point of departure for further ideas. This can be done by writing the idea in abbreviated form on the board while at the same time asking for a different plan or idea. If one member of a group finds fault with another's thinking, he should be asked, "How do *you* think it should be done?" If he has a different idea, it also should be posted on the board. However, if he merely wishes to register an objection, the leader may accept the objection by placing a question mark after the idea to which

[7] N. R. F. Maier, *The Appraisal Interview.* John Wiley & Sons, Inc., New York, 1958.

he objects and then pointing out something along the following line: "Later on we will want to go over all of the ideas and evaluate them. For the present let's concentrate on getting as many ideas as we can. Even some ideas that appear impractical may turn out to be suggestive and lead to the unusual." The leader need not be afraid of poor ideas since listing them does not indicate that they will be adopted.

This process will be recognized as akin to brainstorming,[8] which derives its value from the fact that evaluation inhibits the expression of opinions, restricts the freedom of thinking, and prevents others from profiting from different directions in thinking.[9] It has been found that groups made up of persons differing in personality produce better solutions than groups made up of persons of like personality.[10] By probing for a variety of ideas the leader can introduce some of the stimulation that people of differing personalities exert on each other.

Dealing with agreement and disagreement: As already indicated, disagreement in a group can either lead to hard feelings (thus creating a new problem), or it can stimulate thinking and lead to innovations. When members of a group are too much in agreement, the function of the leader is to stimulate disagreement. For example, everyone in the Change of Work Procedure case might agree that the job as now performed is better than the work method suggested by time study. If the foreman asks the men what they think the ideal situation would be or what bothered them most, he might find differences in opinion. Thus it is common for peo-

[8] A. F. Osborn, *Applied Imagination: Principles and Procedures of Creative Thinking.* Charles Scribner's Sons, New York, 1953.

[9] N. R. F. Maier, Reasoning in Humans: I. On Direction. *J. comp. Psychol.*, 1930, **10**, 115–143; II. The Solution of a Problem and Its Appearance in Consciousness. *Ibid.*, 1931, **12**, 181–194; An Aspect of Human Reasoning. *Brit. J. Psychol.*, 1933, **24**, 144–155.

[10] L. R. Hoffman, Homogeneity of Member Personality and Its Effect on Group Problem-Solving. *J. abnorm. soc. Psychol.*, 1959, **58**, 27–32. L. R. Hoffman and N. R. F. Maier, Quality and Acceptance of Problem Solutions by Members of Homogeneous and Heterogeneous Groups. *J. abnorm. soc. Psychol.*, 1961, **62**, 401–407.

ple to agree on what is good or bad, but possibly to disagree on what is best or worst. This approach, therefore, serves to encourage disagreement.

The value of increased disagreement in stimulating innovative solutions in the Change of Work Procedure problem was experimentally demonstrated by Hoffman, Harburg, and Maier.[11] In these experiments the level of disagreement between the foreman and the workers was varied. For example, the job was made much more boring for one set of groups than for the other set. This change caused the men in these groups to become more determined to keep their rotation and to more strongly resist the solution supplied by the foreman. One would expect the strong opposition groups to resist change, but what effect would this have on the integrative solutions?

The results obtained are shown in Table 14. The weak

TABLE 14. *Solutions Obtained with Different Levels of Disagreement*

Experimental condition	No. of groups	Per cent old type solutions	Per cent new type solutions	Per cent integrative solutions
Weak opposition	48	14.6	66.7	18.8
Strong opposition	48	22.9	31.2	45.8

opposition groups adopted the solution supplied by the foreman (new type) 66.7 per cent of the time while the strong opposition groups adopted this solution only 31.2 per cent of the time. However, the strong opposition groups did not resist change significantly more often than the weak, as shown by the figures in the first column. What happens is that the opposition introduces more disagreement, and as a result the innovative or integrative type of solution rises from 18.8 per cent in the weak opposition groups to 45.8 per cent in the strong opposition groups (column 3). Strong conflicts are less likely to permit opponents to give in. Innovative

[11] L. R. Hoffman, E. Harburg, and N. R. F. Maier. Differences and Disagreements as Factors in Creative Group Problem Solving. *J. abnorm. soc. Psychol.*, 1962, **64**, 206–214.

integrations can resolve these differences if the conflict does not deteriorate into interpersonal strife. The leader plays an important part in determining the role that increased conflict can play.

Differences in thinking can also be produced by asking the group to discuss the advantages and the disadvantages of a solution or an idea. This listing of two sides of a question causes the thinking to move back and forth on opposite sides of an issue. As a result, the "right" or "wrong" aspects of opinions are objectified and become the bases from which a new idea that capitalizes on merits and avoids weaknesses may emerge.

When disagreement is violent and nonconstructive, the leader may do well to serve in the capacity of a mediator in order to avoid the damage this type of conflict can do. Some group members may disagree to the point of hurting one another's feelings. For example, in our Change of Work Procedure case, Walt might refer to Steve as being a bottleneck. In this case the foreman might restate Walt's point of view by saying "You feel that Steve doesn't get the casting to you fast enough." This type of modification takes some of the sting out of a statement. It is the discussion leader's function to turn a personal attack into a situational problem whenever he can. In the above example, the foreman could protect Steve by saying that everyone has a different work pace and that each person can do some things better than others. If the attack on Steve conveys intense feeling, the discussion leader might indicate that Walt apparently feels strongly about something on the job and is bothered when held up. He might add, "Talking about the job may indicate how we can change it to get rid of irritating conditions." If the situation can be blamed for an outbreak, if the foreman restates an attack so as to remove the sting, or if he protects the person who might otherwise go to his own defense, disagreement may be prevented from disrupting constructive problem solving. The leader must be sensitive to hurt feelings and make it unnecessary for a person to come to his own defense. This means that it is best for him to step in before an unfortunate turn in events causes things to go from bad to worse.

Periodic summarizing. A summary is not to be viewed as a procedure confined to the end of a meeting; rather it has several valuable functions, and the leader who effectively makes use of the summary can do much to upgrade the efficiency of any problem-solving conference. Some of these functions are described below.

Getting a discussion back on course: The leader may indicate briefly the various topics that have entered the discussion and explore whether, for the sake of time, the group is ready to go on with the central topic of the meeting. He may then summarize the main objectives and issues of the conference if this seems needed. If he has accurately diagnosed the situation (that the participants have merely been distracted), they will agree to, and even welcome, the opportunity to get down to business. A leader who fails to do this will find that a group member often does it for him. If he is in error, then it may be necessary to explore the side issues and tangents. Perhaps some problems raised are actually relevant, and the leader was unaware of their connection with the discussion topic. It is important that the leader avoid using this function of keeping the discussion on the topic as a way of dominating or controlling the decisions.

Checking understanding: If a participant talks for a long time, it may be difficult to determine just what is important to him. In many instances it is not clear whether he is talking for or against a particular issue. The leader may ask, "Before you go any further, let me see if I can restate what you mean," and then proceed to summarize the view expressed. This function of the summary is similar to the method of reflecting feelings; except that, in this instance, factual and conceptual considerations are the important content.

A restatement should be made in the leader's own words, and it may be reduced to a sentence or two. If the leader's summary is inaccurate, the participant can clarify or elaborate. If the summary is accurate, it demonstrates the leader's insight and his desire to understand. His focusing or understanding rather than evaluation sets a precedent for the participants to follow. Frequently the same idea expressed in different words clarifies it as well as distinguishing it from similar ideas. A restatement might also make the need for further refinements apparent.

In our case of the Change of Work Procedure, Walt might suggest that the rotation be reduced to rotation between two rather than three positions and changing positions once every two hours rather than hourly. The merit of this viewpoint might not be apparent to everyone and hence might be opposed as inadequate. However, the leader might summarize this idea by saying, "In other words, you'd suggest rotating each person's two best positions, while the frequency of exchanges could be reduced or might even be kept the same." This summary brings out the gains in Walt's suggestion and at the same time separates and reveals the two aspects of his idea. Unless Walt had an entirely different idea, this summary would be welcomed by him, since it makes his idea stronger because it separates two parts, either or both of which may be accepted or modified independently.

Increasing communication within the group: Closely associated with the improved understanding that a summary may contribute is the increased communication to other members of the group. A single statement might mean quite different things to every member of a group. However, this range in meanings is rapidly narrowed down when two different statements of the same idea are available. Any apparent conflict in meanings between a participant's statement and the leader's restatement that the participant has failed to note will cause others to raise questions and result in better communication. In so far as others are brought into the activity of interpreting one person's idea, group involvement in the process of understanding is stimulated.

Improving the leader's listening skill: The process of summarizing forces the leader to listen and pay attention in a manner that may have been somewhat foreign to him before. When a leader listens to evaluate, he looks for weaknesses and instances in which the idea would not be appropriate. This is a critical and evaluative kind of listening. However, when he listens to summarize, his attention is on grasping the meaning the participant is striving to express. This effort at understanding is constructive and encourages further participation because the leader is helping the member to think through an idea that may actually be somewhat vague to him. When persons feel their thoughts must be clear before they contribute, they become reluctant, and many potential spontaneous contributions are lost. It should be understood that the purpose of discussion is to clarify thinking, and in this function all participants can contribute. It is not uncommon for a person to reject his own idea as inadequate when he has a chance to fully examine it with a group. This opportunity should be afforded to everyone because it completely avoids the need to save face.

The discussion leader sets the stage for improved communication when he makes an effort to understand. The writer has seen a whole group of men actually perspire while trying to understand someone in the group who had a vague but unusual viewpoint.

Periodic reviews: Discussions in which many angles or ideas are explored may cause participants to feel that their ideas have been lost or ignored. This is especially likely to occur if a blackboard is not used to record ideas. The leader who periodically inventories the contributions not only indicates that they have been accepted, but permits the various ideas to continue to exert an influence on the thinking of others. Often the trend of thought follows a chainlike pattern, but with the aid of such summaries a quiltlike pattern may be woven.

In using such summaries it is also possible that the contributions may be grouped according to similarities and differences. This function of the summary will encourage the group to make progressively finer distinctions and require participants to clarify their previously expressed views. Discussions that evaluate in terms of likenesses and differences tend to refine a group's thinking, and a leader who effectively uses this process can cause a group to problem-solve beyond its normal level.

Indicating and measuring progress: After a statement such as "We seem to agree on a number of points even if we do not agree on others," it may be in order to summarize the points of agreement.

Restlessness is not uncommon in group discussion, partly because each person's interest tends to reside in his contribution and because conflict disturbs many persons. In summarizing progress from time to time, the group not only gets to experience the several points of agreement but also is relieved and assured by the leader's acceptance of disagreement as a constructive force. Such summaries not only reduce anxiety but serve to make the progress a group product, and this heightens interest in the discussion.

Separating a problem into its several parts: Frequently some parts of a problem have been solved and therefore can be set aside so that the remaining ones may be considered without the agreed-upon aspects being held over to complicate matters. For example, a works manager made the statement, "We seem to agree on the need for a reduction in some of our lines, but the question of which items to cut out without creating a hardship seems now to be the problem." This statement shifts the discussion from one in which each participant is arguing against a cut in his area to one having to do with the problem of how to cut lines without its being done at someone's expense.

Sometimes a discussion on the advisability of promoting a certain man confuses the evaluation of the candidate's proficiency on his old job with an estimation of his capabilities and potentialities on the new job. If a group of superiors agree that he has certain strengths and a few weaknesses on the old job, the question of whether the new job will utilize the same strengths and avoid his weaknesses may well be raised. If agreement is reached on these points, they may be summarized and disposed of for the time being. This allows the remainder of the discussion to deal with the added requirements on the new job, regarding which there may be little objective basis for opinion in evaluating the candidate. This speculative aspect of the discussion should be clearly separated from the portion related to performance on the old job and its similarity to the new job.

This function of the summary, therefore, is to dispose of settled issues in order to clarify the relevance of matters that remain. Intelligently used, it becomes one of the most important aids in moving a discussion forward.

NEED FOR CONTINUED SENSITIVITY

The treatment of the two discussion procedures—dealing with feeling and aiding problem solving—has been such as to make them appear as first and second stages of a discussion. In one sense this is correct: problem solving should not begin until feelings have been properly recognized and respected. However, this precaution does not prevent feelings from being aroused during the discussion of the various aspects of the problem. When this occurs, the leader must be ready and willing to adapt his procedure to the condition (emotional or intellectual) of the group.

It does seem appropriate, therefore, to regard the discussion procedures as two general types rather than as two stages of a discussion. In some instances, when emotional involvement is at a minimum, the whole discussion may be of the problem-solving type. A group of persons solving a puzzle will tend to work together without any apparent emotional investment. This purely objective involvement is perhaps more rare than is usually supposed. It is probable, however, that the presence of emotional investment in ideas and in decision outcomes is frequently overlooked. Conference leaders, in general, tend to underestimate the degree to which face saving and recognition needs cause persons to rationalize their biases and give them intellectual support. People seldom claim that they fear a change; instead they attempt to prove that the change is for the worse. Discussions that do not get at the real causes bear little fruit because they deal with irrelevant facts and issues.

The discussion leader must be sensitive to the feelings behind the remarks and be ready to explore them whenever they appear. This requires the leader to devote attention to the group's behavior rather than be blinded by an agenda. Practice and postmeeting reviews of events will do a great deal to develop sensitivity in discussion leaders. Formalized training can do still more in this regard.

CHAPTER SIX

Reaching the decision

DECISIONS SPECIFY ACTION

When the process of *idea getting* has run its course, the group effort may be turned to the processes of *evaluation* and the selection of a final solution. In some cases the possible alternative actions are limited in number so that the process of selection may occur after a relatively brief period of problem solving. The important consideration is not to begin the evaluation process before the group members have had ample opportunity to contribute as much as they desire and to the extent of which they are capable. The leader may wish to test the group's willingness to proceed to a final stage of the discussion before leaving the *idea getting* part of the conference. It should be apparent that this final stage is concerned with the action-steps the group feels are appropriate. The actions agreed upon might include any number of the following: (1) a basic change in the job, (2) a recommendation to higher management, (3) an agreement to hold another meeting, (4) an agreement that participants will hold meetings with their subordinates before settling on a decision, (5) a decision not to take action at this time, and (6) a plan to experiment with several alternatives.

There are a variety of approaches the leader may take in handling the evaluation process. The procedures discussed below are suggestions and should not be regarded as stages in the evaluation process. However, it will be apparent that some of them represent initial steps, that others may be later steps in the evaluation process, that still others are limited to certain conditions, and that the remaining represent alternative procedures. The choice of evaluation procedure depends on the complexity of the problem, the amount of disagreement, and the number of alternative decisions available. Suggestions for the proper use of the procedures will be made in connection with the description of the procedure.

EVALUATING CONTRIBUTIONS

After a variety of ideas has been contributed and the group seems unable to make further additions, the evaluation procedure may be initiated by the leader. This change in agenda does not preclude the possibility of adding further items to the list in the event the evaluation process suggests a new idea to someone.

Examining the advantages and disadvantages of each solution. In complex situations a particular idea may have both advantages and disadvantages. Persons who favor a particular solution tend to present the favorable arguments, while those opposed present the unfavorable. As a consequence, the group is divided into two camps even though they may differ with each other on a friendly basis. If, however, the leader asks the group as a whole to consider both sides of the argument, the group is made to work together in exploring the merits and demerits of the solution. This makes it unnecessary for anyone to take a firm stand which he must defend against an opposition. The procedure of letting the group explore the pros and cons together greatly reduces the face-saving problems and reduces the tendency for participants to take premature positions.

In following this procedure the leader makes two columns for each of the suggested solutions that has been listed on the blackboard. Over one column he places the heading "Advantages" and over the other, "Disadvantages." Anticipated results and arguments can now be contributed in any order. It is the leader's job to abbreviate each point and place it in the appropriate column. Skill in abbreviating and in grasping the core of the argument will contribute to the speed and success of this process. (For further details see pages 166 ff. and 178 ff.

It should not surprise the leader if he sometimes has difficulty in determining the column in which a particular contribution belongs. This confusion can be clarified by asking the contributor whether his point represents an advantage or a disadvantage. A question of this kind may cause the contributor to clarify his meaning by indicating the column in which it belongs or making further additions. Frequently he will answer "Neither." If this is the case, it is probable that there are two or more points in his argument. These points should then be separated and each one placed in its proper column.

It may be argued by someone that one advantage can offset five disadvantages. This opinion should be accepted as sound, and the leader may then explain that the lengths of the lists are irrelevant since the purpose of the analysis is to look at both sides of a question so that everyone will have a better basis for evaluation. It will be found that some disadvantages can readily be removed or avoided; others may be improbable; and still others may represent insurmountable obstacles. This appraisal of the importance of a solution's merits and weaknesses should be made by the group before attempting to reach the final decision.

This two-column procedure is recommended for situations which yield several solutions and for which there are no clear-cut advantages of one solution over others. When one of the solutions has the character of elegance, it would be somewhat of a boring routine to go through this process. On other occasions, it may be agreed that some of the alternatives are too silly to analyze. In such instances the leader may cross out the items, providing, of course, that the group agrees to the elimination. One objection to the removal of an item, however, should be enough to retain it in the list.

Exploring supporting evidence. Frequently solutions that are offered for the problem at hand actually are solutions for some other problems. People become attached to certain solutions and tend to use them whenever they have a problem. One department head found that a particular employee ceased having accidents (collisions) when he was given a different make of truck to drive. As a consequence he supplied other accident-prone drivers with this same make of truck. It became his solution to making a driver safer. Not taken into account was the fact that the first man had short legs and therefore couldn't apply the brakes adequately on the truck he had been driving. In the new truck, the brake pedal traveled through a shorter distance, and he ceased having collisions.

Solution preferences dominate our thinking more than is usually supposed. Persons who have had success with improving production by the use of music see it as a solution to many other problems, while time-study engineers see improved work methods as a general solution. It is not surprising, therefore, that specialists in accounting, psychology, engineering, and investment might suggest quite different solutions to a problem that is presented. Without doubt each may recommend something that will lead to an improvement, but all may fail to solve the particular problem at hand.

In order to solve a particular problem its solution must make use of the specific facts that are known. Seldom are all of the desired facts available; yet it is under conditions in which few facts are known that the tendency to ignore facts is greatest. This failure to use what is known arises when a group finds that no single solution's superiority can be proven to the satisfaction of all members. Since the solution

seems to be a matter of opinion, each person tends to think
that his opinion is as good as anyone else's. Yet it is clear
that solutions based upon the facts that are known have a
better chance of succeeding than those that have a lesser
basis in reality.[1]

In order to focus on the facts that are known, the leader
may turn the discussion into an evaluation of the various
solutions by asking members to indicate the supporting factual evidence. The facts supplied can then be placed in conjunction with each solution. Solutions lacking supporting
facts might be circled and in this way set aside or tabled for
the time being. It is apparent that a good-sized blackboard
would greatly aid in this evaluation procedure.

It is essential that the leader distinguish between supporting facts and proof. If an accident occurred during in-
clement weather, this does not prove that the weather caused
it or even contributed, but the fact that such a weather condition prevailed still can be retained as supporting evidence.
It may take many facts to prove a point, but this does not
justify ignoring those one has because they are insufficient.

Using the stalemate constructively. When evaluating
evidence in support of a solution, it frequently happens that
one person argues for a solution by referring to a fact in the
situation while another person disagrees by furnishing an
opposing fact. For example, one person may claim that a reduction in talking will increase production by pointing to
the fact that rejects are higher in units where talking occurs
the most. This fact may be countered if another participant
refers to the fact that production is higher in these same
units.

This conflict in evidence can lead to a great deal of
fruitless discussion. A good way out of this conflict is for the
leader to suggest that the two views produce a stalemate
since each is based upon acceptable but opposite supporting
evidence. This method of canceling conflicting alternatives

[1] A systematic method for selecting a solution under conditions
of uncertainty is described in Chapter 8. For our present purposes, the
more simplified approach described here is adequate.

permits the discussion to proceed to a consideration of other facts that may support the solution under consideration or to proceed to a different solution.

It is helpful to regard a solution as a structure built upon foundation posts of facts. A single fact may be a supporting post, and a single foundation post as a support is better than none.

It is important to distinguish between conflicts in the supporting facts and mere disagreement. A person should not be regarded as having set up a stalemate if he disapproves of a solution or if he claims that a supporting fact is insufficient to prove the merits of a particular solution.

This type of discussion procedure is most apt when there are many solutions to a problem and when there is a great deal of controversy over the relative merits of a few solutions. For details on this method see Chapter 8.

Exploring the new problems created by solutions. Up to this point, solutions have been evaluated in terms of the degree to which they achieve objectives and the desirability of the accompanying by-products. Remaining to be considered is a determination of whether or not the solution creates a new problem. New problems created by proposed solutions range from minor ones to some that are more serious than the original one.

The cost of implementing a solution is the most obvious new problem that may be created by a solution. For example, increasing the lighting may solve a problem of excessive errors in inspection, but the cost of the lighting introduces a new problem. If the improved inspection is worth more than the cost of the lighting, the solution represents an improvement. However, the possibility that other solutions might accomplish the same thing for less should encourage further comparisons. Skylights, better placement of lights, better contrast, etc., are examples of other possibilities.

If a solution creates a serious new problem, the feasibility of solving this new problem should be explored. Suppose the cost of the lighting in the above illustration exceeds the value of the gains and none of the alternate solutions adequately achieves the objective. The failure of the alternatives to solve the problem lends new value to the desirability of improving the lighting. Reducing the cost of the lighting may then become the problem worthy of consideration. Problem solving in this area could conceivably lead to the utilization of available waterpower or even to a new way to produce electricity.

The possibility that new problems may be created by a solution to an initial problem is often overlooked, and it is for this reason that the discussion leader should introduce a systematic evaluation of solutions with respect to the new problems they may create. The cost of a solution is an obvious consideration, and in some discussions it may have already been considered in connection with the listing of advantages and disadvantages.

Suppose, however, that a solution involved the introduction of laborsaving equipment. The cost of this new machinery would be a first consideration, and it might readily be apparent that this investment was a small one when the potential production increase was considered. The cost of retraining the men might be a new problem which also might be viewed as a minor cost. Another new problem might be the need for a new time study since production standards would be affected by the change. The actual cost of time study also might be small, but if one raised the question of employee acceptance of the new standard, a complex problem might be discovered. During periods of labor shortage, laborsaving machinery would be given a different kind of reception than during periods of unemployment. Thus the employment situation and industrial conditions as a whole might influence the extent to which a major production improvement might introduce side effects and new problems.

Depending on social and economic conditions, the new problems that might be created by solving an industrial problem include (1) prevention of a strike, (2) avoidance of featherbedding in a new labor contract, (3) maintenance of good morale, (4) prevention of future opposition to changes, and (5) regaining a reputation in the community. These new problems would have to be examined in the light of their solubility before the merit of a particular solution could be fully assessed. The supposition that time will take care of the bad feelings a solution may arouse is an oversimplification. In many situations an unpopular act creates enemies, and a few such enemies can exert enough persistent effort in obtaining revenge to more than offset the goodwill efforts of many friends.

SELECTING A SOLUTION

The complexity of the process of selecting a solution will vary greatly depending on the size of the group, the variation of interests among group members, and the richness of the supply of alternatives from which to select. In some situations the superiority of a particular solution may be so obvious that the selection problem is nonexistent; yet even in such instances the possibility that other good alternatives may be created should not be overlooked. Just because a particular change represents an improvement does not exclude an evaluation of its merits and demerits.

When the supply of alternatives is fairly rich, the selection process is more complex and more satisfying. Undesirable alternatives should not be discredited, no matter how faulty, because this process may reflect unfavorably on the persons who suggested them. As long as good alternatives are present, they have the best chance of being selected so that the poor ones need not be actively rejected. This simple process of positive selection instead of rejection avoids defensive behavior and the need to save face.

Conservative versus liberal alternatives; action versus no action. In some instances the alternatives available may be whether or not to take action. For example, an executive group might have to decide whether to expand production facilities at this time or to wait and see if the market forecast is correct. The second possibility is the conservative choice in that it will result in fewer obvious dangers and less extensive gains. In one sense it leaves the outcome to chance and hence represents reluctance to take command of a situation. It represents defense rather than attack. Obviously this is sometimes wise, but at other times it represents lack of confidence. Since security is a predominant motivation, conservative opinions are likely to be represented in a discussion. It is for this reason that individualism can lead to more imaginative decisions than group decisions. True also is the fact that some of the great individual leaders in history verged on insanity and obtained their confidence from this source. Perhaps chance rather than wisdom made them great.

In order to offset the disadvantages of overconservatism in group decision the leader must leave ample opportunity for conservative members to voice their fears. Expressing fears brings them into the open where they can be examined and realistically appraised; at the same time some lessening of the fear is gained from mere expression. A discussion of fears also forces the liberal members not only to become aware of the risks, but also to suggest safeguards. In any event it is up to the leader to make the group realize that an unwillingness to take action is, in effect, a decision to (1) postpone action on the supposition that the passing of time will make the decision easier or unnecessary and (2) turn the control of events over to circumstances outside the group. This reluctance to act may or may not be desirable; the important thing is to realize that indecision is actually a decision regardless of whether or not one wants it to be. The following illustration makes this clear.

The management of an Ohio company had difficulty in deciding which of three parcels of land to purchase for a new plant site. Each location had advantages depending somewhat on which of several product lines would be enlarged. Since no agreement was reached, the decision was delayed with the expectation that more information regarding market trends might swing the choice toward one of the alternatives. In the meantime all three parcels of land went off the market, and a year later the company found itself in the position of having to purchase a property site that was less desirable than any of the other three.

The objective of group discussion is to resolve differences and reach consensus. Sometimes this objective cannot be satisfied, and a minority opinion remains in conflict. Although an unresolved minority opinion is undesirable, one should distinguish between two conditions—when the minority opposes action versus when it favors action. If the minority favors action, the disturbing effects of a majority decision are greater than when the minority opposes action.

Action-oriented individuals are distressed if they cannot carry out their plans, which is the case when they find themselves in the minority. Persons who favor inaction are not blocked if they are in the minority because they can choose between supporting or not supporting the majority effort. This means that for best results in group action, a majority decision to withhold action should be carefully explored lest it be an obstacle to progress. It should be kept in mind that new ideas always begin as minority opinions.

Before a final decision is made, evaluation of the alternatives of action versus no action should include a consideration of the strengths of the individual preferences as well as a determination of the extent to which each participant is able to support and accept each of the two alternatives. Although methods for solving the problem of failure to agree will be discussed shortly, let us assume that these have failed to bear fruit. Full agreement is sometimes difficult to achieve when the alternatives are limited to action versus no action, and it is therefore essential that special efforts be made to assess the opposition. Complex situations permit more opportunities for minds to meet, and the resolution of differences is not as difficult.

Conflicting alternative solutions. A choice between two alternative solutions represents a situation in which action is agreed upon; therefore the disagreement does not represent a desire to avoid a change. Even though one alternative may be more conservative than the other, the conservative alternative is not one of avoidance. This condition permits a number of possible procedures for resolving differences.

Integration: Some alternatives may be integrated. For example, a group of managers might have narrowed a problem down to two choices: (1) discharging a supervisor who is having problems with his staff or (2) placing him in a human relations training program. Even if this group is evenly divided with respect to these two alternatives, a resolution of the differences is not difficult since they may be integrated. The group might unanimously agree to try out the training, and if that failed, to discharge the supervisor. Demotion might be an example of an integrative solution when a group had to choose between discharge and transfer.

Testing alternatives: When two alternatives cannot be integrated, it may be possible to experiment with them. This is often possible when the problem pertains to methods or equipment. The following examples illustrate this procedure: (1) two favored types of billing machines may be tested for a period agreed upon; (2) one method of quality control might be used in one plant and the alternative used in the second; and (3) three ways of cleaning a furnace in a power plant might be tried at monthly intervals. The testing of two or more alternatives may lead to valuable information, and it may create opportunities to save face. When two alternatives receive strong support, it is reasonable for the leader to assume that both have merit and that very little is lost by deciding to use both, if the group wishes.

Treating failure to agree as a problem: Ordinarily a discussion leader is disturbed when a group cannot reach full agreement. He should not regard failure to agree as *his* problem. Rather he should make it the responsibility of the group to determine what should be done if consensus is not reached. When no further progress toward agreement is made, the procedural problem of how to deal with the disagreement should be raised. The group might agree to accept a majority opinion, request the leader to make the decision, or the new responsibility might introduce additional factors or compromises into the situation.

In the event the leader anticipates an unresolved conflict, he may put the original problem to the group with the provision that the group's decision will be accepted providing full agreement is reached. In the event of failure to agree, he may withdraw the problem and make the decision himself.[2]

Protecting minority opinions: Ordinarily a majority opinion is regarded as satisfactory for selecting a decision, and it is the traditional method by which groups reach decisions in a democracy. Although this process leaves a dissatisfied minority, it is a generally accepted procedure. However, it should be recognized that the optimum condition for cooperation is unanimous agreement and that strong majorities are preferable to more evenly divided opinions.

Reluctance to resort to a majority opinion should be apparent from the leader's behavior. In making unanimity of agreement his objective he becomes more concerned with each individual's opinions. The knowledge that a satisfactory majority opinion exists often encourages a leader to hurry a decision to a vote and thereby suppress minority expression. One of the important factors in the satisfaction with a decision is not the mere opportunity to participate, but whether or not the members feel satisfied with the amount of influence they had in the final decision.[3, 4, 5]

The research results clearly show that each participant's satisfaction with group discussions is related to whether he had the opportunity to influence the outcome as much as he wished. Thus satisfaction depends more on a person's felt influence than on how much he talked at the meeting.

[2] N. R. F. Maier, *Principles of Human Relations.* John Wiley & Sons, Inc., New York, 1952.

[3] L. R. Hoffman and N. R. F. Maier, The Use of Group Decision to Resolve a Problem of Fairness. *Personnel Psychol.,* 1959, **12**, 545–559.

[4] L. R. Hoffman and N. R. F. Maier, Quality and Acceptance of Problem Solutions by Members of Homogeneous and Heterogeneous Groups. *J. abnorm. soc. Psychol.,* 1961, **62**, 401–407.

[5] N. R. F. Maier and A. R. Solem, The Contribution of a Discussion Leader to the Quality of Group Thinking: the Effective Use of Minority Opinions. *Human Relat.,* 1952, **5**, 277–288.

It will become clear that a decision reached by a majority vote will leave many members of the minority feeling that they have not had a fair opportunity. Frequently they feel that if they had had more time, they could have changed the outcome. Regardless of whether or not this is true, it is important that the discussion continue long enough to give the minority a realistic assessment of the situation.

The opposite unfortunate extreme is to continue discussions when no further changes or new contributions occur. This condition leads to boredom and general dissatisfaction. It may be argued that if discussion is continued after a group does not reach agreement, personal attacks and social pressures might occur and result in alienating the minority. To prevent this, and in order to give the minority more opportunity to influence the group, it is essential that the leader protect and assist them. Because the minority is weak, such members must be given extra opportunities to express themselves. The majority view is likely to be well known, and many feel free to speak in its support, whereas members holding a minority view are likely to be on the defensive and may even hesitate to voice an opinion. In order to balance the opposing viewpoints the leader must do all he can to protect individuals who are attacked and create opportunities for letting them clarify their views. For example, he can rephrase personal attacks so that the disagreement is made one of difference in ideas rather than a conflict between individuals. Even when it is a leader's inclination to ridicule a vocal minority, he must strive to be patient with them and their thoughts.

A straw vote is a simple way to determine the number of persons preferring each of the solutions. This informal count or show of hands can be used to reveal the number of persons preferring each of the alternatives. A more complete measure of preference would be obtained by having the solutions rated, thereby permitting an expression of the degrees of preference. The degree of objection various individuals have for certain alternates also should be explored. Often the mere opportunity for an individual to express his reasons for opposing a solution assists the group in getting together.

On one occasion the writer was conducting a conference, and it became apparent that an additional meeting was in order. This was a unanimous opinion in a group of twenty executives. Further, it was agreed that the meeting should be on a Friday. Finally the choice of which Friday was posed. The alternative of the following Friday received nineteen votes, while the Friday a week later received one vote. Ordinarily this clear-cut majority is sufficient to make the choice. However, in this case the minority individual was asked if he would be willing to reveal his objection to the majority opinion. He explained that his daughter was being married on that day and that he would like to give her away. As a result, the unanimous choice was to follow his preference since no one had as good a reason for his first choice as the minority individual.

Explaining the problems and inconveniences that minorities may experience can outweigh the preferences of a majority. The least one can do is to explore them and thus increase the satisfaction with the amount of influence a participant was allowed to exercise.

The chronic objector: Sometimes persons who resist compromise and insist on having their own way, regardless of the opposition, do so because they do not feel accepted by the group. Additional attention and protection may aid their social adjustment. It must also be recognized that some persons have personality disorders and serious emotional problems. Such persons often persist in their opinions and fail to be influenced by the wishes of others. A whole group cannot be sacrificed for one poorly adjusted individual. When it becomes apparent that an individual does not respond to considerate treatment, the will of the majority should determine the decisions. However, the leader must always be sensitive, by respecting both individual feelings and group interests and steering a middle course.

The leader may wish to discuss matters privately with an individual who appears to have made a poor adjustment. He should do this in the role of a counselor and should not attempt to give advice since it will not be heeded. Listening to the person's problems may encourage the individual to seek professional help. It might also make the leader more tolerant and understanding.

Reducing a list of many solutions. The situation that most dramatically lends itself to a meeting of minds is one in which a fairly large number of solutions is developed by a group. This condition may appear difficult to resolve because it suggests wide disagreement. However, the opportunities for resolving varied differences tend to be greater in such cases than in balanced conflicts. The first step in this condition is to reduce the list of solutions.

Suppose that ten solutions have been listed and the group consists of ten persons. A simple procedure to follow would be to ask each person to select the three solutions he liked most. If the solutions were each given a number from 1 to 10, then each person would jot down the numbers of the three solutions he preferred. These preferences could readily be tabulated by asking how many persons selected solution number 1, counting hands, and then proceeding in like manner with the other solutions. This tabulation would distribute thirty votes among the ten solutions. Invariably such a procedure reveals three or four solutions that stand out by getting well over half of the votes.

The next step is to examine these high-scoring solutions to determine if and how they may be integrated or combined. Satisfaction results from the fact that every person is very likely to have at least one of his choices among the few that survive. Solutions receiving from zero to two votes can be dropped without protest. Thus no solution needs to be rejected and no one then needs to lose an argument. Rather, some solutions just fail to successfully compete.

The result of this type of participation permits everyone to influence the outcome in a positive manner. When two surviving solutions can be combined, and a third is in conflict with them, the combined solution becomes favored and frequently is a unanimous choice.

An example in the use of this type of selection occurred in a large government military test station. Many scientists were involved. A top level group consisting of eleven persons had a morale problem. They, as well as their subordinates, were dissatisfied with the kind of research they were given to do. Each felt that his department could have more important and worthwhile projects if the station were allowed the time to do them. The obstacle was that assignments were imposed upon them by a government agency, and these assignments interfered with what the group felt were the more important activities. The group, however, had never been able to agree upon the projects they should request from the agency and the assignments that they should attempt to avoid. As a result dissatisfaction with assignments was general, and the government agency was blamed.

In this instance we followed the procedure of listing the research activities that the group members preferred. All contributions were briefly restated and written on the blackboard. A list of fifteen items was obtained. Next we developed a list of all of the activities that were assigned to them by the agency. This list consisted of thirteen items.

When these two lists were completed, the selection procedure described above was introduced. Each person was asked to select the three projects he felt his department was best able and willing to handle. Four projects stood out as being preferred well above the others. Each person had voted for at least one of these four; five persons had voted for two of them; and two persons found all of their choices among the final four.

The same procedure was followed in selecting from the list of assignments given to the station by the government agency. Members were asked to choose the three they would be most willing to handle. Tabulation showed five solutions receiving sizable preferences. It was agreed that the station could avoid some of the assignments, and it was now clear which these would be.

The result of this exercise made everyone realize that by getting together on the activities that were agreed upon as desirable, they would be more than willing to do most of those assigned by the agency. Apparently the problem had primarily been one of finding a way of getting together and agreeing on a combination. Previously each participant felt that other departments received more favored treatment, and as a result all tended to try to get everything they wanted and to avoid as many agency assignments as possible.

The above illustration describes the selection process that may be used to reduce any long list of items, regardless of whether they represent solutions, ideas, or preferences. In some instances one can go directly from the *idea-getting* process to this selection process without spending time on the *evaluation* process. This shortcut is especially appropriate (1) when the value of any item is dependent upon individual differences in preferences rather than a complex pattern of facts or (2) when the facts are common knowledge and need not be explored.

RESISTANCE TO IMPOSED EVALUATION PROCEEDINGS

The evaluation procedures discussed in this chapter require the leader to structure the discussion. The leader may find that his attempts to do this often meet with resistance. Instead of perceiving his efforts as an attempt to be systematic and helpful, participants may see them as a form of subtle manipulation. When this occurs, it is apparent that attitudes and feelings have entered the discussion.

The leader should deal with this attitudinal problem in accordance with the procedures outlined in the preceding chapter. If the leader justifies his actions, he soon will find himself on the defensive. It is unlikely that participants will be receptive to any explanation until they have freely expressed their feelings of suspicion.

In order to avoid the charge of manipulation, it may be wise for the leader to outline evaluation procedures before embarking on them. The method of evaluation may be discussed and even made the subject of a group decision. If a group approves of a procedure to follow, the leader ceases to be in the situation of imposing the structure on the evaluation process.

Since groups are frequently exposed to varied forms of manipulation and trickery on the part of discussion leaders, they tend to be somewhat hypersensitive. They fail to distinguish between procedures that aid a discussion and procedures that control the decision. Both leaders and participants should clearly distinguish between these leadership objectives.

Another way to obtain cooperation in a systematic evaluation procedure is to train the *groups* in the methods. This relieves the leader of the task of imposing the structure. In Chapter 2 it was pointed out that the results of the developmental type of discussion were far superior to the free type of discussion, particularly when the groups, rather than the leader, were instructed to follow the two procedures. When the leader imposed the discussion procedures, the difference in their relative effectiveness was less.

The skill and the attitude of a leader will greatly determine the extent to which a group is suspicious of his motives. The experience of a group with a particular leader also plays an important part, either in increasing their suspicion or in reducing it.

SUMMARIZING THE DECISION

Communicating the decision. Many discussions lead to decisions which later are found to reveal that participants are in disagreement over many of the details. In order to facilitate accurate communication of a decision it is essential that the leader carefully summarize the decision—preferably writing the various details in abbreviated form on the blackboard. These details should be carefully worded, leaving ample opportunity for participants to add, delete, or correct any misunderstandings.

Meetings that terminate in action decisions are the most satisfying and stimulate a sense of responsibility. The failure to settle something leads to the feeling that time has been wasted. When conflict has not been resolved, when the problem is too complex to solve at one meeting, or when further information has to be obtained before continuing, it is the leader's function to summarize these conclusions and treat them as decisions. A decision to gather more information can be a true decision and is treated as such only if the next meeting takes up where the last one left off. In order to ensure this progress, the issues and the reasons for the subsequent meeting should be stated in the summary. Treating the summary as a statement of the decision permits the next meeting to continue from the new orientation.

Unfortunately it is not uncommon for a subsequent meeting to go over the same ground covered by a previous one. This is especially true if a member was absent on the first meeting. Summarizing and stating the problem in its new form reduce the tendency for meetings to lose momentum and move in circles.

When meetings are held merely to discuss something and no action is to be taken, there is little opportunity to experience the feeling of positive accomplishment. Such meetings serve their best purpose when used to disseminate information. The purpose of group interaction in these cases would be primarily to help clarify and improve communication. When such meetings are necessary, they would be improved if some opportunity for decision making could be introduced or incorporated.

Finally something should be said about "fatigue decisions." Some discussions are continued until the group comes around to the leader's way of thinking. When a group arrives at this point, it is not because of acceptance, but of capitulation. This approach trains participants not to waste time contributing and discussing, and unfortunately the leader may feel that his meetings are quite efficient and peaceful. He may never become aware of the problem he has created or the yes-men he has developed.

The writer attended a committee meeting on the campus in which a topic regarding policy had been discussed for four meetings. After each of the first three meetings, summaries were distributed to the participants. Each summary stressed the failure of the group to agree, despite the fact that to the writer there seemed to be a lot of agreement. During the fourth meeting, the writer again felt that there was considerable agreement, yet the discussion leader showed no tendency to pick out the points of agreement. Finally, the writer asked for a straw vote to test the extent to which the group disagreed. A test showed that, with regard to the main issue which had been discussed in four meetings, there was complete agreement. To the question of why the group should not move to the next problem, the leader replied that he disagreed with the solution. It is not unusual for conferences to be continued until the group reaches the leader's decision. Failure to summarize progress can introduce some of the elements of meetings in which the leader wears the group down until they reach his decision.

Specifying action details. Some good group decisions fail to produce results because certain details regarding the action have not been specified. One decision failed merely because no one knew when to begin the new method of operation that had been agreed upon. The supervisor thought the group decision had been rejected because the men continued the old method, while they in turn waited for him to signal the time for the changeover. It is the leader's responsibility to see that the summary of a decision not only includes the nature of the decision but also (1) specifies the time the decision is to be put into effect; (2) spells out the duties each member is to assume; (3) indicates steps or conditions that may be involved in implementing the decision; (4) describes the kind of follow-up that will be used to test the effectiveness of the decision; and (5) indicates whether or not subsequent meetings regarding evaluation of results will be needed and, if so, when.

An essential part of discussion leadership is to see that these aspects of the decision are fully agreed upon before they are summarized. To assume that the leader should be free to settle these matters on his own or that the group understands and agrees to such details of a decision can be a serious oversight.

FOLLOW–UP MEETINGS

Every group decision should be reexamined after it has been put into effect in order to determine whether it is yielding the satisfactions anticipated and producing the results needed to solve the problem. If a follow-up process has been agreed upon, everyone is inclined to feel free to raise a question if some problem arises. A group decision is subject to change by the group, and this is one of its great merits. A leader cannot readily change his own decisions because his subordinates will question his ability, but the group is its own judge and hence is free to experiment and innovate in the light of subsequent experience. It is through changes, no matter how minor, that a decision can be tailor-made not only to fit a particular group of persons, but also to be altered as the group changes. Confusion with this flexible state of affairs is minimal because everyone involved understands the nature and the reasons for the change. Actually, the existence of the right to change reduces the destructive criticism so common with unilateral decisions.

When group decisions solve unusual problems, it is satisfying to test the way the method is working out. This kind of follow-up gives the group an experience of progress, indicates the leader's interest in the outcome, and stimulates members to think of ways to improve on it. All of these reactions are worthwhile and develop a group's sense of responsibility.

CHAPTER SEVEN

Discussion methods for specific objectives

OBJECTIVE OF PARTICIPATION

As indicated in Chapter 2, discussion *methods* and *techniques* serve a useful purpose in complementing discussion *skills*. The methods described in this chapter serve fairly specific objectives and special conditions. They may be seen as discussion procedures having a rather limited objective and as techniques that may be incorporated into a more general discussion to deal with certain needs or specific problem conditions as they arise. These techniques, therefore, should be regarded as specialized procedures that may be incorporated into a larger discussion pattern or as discussion methods for dealing with specific and limited problem situations.

One objective of a discussion is to permit participants to influence each other. This is in contrast to learning from an authority figure. Although the accuracy of the subject matter taught may appear to be best protected by authoritarian approaches, such learning remains passive, and acceptance is limited. Even the simplest discussion methods permit the social pressure of majority viewpoints to influence attitudes; they permit learning to more closely follow interests and needs; they permit the exploration of ideas that are live issues in the group; and they permit clarification of thinking, because they require participants to express themselves and differentiate between many shades of opinion.

This means that learning through participation not only differs from formal teaching in that the source is different but the content of what is learned is also different. A change in attitude is a form of learning, but it is not something that is memorized. The nature of such learning is emotional rather than intellectual or factual.

Another difference in the nature of learning that is promoted by discussion is the appearance of insight. Insight is an active process; it is something the individual does in response to a situation. These insights cannot be forced. A good lecturer can promote these insights, but a discussion goes a step further. When a person must describe his opinion, he is forced to evaluate it in broader perspective and in relation to the discussion objective. He cannot follow his lecture notes because the order of events in a discussion does not follow a formalized sequence.

The third difference is in the learning of certain skills. These are learnings that are gained through doing and that cannot occur through listening or watching. The application of knowledge is a skill. One can memorize the principle of a hydraulic system, yet be unable to think of it in connection with a problem where its application might lead to an invention. In order to use such knowledge it must not only be thoroughly understood, but it must be available in a great variety of settings. A good teacher assigns many varied problems for his students to solve so that they experience a basic principle at work in a variety of relationships. This kind of teaching is a form of participation. Discussions have a similar effect on the uses to which knowledge may be put. The scope of such applications of knowledge may be even broader since a discussion does not furnish a mental set concerning which knowledge to use on a given occasion, as does an assignment to work out special problems. Practice in discussion makes people resourceful not only in their conduct but also in their thinking.

Participation promotes an active rather than a passive kind of learning. Such learning is not only more permanent but also more available. It incorporates skills and attitudes with intellectual content and hence makes such learning a part of the person's conduct and system of values.

It is apparent that the so-called question period is a most limited kind of discussion. One of the earliest forms of participation is that of introducing a question period after a formal lecture or presentation. In some circles this is all that participation means, and to be sure of getting even this degree of participation the questions are often planted in the audience.

However, the limitations of the question period are quite apparent. At worst it means that the authority figure is given another opportunity to make a speech, and at best it permits an exchange between the authority and a few members of the audience. Often the discussants in the audience have motives other than an exchange of ideas when raising their questions.

Group discussions may vary in effectiveness not only because of their size but also because of the type of discussion pattern that the leader initiates. How the leader deals with questions, what kind of interaction he encourages, how he deals with conflict, in which direction he leads the communication channels, and the amount of control he exercises are the issues that concern us here.

TURNING QUESTIONS INTO PROBLEMS

Some meetings are held for the purpose of communicating information, and participation takes the form of a question period. The need for these informational meetings occurs in industry, and it is a common problem in all forms of teaching. It will be granted that this problem is less acute in small than in large groups since a smaller percentage of disinterested persons are a captive audience while the authority answers a question. However, it is a common experience for the leader to fail to answer the question asked.

If the leader does not understand the question, it is quite obvious that many participants also will be in the dark, and this might explain some of the boredom apparent during question periods. In order to prevent question periods from becoming tangential discussions, it is necessary for the leader to require more background from the questioner. Does the questioner request information; is he trying to obtain approval for his own ideas; or is his question a subtle way of disagreeing with the authority? Requests for information should be granted but only to the extent that the questioner wishes. Determining the need for the information might not only interest others but would guide the leader in adapting the information to the need.

Questions that involve approval or disagreement are stated against a background of feeling, and until the attitude is revealed there is little to gain by supplying information. Asking the questioner to elaborate, asking him what his views on the subject are, requesting other participants to express their views, and determining the extent of group interest in the issue raised are methods for evading direct questions that should not be answered.

Let us take the following illustration. A consultant had discussed some of the dangers involved in using punishment as a preventive for accidents. A participant asked, "Suppose a man deliberately violates a company rule, are you saying we should let him get away with this?"

This question clearly is loaded and indicates opposition. If he answers "yes," he will lose the questioner's confidence and perhaps that of others; if he answers "no," he will appear to be backing down and will have to take a defensive position.

Instead of taking a position he may ask for a specific

illustration. One such reply was as follows: A pilot damages the wing of a plane by parking it too close to one of the air-port buildings. The speaker accepts this example with the statement "Let's take a look at the cause of this accident. Granting that he had not properly judged the clearance, what might cause him to make such a mistake?"

The formulation of the problem in this way involved the whole group in the discussion. There was disagreement re-garding the pilot's intentions, his skills, the placement of the building, improper ground signals, etc. Subsequent dis-cussion of how to prevent the recurrence of such accidents caused the idea of punishment to fall into the background. Thus the question of one participant was turned into a group discussion of interest to all present. Neither the questioner nor the leader was placed in a face-saving situation with respect to the role of punishment in correcting faulty be-havior. Rather the questioner as well as the group was caused to think in broader and more constructive terms than that of trying to change behavior by means of punishment.

Most loaded questions can be made subjects for group discussion, and the very fact that they are loaded means that the discussion can be lively. The objective of the leader is to treat such questions as discussion issues and turn them into problems for group discussion. Many questions do not have to be reformulated. The leader frequently need only say, "Let's see how the rest of the group feel about that?"

Questions of a technical nature cannot be so readily turned back to a group. Often they are requests for informa-tion. Even then the leader may present the conflicting views of two experts and let the group evaluate. If the leader wishes, he may express his own views but refrain from trying to prove he is right. Instead he should accept the fact of dis-agreement, encourage others to express opinions, and sum-marize by concluding that some of us feel this way about it while others feel differently.

Controversy is something that should be discouraged while disagreement is encouraged. The expression of opin-ions, a knowledge that group members do not agree, and the feeling that ideas are not imposed or forced, do more to influence attitudes constructively than do facts or the opinions of an authority.

POSTING PROBLEMS

Origin and objective of the method. The method of posting problems was initially designed to protect the discussion leader from premature questions raised by a group. Many questions are out of place and should not be answered because (1) they put the leader on the defensive, (2) sufficient groundwork has not been accomplished, or (3) an answer will put the questioner in a face-saving situation.[1] Instead of dealing with one question at a time, the leader sets aside a period for group participation in raising questions or problems. However, rather than feeling obligated to answer questions or to solve problems, he attempts to summarize the questioner's problem and write it on a blackboard. This procedure makes it unnecessary for the leader to dispose of the problem raised; rather he now functions to collect problems and to assist each of the participants in communicating their problems to others.

The list of contributions can then be made the subject for an organized treatment. A skilled person can build a supplementary lecture around the questions and thus speak to the group as a whole, or he may make the solving of such problems the subject of later discussions. For certain purposes and when circumstances permit, it is desirable to require a group to solve its own problems.

It will be recognized that this procedure not only makes it unnecessary for the leader to defend himself as an expert, but instead allows him to use the group resources to explore problems of mutual interest and even require them to assume responsibility for solving each other's problems. They are surprisingly willing to do this.

The extent to which the problems posted are to be used

[1] N. R. F. Maier, *Principles of Human Relations.* John Wiley & Sons, Inc., New York, 1952.

for later discussion depends on the time available. The mere posting of problems has its value, but the value of the method is greatly enhanced if the list of problems is to be used in future discussions.

The author uses the posting process as one of the first steps in executive training programs. In this way he becomes familiar with the problems of the group, and the subsequent treatment of topics can be guided by the major problem areas represented in the list. However, he never assumes responsibility for solving the problems. If time permits, all of the problems posted are examined at the end of the program, and ideas for solving them are discussed. This gives participants an opportunity to apply the principles taught in the program to their own problems.

When time does not permit an exploration of all of the problems, a few can be selected for special consideration. It is better to explore a few problems thoroughly than to superficially explore all of them. The topics used for detailed treatment should be determined by the group. The leader may ask each person to select from the list three problems for which he feels the program has contributed the most. A tally of the choices usually shows that from two to four of the problems stand out—in the sense that they receive the majority of votes—while the rest receive scattered votes.

Discussion is then turned to a consideration of the problems which received the *smallest* number of votes. A few problems may appear entirely unrelated to the program, but a little thought usually elicits some ideas that suggest how the training program may have been helpful. The trainer may also wish to add supplementary material if it seems appropriate. However, failure to have solved certain problems should be freely granted so that discussion can turn to problems that the group members feel they are able to handle. The objective is to give the participants the responsibility for solving their own problems. By beginning with the difficult problems the group is challenged and usually someone finds an application. By the time the discussion gets to a consideration of the easy problems, the group is full of ideas.

There is a feeling of accomplishment and a development of confidence when the group members get ideas for solving their own problems.

When the posting of problems is used in connection with a single meeting such as a lecture or a conference, the list of posted problems may be used as a basis for formulating a discussion agenda. It may also be used as the basis around which to build a formal lecture. The preliminary posting assures the coverage of topics that are most relevant to the needs of participants. Both discussions and interest in lectures are improved by introducing participation, in the form of posting problems, at the outset. The discussion leader or the expert is thereby brought into closer contact with the group, and distractions in the form of resistance are reduced. Participants and listeners are unresponsive if they are distracted by problems that come to mind. In getting these posted, participants are readier to devote their attention to the immediate activities.

Meetings that are held purely for the purpose of disseminating some information would increase in interest value if participants could raise questions ahead of time and be assured that their problems would be covered. This suggests that question periods would be improved if questions were posted and answered as a group rather than individually.

When to post problems

Stimulating an interest in problems: The method of posting problems has many uses. First of all, it is a good way to stimulate discussion. People are readier to talk about subjects on which they feel confident and on which, with regard to specific problems in their work, they are experts. Once the risk of appearing incompetent (because they have problems) is removed, a group can readily come up with a list of ten to twenty items. Interest grows as the discussion is continued because participants soon discover that they have much the same problems. Ordinarily managers feel that their problems are unique to their own work situations. When personnel in sales, accounting, production, quality control, and personnel find that they have common problems, a good groundwork for better understanding is laid. Even problems with different populations, such as white-collar versus blue-collar groups, male versus female, and technical versus unskilled, become strikingly similar. In using this method in different European countries, with high and low levels of management or with students and managers, the writer has found no basic differences in the content of lists of problems. Two different types of groups of participants will differ no more than two similar groups. Basically such a list deals with problems in the behavior of people, and the same problems recur because human nature is the common factor. If the same fundamental laws did not govern all people, there would be no science of psychology. Situational differences influence behavior, but they do not alter human nature. Although each group feels its problems are unique, the fact that they are less so than expected is a good learning experience in that it becomes apparent that helpful basic principles may exist.

Because people are solution-minded (see pages 242 ff.) and ordinarily look for answers before they really understand the problems, posting becomes a method for developing a problem-solving attitude toward problems rather than an attitude of placing the blame on someone for the problem. Thus the method serves to make problems with people a challenge rather than a headache.

Clarifying job problems: In Chapter 3 we found that the location of a problem may be a rather complex matter. The process of posting problems may serve as an aid, particularly in controversial situations. For example, a manager might ask his subordinates to indicate some of the problems they face in meeting a certain objective. Examples of such specific problem areas are the following:

Meeting deadlines
Giving customers the kind of service they want
Maintaining discipline
Ensuring safety
Providing optimal job satisfaction

A group could contribute many problems in any of these areas, and the mere fact that the superior is interested in the problems his group faces makes them more willing to accept the existing conditions. However, the posting of such problems can go beyond this point. Frequently problems have an emotional loading, and their mere expression seems to relieve the hostility because it takes place in a nonthreatening environment. Once problems are posted and accepted, they are clarified, brought into focus, and made more objective. These conditions promote problem solving so that the mere formulation of the problem often suggests several directions in which the solution might lie.

On one occasion the author was asked to present a program on the subject of preventing office accidents. He decided to post problems. A group of over 100 persons was divided into groups of six to seven, and each group was asked to report what it considered the most acute single problem to solve in dealing with office accidents.

After a twenty-minute discussion, each group reported back, and their problem was posted after it was clarified. Of the sixteen items, twelve were basically different, while four were close duplicates. These sixteen ideas were then generally discussed and evaluated both by the leader and participants, but no conclusions were drawn. The groups were then asked what they had learned about how to reduce accidents. A large number of ideas were contributed, and these were summarized on the blackboard. One of these ideas was that each supervisor could go back to his job and use the same approach on his group.

Although the lecturer gave no answers, it was clear that the group members felt they had learned a good deal about accidents. They not only clarified their problems but learned from each other, and not only in the small discussions but also in the posting process.

The fact that each group was permitted only one contribution forced them to disagree and interact. This limitation on the number of contributions livens up a discussion and makes it more than an additive procedure.

Although the leader may wish to deal with problems that are posted on some later occasion, this need not be a necessary condition. The mere posting of problems serves as a release for feelings, the development of a constructive attitude toward problems, an opportunity to share and compare problems with one another, and a stimulant of ideas for solutions. Often a group is satisfied with these accomplishments. However, a brief evaluation of problems frequently adds considerably more.

Resolving differences: Sometimes discussions break down because there seem to be differences that lead nowhere. Frequently this confusion is due to the fact that participants are not agreeing on the problem. The leader may find it fruitful in the discussion of complex problems to separate ideas for solutions from the analyses of the *problem.* Thus after a discussion has gone on for some time, he may raise the question of whether the group members are working on the same problem. He may then suggest that the participants describe the problem as they see it and then proceed to post each of the descriptions.

Finding several problems in such a discussion is not uncommon. Once the problems are posted, agreement on which should be solved may facilitate the reaching of agreement or of a solution.

Essential skills

Understanding the intended meaning: Posting problems requires many of the discussion skills described in Chapter 5. The leader must be ready to accept all contributions regardless of how he feels about them. His function is to understand what the participant means, and frequently this is quite different from what he says. If a leader can grasp a participant's meaning quickly, he will contribute considerably to the communication between members. We have already mentioned the value of asking for elaboration and examples as an aid to this better understanding.

If the leader has difficulty, he may ask other participants to help out. This takes the focus of attention away from a single individual and gives the group an opportunity to interact.

Emotional factors frequently contribute to vagueness in the perception of problems. Suppose a manager wishes to introduce more efficient work methods and runs into opposition. When he states his problem as: How can I get my employees to work more efficiently? he is blaming employees for opposing some change. An illustration would readily reveal some of the background factors. As a result the discussion leader might rephrase the problem as follows: How can I stimulate interest for improved work methods in my employees? This restatement removes the element of criticism and increases the range of possible solutions.

In some instances the problem raised may be so general that the solution may lie in many directions. A problem such as: What are the major applications of psychology to industry? suggests a purely intellectual interest, but behind it may lie an important problem. It might turn out that the true problem is: How far can you trust a psychologist? Discussion and an example might reveal this feeling, and if it is grasped and accepted, some deep hostility may be released and reduced.

It is also common for two or more problems to be so intermixed with each other as to confuse the whole issue. If the separate factors are isolated, it may be possible to solve each, but not with the same remedy. A person might ask "How can I improve my communications?" When asked whether he is thinking of upward, downward, or lateral communication, he may reply, "All of them." In such a case it would be best to state three problems since the solution for one form of communication might not be appropriate for another. Usually, however, the questioner is concerned with one of these problems more than the others, and an illustration supplied by him will reveal this.

Problems that are posted are clearest if they deal with specific situations. General statements seldom communicate the same thing to different persons. Only after specific instances are understood can problems be stated in general terms that are meaningful to the group as a whole.

Brief restatements of the problem: The ability for restating another person's problem in a brief form readily improves with practice. The restatement is needed because it is the best way to test whether or not the problem is understood. Some problems may be so clear that they might be posted as given, but this is seldom the case. In other instances, only an abbreviation or an addition is needed. Brief but accurate summaries are less likely to be misunderstood because there are fewer key words to misinterpret, and there is less confusion as to which these are. Brevity is desirable if for no other reason than to keep the leader from spending too much time at the blackboard.

It is desirable for the leader to write on the blackboard and talk at the same time when testing his rephrasing of the problem. The written statement gives everyone something tangible to work with and improve. The participant who initiated the problem should be the first person asked to criticize the problem as restated. Sometimes the leader misses the point completely, and this stimulates further explanation; sometimes only a word is unsatisfactory.

Restatements of problems should direct attention away from evaluative objectives and toward more descriptive statements. A problem stated as "what to do with a lazy person" is evaluative in that a person is judged as lazy. After supplying an illustration, the problem might be posted as "how to increase job interest in workers who accomplish less than they are capable of." This restatement might be accepted, or the questioner might object because the man is incompetent. If so, the participant had something quite different in mind when he used the word "lazy," and of course the leader should modify this statement accordingly.

Sensitivity: The pace at which a discussion progresses must be neither so slow as to induce boredom nor so fast as to interfere with participation. In order to keep this balance the leader must be sensitive to his group. This task of diplomatically moving the discussion along without speeding it up requires the leader not only to pay attention to the ideas expressed but to observe the group's interest and attention. If he is not sure about the group's state of mind he might ask participants whether they are progressing fast enough.

Usually it requires about an hour to post approximately fifteen items. For many types of discussion this length of time may not be needed to explore a problem, while for others interest may be maintained for more than an hour.

When additional problems are not readily forthcoming, the leader might suggest stopping after one or two more items. He may use this approach with a time limit to give those who have not contributed a problem a special opportunity. He should not terminate the discussion without waiting out a good pause, because some of the most emotionally involved problems come only after the discussion leader has demonstrated by his performance that the climate is acceptant and nonthreatening. If a new batch of problems is forthcoming, he should not hold to the suggested time limit.

Preventing evaluation and problem solving: Initially groups of persons make evaluations of the contributions made by others. Although this type of interaction is desirable for problem solving, it interferes with the process of posting problems. The objective of the method of posting problems is to clarify problems. The type of interaction needed is support and understanding. If one participant is inclined to be critical of a person who poses a problem or if he tries to alter or improve on the problem, it is the discussion leader's function to see that the original contributor gets the problem stated as he wants it. A person who wishes to alter another person's contribution can be asked to state what he has in mind, and this problem can be made a separate entry. It can be made clear that everyone need not agree on whether or not something is a problem. It is sufficient that each entry be the problem of someone in the group. Disagreement in the group would be used to get new problems, not to change someone's mind.

Participants also are inclined to think of solutions while problems are being posted. It is permissible to allow some discussion along these lines and then indicate that, on a later occasion, finding solutions will be the prime objective. It can also be pointed out that the effective statement of a problem suggests solutions and makes problems which may have seemed to be due to the contrariness of human nature appear soluble and interesting. The leader can then indicate that for the time being it is profitable to collect more problems.

The accomplishments of posting problems. Improved participation is one of the most immediate gains. Once a group becomes involved in locating problems, the climate of trying to understand rather than evaluate one another becomes established. The result is improved cohesiveness, better communication, and the finding of common objectives.

Problem solving is enhanced in that problems are clarified; the attitude toward problems changes because problems are seen as challenges rather than headaches or the fault of other persons; and self-assurance increases because participants discover that they are both helping others and being helped by them.

The attitude toward the discussion leader also improves because he is seen as an aid rather than as a critic or judge. The group members feel responsible for solving their own problems rather than having an outsider give flippant formulas that he doesn't have to live with himself. When the leader doesn't have all the answers, the participants have an opportunity to grow rather than defend themselves from feelings of inferiority. The best improvements in supervision are better achieved through growth in problem-solving ability than through the learning of solutions that experts suggest.

The above-mentioned accomplishments of posting problems are those that participants usually contribute when the question is put to them after participating. Additional gains frequently are mentioned, but these usually are specific learnings. Mention is made that they now know what to do about some particular problem. In general, the method arouses more enthusiasm and interest than is anticipated. Apparently there are a number of personal gains that differ from one person to another. Perhaps some of the satisfaction is due to a welcomed change from the kind of discussion where the leader remains the expert.

THE RISK TECHNIQUE

Origin and objective of the method. The risk technique may be regarded as a procedure for aiding a group to express its fears and hostilities about some situation or problem. This method is based on counseling principles which advocate the value of letting people release their feelings in a non-threatening situation. The relief gained from such expression is commonly called catharsis. The values of so-called gripe sessions are largely derived from this same process.

As pointed out in Chapter 5, problem-solving behavior does not occur until interfering feelings have been dealt with. Frequently the fear and hostility are aroused by an action the management of a company wishes to take; consequently the opportunity to express opposition is not readily available. Persons who express opposition are judged unfavorably by those responsible for the action, but even if criticism is welcomed, a leader who is involved in the action finds it difficult to lend a sympathetic ear. It is easier to listen to complaints about others than about oneself or the group with which one identifies. The risk technique was developed to aid the emotionally involved discussion leader in listening, accepting, and understanding.[2]

In essence the risk technique is a procedure for posting objections to, or feelings of doubt or fear for, some action or plan that is under consideration. The discussion leader is less inclined to be on the defensive if he sets aside a special period to have the group raise objections, and it is his function to restate them, post them, and develop as many different anticipated risks as possible. The longer the list the more successful and worthwhile the discussion. In this role of posting, the leader feels no obligation to reply to questions and ob-

[2] N. R. F. Maier, *Principles of Human Relations.* John Wiley & Sons, Inc., New York, 1952.

jections. This attitude on his part encourages participants to feel freer to reveal their true feelings than to hide behind rationalizations.

Once a list is posted, the discussion can proceed to ways in which the dangers can be reduced or avoided. Only the important ones may need to be considered since some will be reduced by the mere opportunity to voice them.

The writer has found the risk technique invaluable in introducing new management concepts in training programs. New ideas are threatening to persons who are supposed to use them. The concept of group decision, for example, represents a basic change in a manager's function and, therefore, arouses both fears and hostilities. Thus, any discussion regarding the merits or demerits of this type of management tends to be colored by strong feelings.

During an introductory presentation of group decision and its application to management, many questions are aroused in the minds of the participants. This is when the writer finds it advisable to permit an airing of the negative side of the controversial question by asking the group to explore the risks that group decision would introduce. Regardless of whether the risks expressed are due to misunderstanding, imagined dangers, false assumptions about human nature, or real dangers, they are accepted and posted. The risks include such factors as (1) too much time would be required, (2) groups would fail to agree, (3) poor decisions would be caused by lack of knowledge, (4) decisions would be contrary to company interests, (5) management would lose control of company, and (6) higher management would reverse group decisions. Usually the risks posted fall between sixteen and eighteen in number.

The list of risks, when completed, is reproduced and distributed for later action. As in the case of posting problems, the participants are later given the responsibility of deciding how to guard against the risks. Actually, many disappear as new information is gained; others require careful understanding of the appropriate uses of the method and the development of conference skills such as those discussed in Chapters 3 through 6.

When to develop risks

An antidote to selling: Many conferences are held for the purpose of informing subordinates of a change either being adopted or considered. In presentations of this kind it is almost inevitable that the merits of the change will be presented. Before long the group may become concerned with certain mental reservations, and until these can be expressed, they remain as distractions so that participants cease to be further informed. Such conferences may profit by incorporating a period for posting risks. The problem for discussion could be introduced with a question such as "What are some of the risks we must guard against in setting up this plan?"

In discussing the dangers, participants can talk about possible abuses, e.g., mishandling because of lack of communication, training, or skill; possible favoritism; disadvantages suffered by certain groups; loss of job satisfaction; and any number of possible or imagined outcomes.

Once the leader knows the resistance points, he may present further information (often repeat information already supplied) that may be relevant to some of these risks. This presentation will be received with greater interest and attention because it follows the participation. However, the new points should not be presented as replies, but as information that may or may not have something to do with the risks. After the additional information has been given, the discussion can be turned over to the group, the objective being to determine the extent to which the added information guards against certain risks.

It is not to be expected that all fears can be removed. The leader's mere acceptance of the existing feelings of danger, the opportunity for subordinates to participate in reducing the dangers, and the success achieved in reducing some of the dangers is sufficient to remove much of the resistance to change. Reducing fears, recognizing that some problems still exist, and respecting the fears and the problems that remain are adequate bases on which to build improved acceptance.

Reducing general anxiety: Impending decisions such as mergers, a large move, a change in company policy, new legislation, and a reduction in work force arouse many fears. These fears harassed the airline companies when the jet began to replace conventional equipment, and some of the unresolved fears still plague them. Often it is impossible for any one person either to supply answers to questions or to give reassurance of any kind. Not only is information lacking, but managers fear that, if discussions are held, embarrassing questions will be raised. As a result rumors characterize the form that communication takes.

The leader of any work group can post risks since he does not place himself in the position of having to reply to them. His objective is to explore some of the bad things that might happen when the company makes certain changes.

In one company a merger was pending for several months. During this period there was evidence of a considerable amount of anxiety in the middle management of the company that was absorbing the smaller one. This became apparent during some of the training conferences. In these conferences, a group of men from all departments and from all sections of the country met together for a period of a week.

Risks were posted with two such groups of middle management personnel. In order to obtain the first risk from each group, a long pause was required. After the first risk was posted, there was little difficulty in obtaining others. In the first group, consisting of twenty-two persons, a total of seventeen risks were posted. The risks ranged from fear of being downgraded to fear that the company would lose money by taking over a less profitable organization. Several participants indicated that they felt better immediately. The risks were reproduced and distributed to the group the following morning. After the group members had read them over, a poll was taken to determine how the group felt. Eleven participants indicated that they were less anxious; none indicated increased anxiety; and eleven indicated no change.

The second group consisted of 28 persons and it posted 23 risks. After going over the list the following morning, 10 members felt better, 16 felt the same, and 2 felt somewhat worse.

There was strong approval for having gone through the experience even by those who felt no better or even worse. The values of talking it out, seeing that others felt the same way, and clarifying their feelings were mentioned most frequently.

Some months after the merger had taken place, two similar groups were asked for risks, but on these occasions the anxieties were more in the form of unsolved problems than anticipated injustices. After posting the risks entailed in the merger, these groups felt neither better nor worse. Nevertheless, most of them felt that the exercise clarified matters and suggested solutions. However, until they got back home and licked the problems, they felt they had no grounds for feeling better.

Essential skills. The skills for posting risks are essentially the same as those for posting problems. The ability to summarize and restate the fears so as to create a receptive climate is essential to the success of the method. The leader must also be sensitive to gauging how long the posting process should be continued. There is no set duration for such a discussion since the length of time required depends on how much and how quickly the fears are expressed.

Ordinarily the initial fears may be more logical and plausible than some of the later ones. People are most ready to reveal the fears they can justify or which are likely to be shared by others. When these contributions are accepted without being criticized, the fears less well founded in logic will be expressed. These irrational fears are the important ones, and they are the least likely to be shared because the person may not have discovered or understood them himself. Only after some of the superficial feelings are expressed do the more deep-seated ones come to the surface.

Another factor that assists in the expression of deep-seated feelings is the interstimulation that occurs. The free expression of one person not only encourages others, but it arouses related anxieties in them and helps them to recall and clarify their own feelings. The leader must permit these feeling-provoking processes to occur, and this means that he should learn to tolerate long pauses, especially during the early stages of the meeting.

The skill in outlasting a pause requires sensitivity on the part of the leader. He must avoid talking and attempting to hurry the process. Only by living through these pauses can a leader successfully get the deeper and truer attitudes revealed.

However, pauses are only meaningful when there is something to be brought to expression. To use pauses when the group wishes to move forward merely creates boredom, and this condition tends to arouse discussion simply for the sake of avoiding boredom. In other words, the leader must be able to perceive when his group is introspecting and when it is waiting for the leader to move forward.

Sometimes the group may be divided in that many wish to move faster while a few wish to belabor a point. If the leader responds to the majority, he may have to curtail the discussion of a few talkers, but if he remains too permissive, the majority may become bored. He must strike a middle course, and to do this he must be sensitive as well as tactful. Practice and careful analysis of his successes and failures improve these skills.

Accomplishments

Reduced tension: Anxiety differs from fear in that it is general and its object or cause is vague or unknown. The emotion of fear incorporates a fear object. The existence of a reference object permits fear behavior to be directed along particular lines—avoiding the fear object or guarding against it. It is difficult to escape or guard against the unknown source of fear. Thus anxious behavior lacks direction and organization and hence is general and diffuse.

One of the values of discussion is release of tension through expression (catharsis). The mere expression of hostility or fear under conditions that do not threaten and aggravate the fear condition has a value in itself and is a part of therapeutic procedures.

A second value derives from the fact that the anxieties and vague fears are clarified through expression and posting. This adds further relief because fears that are understood lend themselves more readily to problem solving.

A third value of posting is the insights gained. Often the fears are found to be based upon remote possibilities, and the very fact that they are understood and posted places them in a frame of reference where they can be viewed more objectively. In some instances participants discover their own exaggerations; in others they discover the childish nature of their accusations. Seeing things in broader perspectives gives them insight into their own fears.

Finally there is a value in the sharing and exchanging of feelings. Persons often keep their feelings to themselves because they imagine their own problems are unique—perhaps abnormal. Many fear that they will make fools of themselves if they really expose their true feelings. Public expression makes participants realize that others have similar feelings, and this develops confidence in oneself as a normal person. It is always reassuring to find that others share our feelings.

Often managers hesitate to let subordinates express themselves freely because it is assumed that they might make unreasonable requests. However, failure to permit expression tends to heighten tensions rather than resolve them. Expression reduces tension and aids the resolution of conflicts. Unreasonable and unrealistic feelings are reduced through expression, whereas intellectual content tends to be furthered by expression.

The above values of the risk technique are based upon principles of nondirective counseling,[3] a therapeutic approach that is supported by a great deal of sound research.

[3] C. R. Rogers, *Counseling and Psychotherapy*. Houghton Mifflin Company, Boston, 1942. N. R. F. Maier, *Frustration*. McGraw-Hill Book Company, Inc., New York, 1949. Reissued by Ann Arbor Paperbacks, The University of Michigan Press, Ann Arbor, Mich., 1961.

THE TWO–COLUMN METHOD

Objective of the method. When people engage in controversy, the usual pattern of interaction is for one side to present evidence in favor of their position while the opposition presents evidence in support of the opposite position. This is the characteristic pattern when people argue. Each struggles for time to get his side represented, often interrupting one another. A somewhat more polite version of the same process is the "yes-but" discussion in which the conflicting parties get their opponents to stop talking with the "yes" and then counter with the "but" and a report of the errors in their thinking. Debates are even politer ways of disagreeing in that the conflicting parties are allowed equal time.

Even the *selling* approach follows the pattern of taking sides. The person who is trying to sell presents the favorable evidence while the listener asks doubting questions.

The common methods of persuasion mentioned above have one thing in common: all present facts and evidence carefully selected to build up one point of view at the expense of the opposite point of view.

Experimental evidence shows that even when people try to stay out of an argument, they soon get trapped into one because it is difficult for them to listen to a one-sided point of view without taking exception to it.[4] The fact that people let their attitudes select the facts they use in a discussion, rather than letting the evidence shape their opinions, explains why argumentation fails to change attitudes. People who have an unfavorable attitude toward a company can find facts to bolster this position, while people with a favorable attitude will find other facts that support theirs. Thus people can engage in an argument even if no disagreement over facts or their interpretation exists. However, it must be granted that disagreement over facts or the interpretation of facts would contribute to the argument if not to the outcome.

[4] N. R. F. Maier and L. Lansky, Effect of Attitude on Selection of Facts. *Personnel Psychol.*, 1957, **10**, 293–303.

If we grant that attitudes select the facts people use as evidence to support their own opinions, it becomes apparent that even if the facts are refuted, the opinion remains intact and hence can function to select a different set of facts. Only when facts cited *cause* the opinions entertained will a change in them alter opinions or attitudes. Since peoples' attitudes, especially when challenged, influence the evaluation and selection of facts, it becomes evident that arguing must have limited effectiveness.

Actually disagreement, instead of serving to persuade another, stimulates him to find support for his own position. Thus an opponent attempts to refute or obtain counterevidence when he is confronted with an argument designed to persuade him to change his views. Such a situation, therefore, stimulates each side to listen for the weakness in the evidence supplied by the other.

Instead of listening in order to understand, each side of the controversy listens to refute and to judge unfavorably. Of necessity, this kind of discussion leads to two positions— each side contending their position has all of the virtues while the other has all of the faults. The result is to cause people to create absolute rather than relative value systems. Thus ideas are classified as good versus bad, right versus wrong, black versus white. Actually these absolutes seldom fit the realities. If two groups can disagree so strongly, it is probable that each position has both strengths and weaknesses. The truth may lie in neither position.

The two-column method is designed to deal with controversy constructively and lead to an appreciation of the fact that each position has merits as well as weaknesses. Controversial questions such as the admission of Communist China to the United Nations, a merger between two companies, the passing of a law restricting the strength of unions, and the selection of a political candidate in a two-party system are topics that often are seen in terms of black and white extremes, yet eventually a decision between them must be made. This final choice does not allow one to take a position between the two alternatives. The choice is an all-or-nothing phenomenon. However, if this final choice can be delayed through a consideration of intermediate greys, it might permit the development of better alternatives and more realistic decisions.

Procedure. The procedure is still another variation of posting, but in this instance the conflicting ideas are posted in separate columns. If the issue is between alternatives such as procedure A and procedure B, one column is given the heading "Favorable to procedure A" while the other column is given the heading "Favorable to procedure B." The leader then requests ideas or arguments in support of each of these alternatives. Note that this approach gives the group an opportunity to contribute positively to either alternative, not to talk against either of them. [The reader will recognize that this procedure has already been described, in part, in connection with the evaluation of alternative solutions (Chapter 6). Here it is treated as a type of discussion.]

It is the leader's duty to post each contribution in its appropriate column. If one member argues against a contribution made by other members, the leader should attempt to reformulate the point so as to make it a positive contribution to the other column. If the same argument appears in both columns, which is not infrequent, they may be regarded as canceling each other. The leader's objective is to collect as many listings as quickly as possible. Now and then some discussion will occur regarding an entry. If differences are resolved, he can proceed according to the group's wishes. If a contribution is protested, it may be listed with a question mark to indicate that a protest was raised. However, a protest should not allow an item to be removed. The leader should make it clear that the lists represent ideas that *some* members of the group consider relevant and that the contents of the lists will be evaluated later.

Sometimes a controversy takes the form of arguments for and against an action under consideration. In such cases, the two columns are given the headings "For" and "Against," and the same procedure is followed.

Once the two sides of the issue have been posted, the discussion should turn to a consideration of the problem of how to resolve the differences. If the merits of two alternative solutions have been posted, the discussion question becomes one of how to capture the major advantages of each. If the positive and negative aspects of a particular action have been explored, the discussion question becomes one of how best to avoid the disadvantages without losing the major advantages.

These discussion questions have a mutual interest for all of the participants and therefore can become the basis for cooperative problem solving. Thus, what begins as a conflict in interests becomes the core of a mutual interest.

Essential skills. The skill requirement of the two-column method is essentially the same as that for posting problems and risks. Brief summarized statements are needed for posting. The leader may sometimes be confused with regard to which side of an issue a participant is contributing. Asking him which way he is arguing often aids him in clarifying his point. Some participants claim to be arguing for both sides. Usually this uncovers two or more aspects of the participant's idea. When these are separated, entries may be made in both columns or in neither.

The conduct of the evaluation stage of the two-column method represents a departure from the posting process. The question of locating the problem and conducting the discussion may follow the principles discussed in Chapters 3, 4, and 5.

Beneficial effects of the method. The merit of the two-column method is that the controversial aspects of the issue become objectified in the posting process. Instead of the group dividing into two camps, the group as a whole can be making contributions without some members attacking or disagreeing with others and without being attacked or criticized. This removal of personalized issues results in obtaining a more complete appraisal of the two aspects of the controversy.

As entries in the two columns are obtained, it soon becomes clear that all of the virtues are not on one side. The question of *absolute* values—black versus white—turns into a more reasonable consideration of *relative* values. It is not uncommon for the same person to contribute items to both columns.

Many controversies continue to be nonconstructive in character because a change in one's point of view suggests weakness or loss of face. These personal problems, so important in many discussions, stand in the way of resolving differences. The posting process directs the arguments into columns and not toward persons and avoids the need for a person to take a stand.

The value of catharsis is also likely to be felt. Many of the reactions to controversy are based on fears, and the opportunity to explore them freely reduces tensions. The threat of the opposing viewpoint is also reduced because, in exploring the issue together, participants discover that those who are in disagreement actually have honorable motives.

It is common for persons engaged in controversy to ascribe malicious motives to their opponents. For example, a union might claim that management is trying to take from them the gains they worked many years to achieve. In reply the management may accuse the union of attempting to whittle away management prerogatives. The behavior manifested by each might support these charges. However, an alternative interpretation fits the facts just as well. The union might fear the loss of its gains and hence try to strengthen them. This would explain why they demand a union shop and require that all workers belong. In striving for security they are asking the company to hire through the union. The company in turn fears that the union is striving to gain control of the company and therefore does all it can to prevent the union from having a say-so in hiring. The company fears that it cannot hire competent workers if the union controls employment and believes that the union wishes to lower standards. The company does not wish to let the union examine its books for fear that it will demand an unfair share of the earnings. Regardless of where the truth lies, a controversy raises fears. These fears become projected and are made the motives of the opposition. Problem solving would be enhanced if the real motives rather than the alleged motives were dealt with. As a matter of fact many problems might better be approached from the question of what each side of a controversy can do to reduce the fears of the other side.

In international relations this problem of projecting fears and making them the motives of others is common. When is a military "build-up" a defense, and when is it a preparation for attack? Each side claims its own action is a defense against the aggressive designs of the other. Both might be motivated by fear or by a desire for territory. The outward appearances might be the same in either case, but the solutions would be different.

The two-column method tends to clarify the complexity of a motivation pattern. The reason for an action may include a variety of positive gains, protections against certain dangers, ways of punishing the opposition, etc. Which of these are real, which are alleged? Once they are assembled in columns, they lend themselves to realistic appraisal by the group as a whole. Both sides of the questions thus are then appraised in turn and in cooperation.

NONDIRECTIVE AND FREE DISCUSSIONS

Permissive discussions. Most discussions have a fairly specific objective such as solving a particular problem. The nondirective discussion is group centered.[5] It is basically an extension of nondirective counseling [6] procedure, adapted to a group situation. Since client-centered counseling is a form of individual therapy, it is clear that group-centered leadership has implications for group therapy. It immediately becomes apparent that the basic value of nondirective or group-centered discussions resides in effectively dealing with

[5] T. Gordon, *Group-centered Leadership.* Houghton Mifflin Company, Boston, 1955.

[6] C. R. Rogers, *Counseling and Psychotherapy.* Houghton Mifflin, Company, Boston, 1942; and *Client-centered Therapy.* Houghton Mifflin Company, Boston, 1951.

feelings, as described in Chapter 5. The leader's function is to encourage discussion among group members by promoting understanding and acceptance of one another. Gradually the leader withdraws from his role as a leader and shifts responsibility for discussion to participants. The leader sees his role primarily as one of withdrawing from the center of things and fading into the background after he has established the permissive nonthreatening climate.

The designation "group-centered" describes the objective of such discussions. It is whatever the group wishes to discuss. The leader imposes no structure but permits the structure to emerge from the group itself. Satisfaction of group needs, solving of group problems, and resolving of interpersonal conflicts gradually become the agenda.

This type of group process has much to contribute to personal adjustments. A group of alcoholics would receive a great deal of benefit and personal insight from a permissive situation of this type. However, its applications to disturbed work groups also become apparent. It could become the pattern for gripe sessions, grievance hearings, and emotional upsets of a temporary nature.

A further application would be its extension to work groups in order to mold them into more cohesive units. Meetings might be scheduled from time to time in order to deal with problems unrelated to job objectives. The supervisor in such cases would merely schedule time for the discussion of whatever matters the group would like to pursue. The justification for such meetings would be based on the assumption that a cohesive, well-adjusted group is a more valuable team than one that has unresolved emotional conflicts.

A discussion leader of this type gets closer to his group and develops new insights into the workings of a group. Their needs, worries, satisfactions, frustrations, and relationships with one another become valuable bits of information which contribute to a better understanding of their behavior.

Degree of leadership control. The objective of the leader may be either to withdraw from the leadership function or to retain leadership while restricting its function to that of conducting the discussion in accordance with the group's needs and feelings. Instead of determining the topic, imposing a structure, or representing a point of view, his leadership function is to see to it that communication is facilitated, that hard feelings are dissipated, and that persons with minority opinions have a chance to be heard and understood. In the first instance (nondirective discussions), he performs a passive role; in the second (free discussions), an active role with respect to the discussion leadership but not with respect to the contents or the thinking processes.

In both instances the leader is permissive with respect to what is said and what actions or decisions are made. However, in the free discussion he assumes responsibility for the success of the meeting in so far as group satisfactions are concerned; in addition, he feels free to contribute helpful knowledge or information. In neither case does he impose his views or attempt to influence the decision.

Both types of discussion lend themselves to dealing with emotional problems. The nondirective or group-centered discussion, being more therapeutic, would be more adapted to handling interpersonal conflicts within the group, while the free discussion, being less passive, would be appropriate for solving a problem involving conflicting objectives, such as problems associated with satisfactions and acceptance of group decisions. For example, the problem of fairness relates to a job decision rather than to therapy. It is concerned with a problem involving attitudes and feelings rather than emotional maladjustment. It would seem more efficient for the leader to retain control of the discussion, and see to it that it remained free and was directed toward a resolution of the conflict.

DEVELOPMENTAL DISCUSSIONS

Origin and objective of the method. The purpose of the developmental discussion is to introduce some structure into group discussion so as to increase the quality of a group decision but not to determine its nature. The leader's objective, therefore, is to improve the group's thinking in reaching a better decision, not a preconceived decision or one that the leader wants. In the sense that the objective of the free discussion is to increase group *acceptance* of a decision, the objective of the developmental discussion is to increase the *quality* of group decisions.[7]

The experimental studies carried out to demonstrate the effect of the developmental type of discussion on decision quality have already been described in Chapter 2. The purpose in citing the experiment at that point was to demonstrate that method as well as leadership skill could influence the outcome of a group's decision. Our present concern is the nature and the place of developmental type discussions in group meetings.

The structure of developmental discussions. Discussions frequently are inefficient because the discussion may follow a somewhat disorganized pattern. One participant may talk about one aspect of a problem while another may turn the discussion into a different channel. For example, in discussing a person's qualifications for a promotion, some participants might talk about performance on the present job, another might mention his fine character, a third might raise questions about the duties on the new job, and a fourth might wonder if the person will be happy on the new job. Recognizing that all of these aspects of the problem are relevant, it must be conceded that no issue is carefully explored by all persons at the same time. In a sense there is interaction between the members but not on the same issues. People may agree or disagree with an action discussed but for quite different reasons.

The developmental discussion is designed to synchronize the discussion of issues so that people will discuss the same aspect of a problem at the same time. This is accomplished by dividing the problem into separate issues, subtopics, or parts. For example, in the problem cited in Chapter

[7] N. R. F. Maier, *Principles of Human Relations.* John Wiley & Sons, Inc., New York, 1952.

2, in which discussion concerned the promotion of Viola
Burns, the subtopics listed were as follows:

1. Duties performed on the present job
2. Appraisal of performance on the various duties
3. Duties of the new job
4. Appraisal of the individual's potential to perform the
new duties (some will overlap with the old job; others may
be different)
5. Selection of the three most important duties to determine whether these are among the duties that are different
and for which we have little knowledge of the individual's
potential or among those that are common to both jobs and
for which we have knowledge of performance.

The breakdown of the promotion problem does not restrict the discussion of topics, and it actually may include
aspects of the situation that might have been overlooked in
a free type discussion. In so far as the topics are similar to
what might have been covered in the free discussion, this
sequence of topics would merely tend to synchronize the
discussion and keep the group from going off in tangents.
All participants would be exploring the five topics, one at a
time and together. In so far as this division includes aspects
that may have been overlooked, the organization of topics
makes for a more systematic and orderly treatment. Experience of progress and a sense of accomplishment would also
be more apparent because there is a progression from one
topic to another.

Many problems can be subdivided into parts which
would aid in synchronizing discussions and making them
more systematic. Both of these gains would be advantages
with respect to increasing the efficiency of coverage, locating areas of disagreement, keeping the discussion on the
topic, and making coverage more complete.

The question of whether the topic breakdown can be
arranged so that a desired outcome is thereby achieved
should also be considered. If the breakdown of the problem
leads to the solution desired by the leader, it becomes a form

of manipulation and ceases to be a helpful factor in improving discussion. Research is needed to determine whether or not different and equally logical breakdowns of the problem can lead to conflicting conclusions. In the meantime, the leader should be guided by a desire to synchronize and to systematize the discussion.

Despite the leader's efforts to be objective in following a developmental discussion, he may find that his efforts to achieve an orderly interaction will be regarded by participants as an attempt to control the outcome. This means that the developmental type discussion requires more skill than the free type discussion. It also demonstrates that emotional factors may be present in some of these situations. For example, some participants may wish to promote a person because they like him. The developmental discussion may be seen as a threat to this objective, and hence the leader may be accused of manipulation when the real objection is the participant's ulterior motive. This merely emphasizes the fact that when feelings are involved, the unstructured or free discussion is favored; structure should not be imposed until the group is really ready to solve problems objectively.

Reducing bias. Solutions to problems are influenced by certain biases and mental sets which reduce the objective quality of thinking. When various members of a group hold different biases and mental sets, these tend to become neutralized through discussion. However, when group members hold similar biases and mental sets, their presence is not apparent, and the final product is therefore lowered in quality.

In connection with promotion problems there are biases and a mental set shared by most participants. A bias is the influence of the impression the candidate makes on the group either from knowing the person or from seeing his record and having a description of the person. The result is some kind of impression. A favorable impression tends to make the group of judges prone to favor promotion despite the fact that all might agree that this personal impression may not be a proper qualification for the position in question. If all have a favorable impression, the bias performs its function without being noticed.

A mental set that is shared by group members is to favor promotions for persons who do well on their present jobs. This amounts to making promotion a reward for past performance. Despite the fact that a group of persons may know that success on a present job may show little or no relation to success on a different job, this irrelevant mental set operates. Performances on different jobs correlate only to the extent that job requirements are similar, yet this similarity is seldom sufficiently explored.

It is true that some persons may argue that promotion should be used to motivate employees. Although motivation influences performance, it also follows that such a policy, if practiced consistently, would lead to staffing all positions with persons who show relatively poor performance. Superior performers are advanced while the others are left on the job when this practice is followed. On the other hand, lateral transfers could make successes out of failures, and promotions should be geared to capitalize on an individual's strengths, while avoiding the requirement of activities in which weaknesses are apparent.

Promotions, therefore, should differentiate the factors of ability and motivation, both of which influence performance in different ways. A discussion that fails to require this differentiation would lead to lower quality decisions. It should also be noted that job satisfaction, which is an important form of intrinsic motivation, depends on good job placement; and good placement permits an individual to utilize his best abilities so that he can have a feeling of success on his job. Promotion to a job for which a person lacks ability does not create job satisfaction even if it pays more. The individual and the company have a mutual interest in having each individual placed on a job that he can master and in which he can develop further. Development is most rapid when a person's strengths are utilized.

It will be seen that the developmental type of discussion tends to reduce both the faulty bias and the adverse mental set. This means that the breakdown of the problem gives its various aspects more complete consideration. Frequently groups reach overall agreement on an issue too quickly. This prevents them from analyzing the situation carefully and thereby avoiding certain traps in the thinking process.

When to use developmental discussions. It is apparent that problems having to do with promotions readily lend themselves to developmental discussions because they can be divided into clearly separate issues and because participants usually are not emotionally involved and hence favor a high quality decision. These problems may be thought of as a model for selecting other problems that lend themselves to logical breakdowns.

The first consideration is a common interest in a high-quality decision. Problems where interest in facts predominates and personal opinions, conflicting needs, and emotional involvement are at a minimum, therefore, should be considered. If a discussion reveals the existence of emotional factors, the discussion should turn to the free type, at least temporarily.

If the leader finds he can break the problem into parts or steps, he should share these with the group and determine whether there are objections to following the procedure he outlines. If questions and doubts are raised, some time for free discussion might be introduced.

The leader may find that the group can assist him in breaking down the problem. In this case he would only be structuring the discussion to the extent that he is asking for a systematic analysis and leaving the nature of the procedural steps to the group.

Essential skills. The important skill in developmental discussions is the leader's ability to sense when a structured approach is welcomed and when it is resisted. Groups will appreciate the injection of organization in a discussion when intellectually stimulated. At these times they are task-oriented, want to make progress, and are interested in an end product of which they can be proud. Under such circumstances a free or nondirective discussion would be boring, if not irritating.

A second skill involves the ability to make a systematic analysis of a problem. Unfortunately this same ability qualifies the leader for being a good problem solver himself, which in turn makes him impatient with respect to letting a group think their way through the problem. Such leaders must learn to use their talents to ask stimulating and provocative questions that take the thinking out of a rut (see Chapter 5) and develop an appreciation for the values of participation. A creative problem solver can learn to upgrade group thinking and suppress the tendency to think for the group.

Some leaders may find that they obtain better acceptance for the structuring of developmental discussions if they ask the group to decide on the organization to follow. If a group becomes defensive or asks questions that indicate doubt of the wisdom of following a series of steps the leader recommends, this will be his cue to invite participation in formulating an acceptable procedure.

Finally, the ability to pace the discussion to fit the group should be mentioned. The leader must focus on progress yet not force it. Discussion time should not be wasted on minor differences in opinions when these can easily be resolved.

Suppose the promotion problem described on pages 28 ff. is being discussed. Step 1 requires the listing of duties performed by the candidate Viola on her present job. One member might contend that the ability to work as a member of a group is a job requirement while another member might strongly disagree. Such disagreement might be strong and yet be quite unimportant for the objective of the discussion. The leader might help things out by asking, "Would a person ever be discharged for not getting along with others?" After some discussion, the group might reach the conclusion that even if getting along with others was not in the job description, it should be there or at least is relevant. If some members accepted the duty and others did not, the leader could resolve the matter by merely putting a question mark after the controversial duty. Skill in preventing discussions from being sidetracked, without sitting in judgment, involves sensitivity and intellectual insight.

In evaluating performance (step 2, page 30) one might expect members to show some disagreement. The leader in such instances can strive for an average opinion and avoid lengthy discussion. If this quick approach is questioned, he can use plus and minus signs or even indicate a range of opinion to register the fact that wide and strong differences are present. The important thing is not to let the discussion become a debate over a small difference.

Disagreement over potential duties and performance (steps 3 and 4, page 30) might be fairly large. Here question marks, striking an average, or indicating the range of opinions should be freely used. As a matter of fact, the difference of opinion becomes an essential fact in the final decision.

In selecting the important duties (step 5), the important skill item is to poll the group opinion. Each person can be asked to select the three duties that are most likely to spell success or failure on the new job. These can be tallied, and, as indicated in Chapter 6, two to four duties will stand out.

The discussion next naturally turns to examining the candidate's anticipated ability to perform these important duties. If they are associated with question marks, wide range in opinion, or relatively poor evaluations, it becomes evident that the candidate is not well qualified. It is clear that this part of the discussion should not be hurried and should follow the free pattern.

Although the above description indicates the need to move the discussion along, the leader should not hurry it. The pace set should be designed to prevent time from being wasted over minor differences, not to *prevent* disagreement and the raising of questions. Thus again the discussion leader is advised to steer a middle course between one that makes for boredom and one that makes for rapid progress. The leader's ability to sense these differences will help him to guide discussion along this middle course.

PHILLIPS 66

Origin and objective of the method. Discussion methods may be viewed in accordance with how much they spread the participation in the group and the extent to which participants become involved in their attempts to influence one another. The discussion pattern known as Phillips 66 [8] was initially designed to involve more persons in an audience in framing questions for a speaker to answer. The technique was to divide an audience into groups of six and have them spend six minutes to formulate a question for the speaker. This permitted all persons to participate in asking questions and also to become more interested in the speaker's answers. The technique, however, had other values and is frequently used to let small groups work on problems with each other. This method is primarily one of permitting large groups to obtain some of the benefits of small group discussion.

Uses of Discussion 66. There are many situations that lend themselves to the method of this type of discussion pattern, sometimes called "buzz" sessions. Everyone cannot participate if a group is large, but by subdividing the group into small ones everyone is given an opportunity to interact. Each small group causes various points of view to come to expression so that the various phases of the problem are subjected to interaction. Thus each person has an opportunity not only to express his opinions, but to experience the reception of his contributions in comparison with those of others. Through interacting with one another, participants experience social pressure and learn that some opinions are more popular than others.

In addition to the participative experience, Discussion 66 permits groups to report their conclusions. This introduces a second kind of experience. Various groups may come to an agreement, but the thing agreed upon might be different from one group to another.

[8] D. J. Phillips, Report on Discussion 66. *Adult educ. J.*, 1948, **7**, 181–182.

In examining the group results of the promotion problem, discussed in Chapter 2, it was found that the majority of the groups reached unanimous agreement despite the fact that the discussion leader was unskilled.[9] For the free discussion groups, 80.5 per cent of the decisions were unanimous while for the developmental discussion groups, 64.4 per cent of the decisions were unanimous. Typically Discussion 66 is of the free type and is most likely to produce consensus, unless the leader is domineering. Structuring discussions, such as the developmental type, must be well done; otherwise the leader may stifle the discussion and make the group less able to resolve differences.

In a more recent unpublished study, twenty-five groups of three and four persons each were given the promotion problem and were asked to decide on one of three alternative decisions. These alternatives were:

1. To encourage the candidate to take the job
2. To discourage the candidate from taking the job
3. More information needed to make a decision

In this case thirteen of the groups were instructed to follow the free discussion while the other twelve were instructed in the developmental discussion. No discussion leaders were assigned.

The results are shown in Table 15. It will be seen that 84.6 per cent of the free discussion groups reached unanimous decisions even though all three alternative decisions were represented. In the developmental discussion groups all of the decisions were unanimous. If we combine the groups, we find that all but two of the twenty-five groups (92 per cent) were unanimous in their decisions. Nevertheless, 28 per cent of these favored alternative 1, 40 per cent favored alternative 2, and 24 per cent favored alternative 3. Thus groups tend to resolve their difference through discussion, but they may be in complete disagreement with other groups.

The fact that groups discussing the same problem can

[9] N. R. F. Maier and R. A. Maier, An Experimental Test of the Effects of Developmental vs. Free Discussions on the Quality of Group Decisions. *J. appl. Psychol.*, 1957, 41, 320–323.

agree within the group and yet arrive at different conclusions is an important learning experience. It gives people a real life demonstration of how they can influence each other through discussion without arriving at the truth. Certainly all three alternatives cannot be correct. In obtaining reports of discussions from small groups, the audience is confronted with data that are very challenging because the participants

TABLE 15. *Frequency of Unanimous Decisions (Groups of 3 or 4)*

| Group number | Decision in free discussion groups | | | Group number | Decision in developmental discussion groups | | |
	En- courage	Insufficient information	Dis- courage		En- courage	Insufficient information	Dis- courage
1	1	2	0	2	0	0	3
3	0	0	3	4	0	0	3
5	0	0	3	6	0	0	3
7	3	0	0	8	0	0	4
9	0	3	0	10	0	0	4
11	3	0	0	12	3	0	0
13	0	3	0	14	0	0	3
15	0	3	0	16	0	0	3
17	0	1	2	18	3	0	0
19	0	3	0	20	0	0	3
21	0	3	0	22	3	0	0
23	0	3	0	24	3	0	0
25	4	0	0				
Total ...	11	21	8	Total ...	12	0	26
Per cent ..	27.5	52.5	20.	Per cent ..	31.6	0	68.4
Per cent unanimous, 84.6				Per cent unanimous, 100.0			

themselves created the data. Research reports have an intellectual appeal, but data derived from one's own behavior are not readily dismissed or rationalized.

Essential skills. The success of this method depends greatly on how appropriately it is used. The two sixes in Discussion 66 have limited meaning in that they call for a six-minute discussion among six persons. Some problems require more than six minutes, and the number of persons may range from three to eight.

There are a number of principles that should be followed

to achieve best results. Skill in applying these to the situation is vitally important.

Choice of problem: The success of a discussion requires a problem or question the participants feel both qualified and justified to discuss. An international problem might be a good question for students in political science but not for foremen. The topic should fit into the group's experience or interests and be relevant to the general program. Participants will not feel qualified to discuss a technical problem as a substitute for a lecture. Such discussions are never to be substituted for informational lectures. People learn most from each other when each has something to contribute.

Questions such as what is fair, feelings toward discipline, important needs or goals, causes of poor morale, etc., are matters of experience, and everyone has learned something from his experiences.

Good discussion issues should also be matters over which people differ or disagree. All persons might agree that delegation of authority is a good thing, but how much and when to delegate would stimulate disagreement. Thus the formulation of a question should be specific enough that the discussion goes beyond vague generalizations.

The magnitude of the problem issue should be limited so that all groups will be forced to interact on the same matters. Groups discussing a broad question of higher education may go off in different directions so that their conclusions may reveal few common elements in discussion content. Such a discussion would be improved by selecting a controversial aspect of education.

Clear assignments: What the groups are expected to do and report should be made very specific. Many failures in Discussion 66 occur because groups are unsure of what they are to do. Requesting a decision or a conclusion is more specific than asking groups to report their opinions about something. Requesting groups to report on what they consider the most important cause of something is more specific than requesting them to determine the causes of something.

The purpose in narrowing the issue is to force the group

to come to grips with their disagreements. In some discussions the group members add their opinions together and in their report merely summarize a list of contributions. This type of discussion is an additive process and lacks vitality because it requires no resolution of differences. Group members learn and profit most from resolving differences, not from accumulating ideas or facts.

Size of group: The proper size of the group depends upon a number of environmental considerations. A group should be small enough so that each person can hear the others and feel he has the opportunity to express himself. Whether chairs can be moved or whether seats are fixed will influence these requirements. In fixed seats two persons can turn and discuss with three behind them. Thus five-person groups are ideal. With movable chairs or tables, seating groups of as many as eight may be practical.

Another factor to consider is the size of the audience. When the number of group reports exceeds twelve, the reporting aspect of the discussion becomes monotonous. Thus, with the same topic, groups of eight or more might be desired in an audience of 100 persons, while groups of three or four might be appropriate in an audience of twenty-five.

When audiences of several hundred are used, some short reporting method is required. For example, the conclusions might be classified. The leader then polls the groups to determine the number of groups reaching each of the decisions. Discussion can then be used to explore exceptions or unique conclusions.

Proximity of groups: It is best to have all groups discussing in the same room, rather than send them to small discussion rooms. The activity and excitement of one group's discussion is contagious and causes others to interact. The more the discussion noise the better, because the noise requires the group members to get closer together and listen harder.

Time limit: The amount of time allocated for discussion depends on the topic and the size of the group. Groups should be given enough time to resolve differences, and six minutes is seldom enough. Best results are obtained when groups have a problem of sufficient complexity to require from twenty to thirty minutes. If discussion requires more than an hour, it is safe to conclude that the topic is not a good one for Discussion 66.

In general, groups finish in pretty much the same time. It takes a group of six persons a certain amount of time to discover their differences and to resolve them, and this process is very much the same from one group to another.

Informal climate: A leader can spoil Discussion 66 by talking about it. The important thing is to do it without ceremony. The question is put to the audience as a whole. The next step is to indicate the approximate size of the groups and then let members form their groups without making assignments. The leader and his assistants may give aid when persons seem to get lost. If too large a group forms, he may divide them or move a few persons. The principle here is not to impose too much structure because it will merely add to the confusion. An audience can divide itself into groups of five or six without a lot of fanfare. The confusion that appears initially is a stimulant to informality.

Another factor that aids informality is not to require a discussion leader or a reporter, which Phillips required in his original description of the process. Groups handle those matters in their own way, and the results are best if there are no imposed assignments.

LARGE GROUP DISCUSSION

The limitations of Robert's Rules of Order. In meetings involving large groups (fifty persons or more) the most commonly practiced democratic procedure is that of parliamentary law. The authoritative procedure in this country is known as Robert's Rules of Order.[10] This procedure invites limited participation, and decisions are determined by majority vote. Robert's Rules of Order permit motions from the floor so that the membership may initiate actions as well as

[10] H. M. Robert, *Robert's Rules of Order.* Scott, Foresman and Company, Chicago, 1943.

vote for alternatives presented. Discussions from the floor also permit members an opportunity to attempt to influence one another.

There are three disadvantages to the process: (1) the domination of the majority opinion; (2) the opportunities for trickery in the conduct of meetings; and (3) the abuses created by plotting, exchanging favors, etc., that take place behind the scenes.

The use of the majority rule can be justified by claiming that the will of the majority is preferable to that of indecision or minority rule. In large groups the opportunities for resolving differences are not sufficiently apparent so that the majority opinion becomes a practical substitute.

The fact that the encouragement of trickery, designed to defeat the democratic objectives, is inherent in the process is far more serious. Calling for a vote when the opposition is absent is a common example. Leaders skilled in the use of the procedure can guide the process so as to satisfy their own selfish ends. Unsophisticated members who do not know how to raise objections without being declared out of order become helpless bystanders. Likewise, a few skilled members can confuse an unskilled leader and take the control from him. Some organizations have been taken over by gangsters by this device. Thus influence falls to those who have the procedural skills, not to those who have contributions to make.

Attempts to influence votes by means of behind-the-scenes arrangements, such as vote commitments, the trading of favors, the use of political pressure, threat of exposure, etc., obviously are attempts to defeat the democratic process. Although these procedures may be legal, they are not a part of the process—they are merely its undesirable side effects. The fact that complex procedural rules exist stimulates those with selfish interests to think of ways either to abuse or circumvent them, and the fact that a majority decision is adequate to pass an action encourages the membership to develop a disregard for the dissenting holdout vote.

The parliamentary approach may be an advance over

autocratic rule, and it still might be quite adequate for conducting business meetings, especially when the membership and the leadership are well intentioned. Nevertheless, the search for something better should not be abandoned. Dividing large groups into smaller ones may solve some problems, but the possibility that large group discussions can be improved still remains as a reasonable objective.

Principles for guiding large group discussions. For some years the writer has been trying to devise methods for improving discussions in large groups. The essential feature in these attempts is to permit disagreement to play a major part in discussion and let the points of agreement be determined by a show of hands. There is little point in using up discussion time to have several persons talk in support of, or in opposition to, an issue. Such discussions are intended to persuade others. Yet the fact remains that very few persons change their votes after such a discussion. A straw vote taken before and after a debate will yield little change in opinion. The essential problem seems not to be so much one of changing the minds of peoples who are in disagreement as it is of finding ways to resolve or integrate differences.

This means that discussion time should be devoted, as much as possible, to exploring differing ideas or ways of making concessions rather than in debating the obvious alternatives. It also means that more time should be spent describing preferences rather than in intellectualizing or rationalizing a point of view. Since a majority is strong and has support, its position need not be argued in great detail. A show of hands may give the majority position all the support it needs, while members of the minority might be given more discussion time to explain their position. If their position is a selfish one and they wish to override a majority for personal reasons, the majority can turn them down, but if they have an unusual problem, the majority can be generous. Generosity is a sign of strength, and a majority will consider special circumstances or hardships.

The leader's procedure in large group discussions is to invite the expression of a point of view and then obtain as much participation as possible by giving the audience an opportunity to indicate whether or not they agree or whether or not the point is a valid one. By the use of the question, "How many of you think that this is a sound position to take," the leader can cause members to participate by identifying with the idea. The contributor, in turn, learns whether or not he is having an influence. Once agreement is registered by a show of hands, points of disagreement or alternative views should be requested. These in turn may be evaluated by a show of hands. The important thing is to sort out various ideas and repeatedly invite participation by a show of hands. Discussion is kept within bounds by searching for different ideas instead of being dominated by speeches that support a majority point of view. Endorsement can easily be registered by asking members to participate by a show of hands.

Resolving a controversy over an examination date. The writer has attempted large group discussion to settle a controversial issue such as the date of an examination in a class of 150 or more students. Suppose Tuesday and Thursday are class days and an examination may fall one or two weeks before a vacation or the week following the vacation.

An initial show of hands for a first and second preference might eliminate the week following vacation. Preferences for one versus two weeks before vacation are now opposed for similar reasons. Some persons have other examinations one week before, others two weeks before. Thus their reasons cancel, but one group is in the majority. The question of whether another examination during the same week is a valid reason can be raised, and a show of hands reveals that this generally fails to be impressive. As a matter of fact it will be argued that if the exam is delayed until immediately before the holiday, more time for preparing for both examinations will be obtained. Even persons with three examinations soon concede that this problem is inevitable and that students should adjust by planning. Other disadvantages are then considered. Some want the exam delayed until the week before vacation to obtain study time. Others want it two weeks before to get it out of the way before vacation. A majority favors Thursday, two weeks before vacation, while two minority groups favor Tuesday, on each of the alternative weeks. The solution agreed upon was to let the majority decide the week and let the minority decide the day. On this occasion, the decision turned out to be the Tuesday of the week before vacation. Despite the fact that this date had the most conflict with other exams, this solution was regarded as the most satisfactory. All but two persons felt that the solution was the best possible resolution of the conflict. However, the high degree of satisfaction came only after certain minority individuals had become convinced that they had no better reasons for their preferences than the majority. The major factor in the attainment of high satisfaction was the willingness of the majority to make a concession to the minority.

On other occasions majorities have refused to make concessions to minority groups which they found unreasonable, and in some instances, strong majorities have been willing to let students with special problems take the examination either early or late. The willingness of a majority to make concessions depends largely on the kind of problem the minority individuals raise and the extent to which they show respect for the rights of the majority. It is the majority that holds the upper hand, but when the minority view can be heard, the voice of a worthy minority is respected to a surprising degree.

Posting alternatives. In some large group discussions the method of posting alternatives is efficient. These ideas then can be narrowed down by getting the membership to vote on their most-preferred two (or three) alternatives. Reducing the list brings a group closer together. Usually three or four entries stand out as strong favorites. When practically every person finds at least one of his preferences in the dominant three or four alternatives, participants realize that they have had an influence on the outcome. Discussion can then be devoted to ideas that incorporate as many of the advantages of the three alternatives as possible. This type of discussion, instead of being a struggle for winning, becomes a way of giving as much to as many as is possible. Differences in personal preferences, quality of the solution, hardships created, ability to contribute, and considerations of training or seniority receive recognition as soon as the discussion climate changes from winning over others to that of resolving as many differences as possible. Only a selfish or stubborn minority fails to receive consideration under these circumstances, and they soon learn that they lose more by being determined than by cooperating.

Essential skills

Self-confidence: Perhaps the most essential skill in the use of large group discussions is a state of mind which we might call self-confidence. It takes a great deal of courage to overcome the formal approach to group discussion in which one person after another asks for the floor to make a brief statement of his position on the matter under discussion. After the first expression of a point of view, the leader asks others to register their reactions by a show of hands. Thus, the less aggressive become active participants by taking a stand, either indicating support or disagreement for the contributor's point of view. The objective is to get participants to express different viewpoints rather than to evaluate or select. Many participants are unwilling to reveal their preferences at the outset, but after a short time they become involved.

The leader must be able to withstand the forces of precedent since some persons will insist on following parliamentary procedures by making motions and supportive statements. He should make it clear that the discussion is not intended to follow Robert's Rules of Order and that he is following a problem-solving type of discussion in the hopes of getting the benefit of the group's informal thinking.

Intellectual insights: The ability to break down various discussion issues into separate parts so that points of agreement and disagreement can be isolated is an obvious asset. The more a problem can be broken down the greater the opportunities for testing areas of agreement and points of disagreement. Since much of the progress of such discussions

hinges on the opportunity for members to participate by a
show of hands, it is desirable to create a sequence of choice
points and thus progress by a series of steps.

Discussions that do not permit this type of participation
would proceed better by subdividing the group, but a skilled
analyst will find that many complex issues can be systemati-
cally explored by finding points of agreement and locating
the nature and the sources of differences. Especially important is the thorough exploration of differences, since it is these
that must be resolved if a group is to reach agreement.

Summarizing skills: Summarizing and restating ideas
(discussed in Chapter 5) are highly important in facilitating
communication in a large group. In small groups the leader
will be readily corrected if he misinterprets something. If he
has difficulty in understanding an idea, he can request assistance from others. In large groups these important aids are
less available, so a greater burden is placed upon the leader.

Blackboard skills: A blackboard is essential for posting
alternatives and registering votes. The ability to write legibly
and quickly, to use abbreviations, and to continue talking
while writing is invaluable. A leader cannot afford to lose the
attention of the audience while his back is turned.

Sensitivity: Sensitivity to audience cues becomes important in large meetings, while sensitivity toward individuals
as persons is more important in small meetings. The leader
must sense the preponderance of feeling, paying attention
more to the group than to individuals. The forest, rather than
the trees, becomes his focus.

Opportunities to escape participation are greater in large
groups, and this means that the leader must readily sense
the audience's reaction to this new responsibility. An audience can punish a leader by withdrawing or by taking a stand
in favor of a participant who seems to represent a majority
view and wishes to settle matters by taking a vote. The leader
must avoid taking a defensive position because recovery from
this is especially difficult in large groups. Avoiding replies
to leading questions and turning them into discussion issues

will aid the leader, providing he senses the problem soon enough.

Selecting the problem: Some problems lend themselves to group analysis more readily than others. It is apparent that points of view that differ in degree are more readily reconciled than those that differ in kind. For example, setting safety goals, production standards, differential pay rates, and hours of overtime are representative problems that permit large group discussion because the differences may be largely those of degree. Problems involving justice or fairness, finding the best plan of action, and thinking creatively may raise situations that cannot be compromised. In such cases it is important to find additional alternatives and discover ways to trade concessions. If a decision involves a series of choices, the majority may make the important first choice from the several alternatives and grant the minority the second choice. Problems that permit a series of successive decisions thus introduce ways for settling problems without making the majority the victor and the minority the loser.

CONCLUSIONS

It will be apparent to the reader that the various group discussion patterns described in this chapter are variations of the central theme of this book. Once the reader thoroughly understands the theme, he will find that he can adapt it to meet his own specific situations. As an aid to the process of generalizing the central theme, it might be desirable to describe some of the parts, recognizing that, taken by themselves, they may have quite a different meaning than when placed in the setting of the theme.

The writer sees the basic elements that characterize the underlying philosophy of this book to include the following general ideas:

1. The objective of problem-solving discussions is for the leader to utilize the resources of a group of people. In an industrial hierarchy, this group would be a superior's immedi-

ate subordinates, and the superior would be the discussion leader. In other groups, it would be the leader who was either designated or elected to serve in that capacity.

In utilizing the resources of the group, the function of the leader becomes one of facilitating the process of group discussion. The assumption that the performance of groups which function on the basis of group decisions in general will surpass that of groups led by the leader is a matter of faith. The leader who does not believe in group decisions that conflict with his own will have difficulty in following this objective.

The use of problem-solving discussions does not preclude the leader from behaving in other ways and in other capacities. Leadership is a function, not a personality trait. The same individual could conceivably play a variety of leadership roles. This volume deals with the leadership function of facilitating group problem solving and group decisions.

2. Two kinds of group resources are recognized: those that have to do with feelings—subjective data and differing attitudes, and those that have to do with objective problem solving—objective data and differing directions in thinking. The first kind of group resource is relevant to the *acceptance* of decisions; the second is relevant to the *quality* of group decisions.

3. The discussion skills for dealing with subjective data and attitudes are different from those for dealing with objective data and directions in thinking. The leadership skills that aid one type of discussion may detract from or even be disturbing to the other. The rationale for this sharp distinction is based upon a large body of research, demonstrating that problem situations may arouse either problem-solving behavior or frustrated behavior, and these two controls over behavior are qualitatively different.

4. Theoretically the point of view is a merging of a number of theories. The concepts of leadership and a group decision grow out of the work of Lewin and his students.[11] Per-

[11] K. Lewin, R. Lippitt, and R. K. White, Patterns of Aggressive Behavior in Experimentally Created Social Climates. *J. soc. Psychol.*,

missive and nondirective methods for dealing with feelings are derived from the work of Rogers,[12] while the qualitative distinction between problem solving and frustration-instigated behavior are derived from the author's researches.[13]

The distinction between the two kinds of discussion processes tends to reconcile the conflicting evidence which shows the value of the nondirective methods in some situations and its failure in others. Data from management surveys are also in conflict regarding the kind of supervisor that is most effective.[14] As long as one searches for a single type of trait for dealing with all kinds of situations, this is bound to occur if, in effect, special procedures are required for different situations. It is in this qualitative distinction between *facts* and *feelings*, between *quality* and *acceptance*, and between *problem solving* and *frustration-instigated behavior* that this volume makes its unique contribution.

1939, **10**, 271–299. K. Lewin, *Resolving Social Conflicts*. Harper & Brothers, New York, 1948. R. Lippitt, J. Watson, and B. Westley, *The Dynamics of Planned Change*. Harcourt, Brace and World, Inc., New York, 1958.

[12] C. R. Rogers, *Counseling and Psychotherapy*. Houghton Mifflin Company, Boston, 1942.

[13] N. R. F. Maier, Reasoning in Humans: On Direction. *J. comp. Psychol.*, 1930, **10**, 115–143; Reasoning and Learning. *Psychol. Rev.*, 1931, **38**, 332–346; An Aspect of Human Reasoning. *Brit. J. Psychol.*, 1933, **24**, 144–155; The Behavior Mechanisms Concerned with Problem Solving. *Psychol. Rev.*, 1940, **47**, 43–58; The Role of Frustration in Social Movements. *Psychol. Rev.*, 1942, **49**, 586–599; *Frustration*. McGraw-Hill Book Company, Inc., New York, 1949. Reissued by The University of Michigan Press, Ann Arbor, 1961; *Principles of Human Relations*. John Wiley & Sons, Inc., New York, 1952; The Quality of Group Decisions as Influenced by the Discussion Leader. *Human Relat.*, 1950, **3**, 155–174; Frustration Theory: Restatement and Extension. *Psychol. Rev.*, 1956, **63**, 370–388; *The Appraisal Interview*. John Wiley & Sons, Inc., New York, 1958; Selector-Integrator Mechanisms in Behavior. In *Perspectives in Psychological Theory*, International Universities Press, Inc., New York, 1960. N. R. F. Maier and P. Ellen, The Integrative Value of Concepts in Frustration Theory. *J. consult. Psychol.*, 1959, **23**, 195–206.

[14] R. Likert, *New Patterns of Management*. McGraw-Hill Book Company, Inc., New York, 1961.

5. Finally some mention should be made of the theoretical position taken with regard to motivation. A good deal of management speculation follows a simple reinforcement theory which stipulates that people repeat behaviors that lead to reward and avoid those that lead to punishment. Thus it follows that managers perform the job in accordance with the way needs are satisfied and rewards are administered. Likert [15] points out that because men are promoted for their ability to get out production, they become production centered in their behavior and overlook some of the long-term gains that employee-centered behavior accomplishes. Haire [16] likewise explains supervisory behavior in terms of the way higher management distributes rewards. Both Haire and Likert recognize that the motivation of supervisors and employees must include more than material rewards and that jobs must satisfy various social needs through recognition, group membership, and supportive behavior. In following the reinforcement theory they make job satisfaction the equivalent of need satisfaction, and whenever a new form of job satisfaction is uncovered they follow the simple precedent of postulating a need that must have been satisfied by the behavior. Thus in recent years many needs have been invented in order to make a prevalent theory plausible.

Our quarrel with this approach is not that it is false but that it is incomplete. The need-satisfaction type of approach overemphasizes the importance of the ulterior motives, which are the consequences of management behaviors, and overlooks the satisfactions residing in the behavior or job activity itself. It likewise fails to explain why the same management reward system produces a divergence of supervisory practices. Both Likert and Haire stress the similarities in management behavior and discount the wide differences.

The point of view in this book places emphasis on the

[15] *Ibid.*

[16] M. Haire, *Psychology in Management.* McGraw-Hill Book Company, Inc., New York, 1956.

motivational factors residing in the performance of a job.[17] A manager doesn't do things just because he anticipates reward, be it monetary or social recognition; rather he is also influenced by what he likes to do and by what he considers right and fair. If a manager is to practice group decision as a way of leadership, he must derive satisfaction from this method of operation, and he must believe that it is an honorable and good kind of management. Required management practices must fit into a supervisor's system of values to permit him to derive satisfaction from them. In other words, group decision cannot be effectively introduced into a company by rewarding those who practice it. Reward alone will not make it acceptable; it must be believed in for its own sake. If an unacceptable practice is imposed, it may be overtly used but may be so distorted as to produce negative results.

The same logic applies to the value of participation. People are motivated by participative methods because the activity *itself* is satisfying, not merely because the activity *leads* to the satisfaction of various needs. People enjoy problem solving and discussing with others because they enjoy these activities, not just because they lead to ego satisfaction. As a matter of fact, it is not uncommon for participants to become so involved in these activities that they forget to be courteous and lose out on the alleged need satisfaction. Furthermore, the goals set through participation are likely to be challenging because the group believes in them.

The distinction here made is between extrinsic and intrinsic motivation. Extrinsic motivation deals with the satisfaction or the reward gained for having done something, i.e., the payoff is the satisfaction of some need for having behaved in a certain way. It is the kind of satisfaction a man has when he receives pay or praise for working. Intrinsic motivation deals with the satisfaction gained from the activity itself, i.e., the pleasure of walking not for where it

[17] M. Henle, On Activity in the Goal Region. *Psychol. Rev.*, 1956, **63**, 229–302.

takes you but just for the action itself; the pleasure of doing a job not for what it pays but because of its interest. These satisfactions are the opposite of boredom. Boredom is not a form of punishment or deprivation. It is the experience of unpleasant activity itself.

These intrinsic factors cause men to want to do a job the way they think it should be done, and these same factors cause supervisors to behave according to their systems of values. If both aspects of motivation exist, it follows that satisfaction is greatest when intrinsic and extrinsic motivation are consistent with each other.

Managers in general do not enjoy deceiving or punishing people. Above all things they want to be fair. Any management practice that requires behavior in which supervisors do not believe is bound to lack full support, even if it is taught and rewarded. A change in management philosophy cannot be imposed from above. It must be built-in and accepted by those who are to practice it, and this means that training must include a consideration of attitudes and values.

CHAPTER EIGHT

Screening solutions to upgrade quality[1]

INTRODUCTION

This chapter describes a discussion procedure for evaluating a group of solutions supplied by participants. It imposes even more restraints on the discussion process than does the developmental discussion described in the previous chapter. As in the developmental discussion, the restraints are not designed to control or dictate the solution that will be selected; rather they are designed to improve the ability of a group to evaluate solutions to situational problems where quality is important and acceptance is secondary. Despite the fact that quality may be recognized as the important dimension by the participants, their feelings and

[1] This chapter is a modified version of an article by the same name, published in *J. Psychol.*, 1960, **49**, 217–231.

personal biases enter into their preferences, and these tend to distract the intellectual and objective activity.

Since there is a tendency to resist restraints imposed on discussion even when a group is interested in solutions of high quality, the procedure described in the following pages requires considerable skill on the part of the leader. It is suggested, therefore, that the leader begin by acquainting the participants with the evaluation procedure to be followed. The group can be asked to go along with the procedure as an exercise. It can be revealed that restraints will be dropped in the final stage of the evaluation. Thus the final decision will be up to the group regardless of what the procedure dictates.

The restraints may be viewed as a kind of screen which permits some solutions to be rejected while others are selected for later consideration. No claim is made that a rejected solution may not be a sound one or represent a creative idea for some other problem or even for the present one if more information were available. The screen is designed to confine discussion to a consideration of known facts, and in this way it limits the range of thinking.

Although the screening process is to be used for selecting from a number of solutions, it may influence the solutions offered on subsequent occasions. The author already has some evidence that this influence occurs, but if this is verified, its effect is a beneficial one rather than a restraining one.

PROBLEM SOLVING UNDER CONDITIONS OF UNCERTAINTY

The objective of the screening principles described in this chapter is to raise the level of problem-solving discussions when decisions are needed and further information is not available. It is understood that human beings may engage in faulty thinking, but when one cannot prove that such thinking is faulty, how does one prevent it? As a matter of fact, even when proof is possible, it fails to deter many because of the human tendency to persist in a point of view.

Decision making under conditions of uncertainty, according to Luce and Raiffa [2], is the situation in which the outcomes of the various alternatives are unknown. This provision is satisfied by the type of problem under consideration in the present chapter. However, there is also a difference. We are concerned primarily with *problem solving* under conditions of uncertainty. As pointed out on page 118, decision making requires the choosing from a given number of alternatives, whereas problem solving requires that the alternatives be created. Thus problem solving involves both choice behavior and the finding or creating of alternatives. Problem solving under conditions of uncertainty, therefore, involves both uncertainty as to outcomes and uncertainty as to the nature and number of possible alternatives. This type of problem is too complex to be handled by the current type of mathematical models being tested in connection with the decision-making process. The screening process, though less accurate and precise, is a new kind of approach to this complex type of problem.

The potential importance of this approach is not merely one of improving the quality of the product of group thinking, but it also may lead to the exploration and analysis of the nature of the inference process. Human beings make many inferences; they have hunches and claim to have insights. These processes follow logical principles different from those that are pertinent to proof or deductive thinking. As a result one cannot use standard logic in evaluating the inferences made by living organisms, who by nature go beyond what is known. It is our purpose to encourage inferences and inductive thinking yet keep them within the bounds of reality.

THE NEED FOR A METHOD TO SCREEN SOLUTIONS

A deficiency in facts in a problem situation does not discourage attempts to find a solution. As a matter of fact such a free condition often leads to an abundance of solutions so

[2] R. D. Luce and H. Raiffa, *Games and Decisions: Introduction and Critical Survey.* John Wiley & Sons, Inc., New York, 1958.

that a new problem is presented—that of selecting one from among the many possibilities. Whenever the facts in a situation are inadequate, it follows that a good many of the solutions put forth cannot be logically rejected. If an evaluation is to be made, additional procedures must be developed.

Under such conditions it would be desirable either to obtain more information or to test experimentally the merits of various solutions. However, many of life's problems cannot await the evaluation of solutions by these methods so that, for periods of time, there are stages when people can reasonably disagree regarding the merits and demerits of alternate solutions. All persons might agree that the solutions will differ in value when more is known, but until then they cannot agree on the relative merits of various solutions.

In science, conflicting theories are reduced in number, and essential refinements are introduced as research knowledge increases. The function of crucial experiments is to narrow the field. But even in this instance there often is disagreement over the nature of crucial experiments. This means that what one person regards as proof may be insufficient evidence for another. Thus the amount of observational data needed to convince Darwin of man's evolution was not convincing to many others. When a man makes an inference, he takes a "leap in the dark" and makes some additional suppositions. We might say he "makes up" some new facts so that for him his viewpoint or solution is very plausible. If no one possesses facts to the contrary, his "make-believe" facts are acceptable to him, while others may feel cool or even antagonistic toward them.

This disagreement among men regarding the merits of solutions becomes even more marked when we examine some of the day-to-day problems. Actions have to be taken even when the choice made cannot be justified by the facts or circumstances. These actions or solutions to problems may be viewed either as guesses or as hunches. If we consider guesses to be purely a chance selection, then it follows that people should be of equal ability in choosing solutions that will turn out to be effective. However, the term *hunch* implies something more than chance—it suggests a personal logic. People differ in their hunches, and some have hunches that turn out right more often than chance would permit. If people differ in their ability to solve problems when hunches rather than facts primarily determine the solutions developed, it is possible that this difference represents the contribution of creativity. Our immediate objective, however, is to determine whether solutions can be evaluated by procedures that do not make use of experimentation, logical proof, or probability analysis. In other words, when facts and proof cannot be used to select the best solution from a group of possibilities, what sort of methods or skills can operate to ensure better than chance solutions?

The problem is further complicated by the fact that people prefer solutions that they played a part in formulating, and this may lead to popular choices rather than ones that eventually may be supported by additional facts. Selecting wise solutions under these conditions introduces numerous subjective factors so that questions of utility, statistical probability, and rational behavior are only a part of the total problem-solving process.

At present the hypotheses of man-made machines will be probability predictions rather than hunches. Perhaps this is their greatest virtue. In the meantime it is of interest to determine whether solutions to problems, particularly those involving people, can be screened so as to upgrade the quality of a group discussion outcome.

ILLUSTRATIVE CASE

In order to describe the screening process it seems best to use a specific problem so that the solutions recommended can be evaluated. In working with this material, the solutions were obtained by dividing experimental groups of ten to twenty-five persons into teams of three or four persons each. The teams were asked to serve as consulting firms and were given the assignment of reaching agreement on solutions they would recommend. However, recommendations for obtaining additional information, such as talking to the personnel in the case, were not acceptable as solutions because these were merely a means to the final solution. Each team was limited to solutions with no more than three action-steps. The request for having solutions stated in terms of actions to be taken was included because some groups state solutions in terms of objectives, if not carefully instructed. A limit was placed on the number of steps so as to force groups to select from among the ideas that came to mind.

The case of the Sewing Machine Operators [3] was then presented. The situational description was read by the leader, after which two persons in the group were appointed to read the dialogue. These materials are given below. The final step was to supply each team with a copy of the above-mentioned materials and a copy of the plant layout shown in Figure 7. A half hour was allowed for obtaining consensus on three action-steps.

The situation. For the past six months Bill has been the supervisor of a sewing room of twenty-five girls in a garment factory. The girls are all union members. Until recently, his main problem was that of getting out enough production. Three months ago, however, all sewing machine operators were changed over from hourly to a team piece-rate system so that production has become fairly satisfactory. Quality is now the big problem; not only are there too many rejects, but serious complaints are coming in from salesmen in the field. Since the girls are not paid for rejected items, it is difficult to understand why they are not more careful.

Bill has been called in by his department foreman, Mr. Johnson, to discuss the matter.

The dialogue

Mr. J.: Bill, I want to talk to you again about the kind of work your unit is turning out. What's the matter down there anyway?

Bill: Darn it, I don't know. On the old hourly rate the girls

[3] Taken from N. R. F. Maier, *Psychology in Industry.* Houghton Mifflin Company, Boston, 1955, pp. 39 ff.

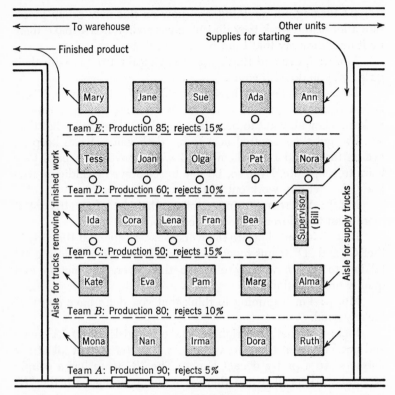

Front of building

FIG. 7. Sewing room layout. Five work teams of five girls each are represented. The supervisor's desk is shown on the middle right. The work flow is from right to left, and the girl at the extreme left in each team is the finisher, i.e., she puts the last touches to the article. The upper part of the figure represents the back of the room, which opens on an aisle connecting with the warehouse to the left and which leads to other units (supervised by Steve and Eddie) on the right. The lower part of the figure represents the front of the building. The small rectangles represent windows.

The names of the teams, their production, and their percentages of articles rejected are shown below each team. The production standard is eighty units per team; the quality standard is 8 per cent rejects. The problem girls are Pat, Nora, Fran, Bea, Marg, and Alma. (*Modified from N. R. F. Maier, Psychology in Industry. Houghton Mifflin Company, Boston, 1955.*)

weren't turning out anything, and now on this new group piece-rate a lot of the work they do isn't any good. When I make them do it over they say that I am picking on them.

Mr. J.: Steve and Eddie aren't having the trouble with their girls that you do with yours.

Bill: Well, I'm not having trouble with all of mine. There is just this small group of five or six who are the real trouble makers. They all want to be finishers and anything but what they are. I've got them spotted next to my desk where I can keep an eye on them, and I tell them that I won't move them until they learn to coöperate. Even so, I'd like to see Steve or Eddie or anybody else get any work out of them.

Mr. J.: You're not trying to tell me that just a few girls out of more than two dozen make your crew look that bad?

Bill: No, but they are the worst ones. I called all the girls in the "C" and "D" teams together last week and gave them a good talking to and now they're worse than ever. Production and quality are both down.

Mr. J.: I'm beginning to think that you don't have *any* that are any good.

Bill: No, that's not right. I'll take the girls in my "A" team and put 'em against any we've got. As a matter of fact all of my finishers are a pretty decent bunch. The "B" team has a couple of good workers in it and there is nothing wrong with the "E" team.

Mr. J.: Yeah, but their rejects are too high.

Bill: Well, that might be true, but those girls certainly produce. Maybe if I can get them to slow down a little the quality will go up. It's going to make them sore, though.

Mr. J.: That's *your* problem. You're not afraid of them, are you?

Bill: No, but they didn't even like it the other day when I got after them for talking on the job. Come to think of it, all that gabbing may be the reason they don't pay any attention to quality.

Mr. J.: Well, tell them that if they don't stop talking you'll break up their little club. You're the boss down there, aren't you?

Bill: Well, you've kind of got me there. I hired everybody in Team "E" in one batch with the understanding that they could work together and I hate to go back on my word.

Mr. J.: Well, give them a good lecture and threaten to do it.

Bill: I know, but it's a headache and those girls stick together and you can't locate the trouble maker. Even when girls don't get along too well they gang up on you. For example, I gave these girls on Team "C" a safety lecture the other day after one of them got her hands caught, and all they did was gripe and pick on me about everything under the sun. I never saw such a bunch of sour hens before in my life.

MR. J.: What's eating them anyway? Certainly there must have been some one thing they picked on.

BILL: Oh, it was the same old yapping about all of them wanting to be finishers. After they've been on the job a few weeks they think they know everything.

MR. J.: Sounds like you've been giving some of those girls a lot of half-baked ideas about the jobs around here. What's there to being a finisher anyway? The pay is the same.

BILL: I don't know. I think it's just a dumb idea they've got in their heads. You know how women are. I know the end job isn't any easier.

MR. J.: Was that all they griped about, or do they want us to give 'em the factory too?

BILL: No. Quite a few of them were sore because they said they couldn't make standard. Most of the girls think the bogey is too hard to hit anyway.

MR. J.: I haven't heard any other complaints about it. After all, 80 isn't so high. Why should your girls complain when none of the rest of them do?

BILL: All I know is that they do. Except for Team "A" and a few others who really turn the stuff out, they're just about the worst bunch of eight-balls I ever saw. I don't know why I have to have all of them.

MR. J.: Bill, we've been over all this before and I'm tired of listening to you feel sorry for yourself. Either get those girls on the ball, or we'll have to put somebody down there who knows how to run things. I don't want to be rough about it, but that's the way it is. I'll give you thirty days to get that mess straightened out, and I'll back you up on anything that seems reasonable. If you can show me some results by the end of that time you can stay; if you don't, we'll have to find something else for you. Is that clear?

BILL: I guess so. But after racking my brains like I have for the past six months, I don't know what you or I or anybody else can do with those girls. I've tried everything.

Examples of solutions recommended. The following solutions are typical of those recommended when groups are limited to three solutions. Solutions numbered 1, 2, 4, and 5 are suggested most frequently.

1. Turn lines 90 degrees clockwise (also counterclockwise)
2. Move Bill's desk so as to give team C more space
3. Discharge Bill
4. Train Bill in human relations skills
5. Rotate girls within a team
6. Rotate positions of teams
7. Post production records of each team
8. Obtain individual scores on rejects
9. Institute music programs
10. Improve lighting
11. Put in air conditioning
12. Put five problem girls in one team
13. Divide up problem girls and place one or two in each team
14. Restrict talking in team E
15. Break up team E
16. Wall up back of room
17. Train Johnson in human relations skills

THE VALUE OF SCREENING PRINCIPLES

It will readily be conceded that the seventeen solutions listed above are excessive in number and vary in excellence. The purpose of the screening process is to reduce this number by eliminating the ones least likely to be successful. In this manner the chances of taking action-steps that turn out to be successful should be improved. This improvement in quality should be accomplished without sacrificing the group's acceptance of the selections made by the screening process if it is to represent a pure gain.

Two of the screening principles developed are designed to reduce the number of possible solutions by rejecting some of them, and two are designed to assist in the process of making a positive selection. Solutions that are neither rejected nor selected may be regarded as tabled.

The reasoning underlying the screening principles has to do with reducing certain common errors in thinking and diverting discussion into constructive problem-solving channels. A good deal of discussion time may be consumed in minor disagreements and in debates over whose ideas are sounder. Frequently a person becomes defensive if another person disagrees with him. As a consequence, discussion time often has to be used to solve an interpersonal problem that was created by the discussion of the initial problem. The screening principles are designed to serve as an impersonal method for rejecting some solutions and supporting others. In this way they tend to avoid or reduce clashes between individuals so as to permit them to cooperate with each other.

Two types of errors are common in group thinking. One of these is to overgeneralize previous experience. A basic principle has value if used under the conditions for which it applies, but knowledge that is generalized without making proper distinctions leads to errors. Past experience can be valuable if the right thing is learned, and it can be detrimental if the wrong thing is learned or if the right thing is applied to the wrong problem. As an illustration we may mention the example of the cat that jumped on a hot stove and as a result never jumped on a cold one. This cat's learning was overgeneralized, and its learning was such that it now avoids the very experience from which it could learn to make differentiations and hence extend its learning. If it avoids all stoves, it can never learn that only hot stoves are bad.

The second common error is the failure to use the facts that are known. Other things being equal, it will be conceded that a group of solutions to a problem founded upon *some* of the facts that are known will be better than a group of solutions having *no* basis in the facts of the case. Although it is possible that one of the latter solutions will be better than the best of the former, this superiority will be purely a chance occurrence and a rarity. In general it would be wiser to use the facts available, even if they were inadequate, than to ignore them.

THE SCREENING PRINCIPLES

In order to clarify how the following principles function, the various solutions obtained in the sewing room problem will be subjected to the screening process. The purpose of the exercise is to clarify the four principles, not to prove the merits of the logic on which the principles are based. The defense of the principles themselves rests on the fact that they (1) eliminate solutions based on personal preference, solutions transferred from dissimilar situations, and solutions lacking foundation in the facts of the problem situation; (2) divert time from debates over questionable facts and conflicting interpretations into a search for better evidence and other ideas; and (3) avoid nonconstructive interpersonal clashes by introducing a depersonalized method of reducing an overabundance of solutions.

In working with the screening principles it is helpful to think of a solution as a structure built on interpretations of facts, which are the foundation posts. It is granted that sufficient foundation posts may be lacking, but this lack does not justify a failure to use those one has. Figure 8 illustrates the relationship between a solution and the interpretation or organization of facts. Solution A rests on two posts while solution B rests on one. Posts 3 and 4 are not supporting structures. The geometrical designs on the posts represent a particular arrangement or organization of smaller irregular blocks which represent facts.

Negative principle 1—solutions transferred from other situations should be rejected. This principle is initially resisted because people believe that you should transfer knowledge gained in other situations. In applying this principle to test a particular solution, the discussion leader asks the group for evidence to support the solution. If it is suggested that the solution solved some other production problem, the leader asks for facts in the present problem that show that the other situation is like the present one. If the conferees suggest that the problems *may* be similar but have no facts to indicate that there are basic similarities, the leader indicates that the solution is screened out because it does not rest on facts in the case. However, he concedes that

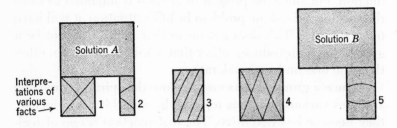

Fig. 8. Relation between solutions and facts. The solution to a problem may be viewed as a structure such as shown by rectangles A and B. The foundational supports of a solution are interpretations of facts shown as irregular figures making up each of the posts. The various interpretations of facts are so organized as to form posts 1, 2, 3, 4, and 5. These posts are available for supporting the rectangular structures.

It should be noted that the posts are made up of geometrical figures, and when arranged in a particular manner, they become supports. This implies that facts must be interpreted or organized in suitable ways in order to become supports. Solution A is supported by posts 1 and 2 while solution B has one post, number 5. Posts 3 and 4 have no structures built on them, which indicates that they have not been used or that they represent different organizations of some of the same facts.

the solution may be a good one, but it just fails to pass the screening principle.

For example, a participant may be an exponent of the use of music to increase production. He therefore suggests that music be introduced into Bill's section. His justification is that experiments have shown music to be helpful. It is clear that support for this solution lies outside the facts of the problem under consideration and hence is rejected. The exponent of music may be asked if the music will help production in Steve's and Eddie's units as well as in Bill's. This is readily granted by the exponent. The leader can now conclude that music is equally good for helping production in all units, and it might be wise to introduce it in the company as a whole. However, it should be explained that Bill has a special problem which is different from any that Steve and Eddie may have. Thus it is granted that music may help production, but since the present discussion is intended to solve the special and unique problem in Bill's situation, it will have to be rejected. This does not mean that music may not be a good thing to introduce, rather that it solves a problem other than the one under consideration.

Once a group of persons gets into the spirit of screening and sees various solutions rejected by an arbitrary principle, they become less defensive. The first reaction is one of feeling defensive; next there is a general impression that all solutions will be rejected; but soon these reactions are replaced by a constructive interest in the new approach.

Let us now turn to the solutions listed on page 220 and see how the first principle deals with them. Solutions 7, 8, and 9 are clearly rejected because they are generalizations from other solutions and hence are based upon ideas borrowed from past experience. They represent attempts to apply knowledge about boredom or motivation to solving the present problem, despite the fact that there are no facts to support the belief that the girls in Bill's unit were bored or lacked motivation. Invariably participants readily agree that there is no basis for these assumptions and that the solutions are uncritically transferred from other situations. Solution 11 also might be suspected to be a borrowed solution, and for this reason the persons recommending it should be asked to give their reasons. If their defense is based upon the success with the solution in other offices, then it is of the transfer type and must be rejected; but if the reason given is based upon the arrangement of the windows, it is retained. For purposes of the present discussion we will assume it passes negative principle 1.

Negative principle 2—solutions supported by facts or interpretations of facts that are challenged by other members of the group should be rejected. It is assumed that each of the solutions not already rejected rests upon facts derived from the problem situation under consideration. Each solution, therefore, rests upon a particular selection or interpretation of these facts, and the various solutions may have identical or different supports.

According to this principle, it follows that if a particular set of facts is seen as fictitious by someone else in the group or if a conflicting interpretation can be derived from the facts in the same situation, it is assumed that the solution rests upon an unsound support. Although a complete foundation is too much to expect in the type of problem situation under consideration, it is reasonable to expect some unchallenged interpretations to support the solution. This does not mean that a particular interpretation must be proven sound; rather it must merely be better than those with conflicting interpretations or facts.

This principle is initially resisted because it first appears that any person can reject a solution by merely disagreeing with something someone else says. In order to challenge a fact or an interpretation, a reason should be given, and this reason must also be based upon a fact in the case. If such evidence is lacking, negative principle 1 is invoked to screen out the objection.

If a participant supported the solution of rotating positions (solution 6) by saying that girls were bored, this fact should be challenged. There is no known evidence in the case. If a person assumed that boredom was present because he would himself be bored on such a job, the evidence would be of his own making, and a solution resting on it would have to be rejected. If, however, a person suggested the solution of discharging the six problem girls and was challenged because another participant did not believe that the girls were problem girls, then the challenger would be asked to supply a fact that supported his challenge. If he said he had no such facts but merely refused to believe that there were sufficient facts to warrant the "problem girl" interpretation, then he would be out of order. There is some evidence in the case to support the interpretation that there were six problem girls, and a refusal to accept this does not constitute a challenge. Thus a challenge of facts or interpretations of facts must have a basis in fact.

Suppose the facts are ambiguous and allow several interpretations. Such a condition is illustrated in Figure 9. The various lines (facts) may be organized to produce a pair of Xs, a W on top of an M, an inverted V superimposed on an upright V, or a diamond with whiskers on the sides. Each of

FIG. 9. Ambiguous interpretations. The lines in this figure may be organized to form two Xs, a V with another V superimposed, a W on top of an M, or a diamond with lines projected from the sides. Which interpretation is correct? Since each interpretation rests on the same facts, they are equally sound, and the correctness of any one of them is challenged by the others. Solutions to problems based upon ambiguous interpretations of facts are rejected by negative principle 2.

these interpretations is based upon facts. If one solution is supported by the interpretation that an X is present, another that an M is present, while a third rests on a V interpretation, then negative principle 2 says that all such solutions should be rejected unless they can be supported by some other unambiguous facts or interpretations.

The underlying logic in this case is that ambiguous interpretations lead to discussions that cannot be resolved and hence are wasteful. Continuing the analogy in Figure 8 we might indicate that such posts or supports are unsound. If the same facts lend themselves to more than one interpretation, each interpretation is less stable and a less desirable support than unambiguous interpretations.

Examples of solutions likely to be rejected by negative principle 2 are solutions 1, 5, 6, 12, 13, 14, 15, and 16. If solution 1 is supported by an interpretation that the window position is desirable because team A is the best team, then a conflicting interpretation might be raised with respect to team E, which is farthest from the window and has the second highest production. If it is argued that all teams should share certain advantages in position near the window, then it is clear that this solution also makes all teams share the disadvantages of being far from the window.

However, if it is argued that turning the lines 90 degrees gives team C more space, this solution should be retained unless it is found that the change takes space from some other team.

Solution 5 usually rests on the interpretation that girls want to be finishers (the last position). The fact, however, is that the girls merely *say* they want to be finishers; perhaps they just want to get away from Bill. However, either interpretation may be used to support the rotation plan. If this is done, then the conflicting interpretation is that rotation within the team places all girls closer to Bill just as much as it places all girls farther from Bill.

Solutions 6, 12, and 13 are subject to similar conflicting interpretations and for this reason are rejected.

Solutions 14, 15, and 16 are based upon the fact having to do with the talking of the girls in team E. The interpretation that talking is undesirable is based upon the poor record of rejects found for team E. It could be argued just as reasonably that talking is good, and this interpretation would be supported by the fact that team E has a good production record. It is this conflict in interpretations that eliminates these three solutions.

Solutions 1, 2, 3, 4, 10, 11, and 17 remain after this screening, although 1 and 11 were questioned regarding some of their assumptions.

Positive principle 1—solutions founded either upon (1) any of the unchallenged facts or (2) unchallenged interpretations of facts taken from the problem situation should be selected for consideration and evaluation. It also follows that, other things being equal, solutions that have more than one fact or interpretation to support them should be considered to be more appropriate than solutions resting entirely on one of these supports. Furthermore, the more different the supporting facts or interpretations are from each other, the more valuable the solution.

Suppose, for example, that there is an interpretation that Bill, in the sewing room case, is a poor supervisor. This opinion might be based upon the punitive responses Bill made in the interview with Mr. Johnson. From this interview it would be unrealistic to reach the opinion that Bill is a good supervisor. Hence the interpretation that Bill is a poor supervisor would represent a supporting post for a solution that was built upon it. Suppose further that we had evidence from another interview, which also led to the opinion that Bill was a poor supervisor. In such a case the opinion would be reinforced by similar evidence, but since a different set of facts were used, a second post would be obtained. Suppose next that an entirely different kind of evidence were available, such as a continued decline in production ever since Bill took over the section. This kind of information would also permit an interpretation that Bill was a poor supervisor and contribute a third supporting post. Such facts, if available for the supporting post, would have an entirely different kind of origin than those used for the first post, which came from the interview. Since the first and second supporting posts are based on interpretations of similar facts, while the first and third posts are based on interpretations of entirely different facts, combination of the first and third posts would be regarded as lending better supports to a solution than the combination of the first and second posts.

This difference in the value of these two pairs of supporting posts can be diagrammatically represented by placing the supporting posts different distances from each other.

The more different the facts that are used to support a solution, the farther apart they would be placed and the more stable the solution that rested upon them would become. Thus the stability of a solution would depend on the number of the supporting posts and the distance they were from each other. In Figure 8, solution A has two well-placed supports whereas solution B rests on one support.

We will now turn to the solutions that have not been rejected and determine whether any of them are favored by positive principle 1. Solutions 2, 3, 4, and 17 can be used to illustrate how this principle selects solutions. Solution 2 has a basic fact to support it: team C has the least space, and it is the worst group. Although it can be argued that this relationship might be pure coincidence, such an argument does not challenge the fact—it merely is a statement indicating the need for more facts. Furthermore, the interpretation that the observed relationship between the work done and the space occupied by team C is a coincidence is based on knowledge obtained elsewhere and hence violates negative principle 1. The facts in this situation place the poor production record of team C and its shortage of space together, and it is unlikely that anyone would seriously contend that team C would do worse if it had more space. It is frequently difficult to convince statistically minded persons to overlook the possibility that errors occur from a failure to give full recognition to chance. Therefore, we wish to remind the reader that we are dealing with situations lacking adequate facts, and no claim is made that solution 2 is correct. It is merely selected by the screening process and will have to compete with other solutions.

Some problem solvers attempt to support solution 2 with additional facts or interpretations. For example, it may be claimed that the crowding of team C creates problem girls. This interpretation can be challenged by the fact that teams B and D have as many problem girls as team C but have the full amount of space. Thus solution 2 rests primarily on one observed negative relationship between space and productivity.

Solutions 3 and 4 are similar in that they make Bill the problem, and as a result they are supported by identical facts. The following observations or posts support these solutions: (1) Steve and Eddie (other supervisors) do not have as much trouble as Bill; (2) the actions that Bill has taken haven't been successful; (3) finishers are the most satisfied, and they are farthest from Bill; and (4) the best teams are farthest from Bill. These interpretations tend to remain unchallenged even though it may be argued that the evidence is not conclusive.

Solution 17 is supported by the fact that Johnson has not been helpful to Bill. This inference usually is not questioned. Sometimes it is argued that training in higher management should precede the training of supervisors. However, this conclusion is based upon facts obtained elsewhere (negative principle 1) and hence cannot be used to challenge an inference based upon the situation under study. Thus solution 17 usually rests upon one support—Johnson's apparent inability to help Bill. If it is claimed that Steve and Eddie work well with Johnson, then the lone support for solution 17 is successfully challenged on the basis of evidence given in the interview.

Positive principle 2—when exceptions to a trend in results can be satisfactorily explained, solutions based upon the trend should be selected for further consideration. Ordinarily an exception to a rule or to a trend in data is regarded as a weakness and hence might result in the rejection of a set of observations. According to positive principle 2 each exception should be examined to determine whether or not it may be associated with some other exceptional condition.

For example, a person might claim that boys in the fifth grade in school can run faster than boys in the second grade. Let us suppose that in comparing ten fifth-grade boys with ten second-grade boys, there are two exceptions to this claim in that two fifth-grade boys were beaten in a race by all second-grade boys. These exceptions would weaken the above claim even if they did not destroy it. Suppose, however, an examination of the exceptions revealed that the two fifth-grade boys who lost the race were cripples. This finding would tend to reinstate confidence in the claim regarding the superior running ability of the fifth-grade boys.

The value of this principle resides in the fact that a general examination of the data may result in the rejection of potentially valuable interpretations. If all of the facts do not fit a particular interpretation, the situation should be explored to determine whether additional facts exist which might explain why certain facts are out of line with the trend. In other words, if exceptional results are obtained under exceptional conditions, the exceptional nature of the results becomes less disturbing and should not be taken as seriously as if obtained under more typical conditions. It is this closer examination of details and the exploration of unusual directions or approaches to problems that characterize the thinking of creative individuals.

When the facts are limited, the appearance of exceptions may cause trends in observational data to be summarily rejected, particularly when no provision is made to give them special attention. Positive principle 2 requires that the exceptions themselves must be defended if they challenge a solution. Any fact in the situation that can explain why the exception occurs therefore becomes relevant to this analysis.

Solutions 10 and 11 usually rest upon trends in data. It is found that there is a general tendency for teams nearest the window to do the best. If we take the production figures for teams A, B, C, D, and E we find them to be 90, 80, 50, 60, and 85, respectively. Figure 10 shows these relationships in graphic form. Exceptions to a general downward trend (broken line) are the figures 50 and 85. Thus team C does too little, and team E does too much. The fact that three teams fit the trend whereas two are exceptions makes the claim for a trend weak. However, let us examine these two exceptions.

Team C, with the lowest production, is exceptional in another way—it has the least work space. This last fact can explain the team's exceptional performance. The second exception concerns the production of team E, since this is too high considering its position. This team is also exceptional in a second way—it is the only team made up of friends. This fact could explain the team's superior produc-

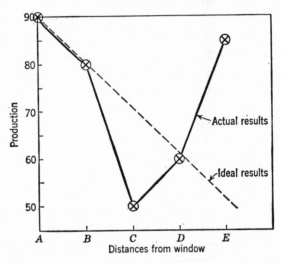

Fɪɢ. 10. Relationship between production and distance from window. The interpretation that a team's production is influenced by its distance from the window is supported by the production figures of teams A, B, and D. If it were not for teams C and E, the relationship would approach that of a straight line (shown as the broken line). Unfortunately, two-fifths of the data fail to support the trend so that the relationship shown in the solid line is obtained. However, before the hypothesis that a trend in results exists is rejected, the exceptional performance of the two teams should be examined further. Team C's conditions are the most crowded, and this could make for poor performance; while team D is made up of a group of friends, which might explain their superior performance. The recognition of these exceptional conditions thus makes the original hypothesis more plausible.

The reader might observe a different trend—that of production increasing as one moves either way from the center of the room. If a meaningful interpretation could be built around these trends, it would be well grounded in the facts of the case. The purpose of this diagram, however, is to illustrate how exceptions to trends in data may be examined to see if facts exist which may explain away the exception.

tion in terms of morale. Granted that nothing is definitely proven, it will be apparent that one exception might cancel another.

Turning now to reject scores of the various teams, we may examine them in a similar manner. We find the figures for teams A, B, C, D, and E to be 5, 10, 15, 10, and 15, respectively. In this instance the rejects of team D may be seen as too low or those of teams C and E as too high. Team D seems not to have an exceptional condition so cannot be explained away. The high rejects of team C can be explained as before, but the high rejects of team E now must be explained by some unfavorable factor, such as "working too fast." It is clear that attempts to explain these exceptions away are not very convincing, but it must also be granted that a contradictory inference cannot be drawn. It may also be claimed that the exceptions to the trend with respect to rejects do not deviate as greatly as do the production figures.

It is possible to argue that the windows serve a valuable function until the middle of the room is reached but that beyond this point the distance from them ceases to be a factor. The strength of this argument will vary somewhat from one discussion group to another.

It will be apparent that the case for the trend in results would be greatly strengthened with only minor changes in the data. For the time being let us assume that even though the case for the trend is weak, the suggestion is present. Let us, therefore, see if a distinction can be made between solutions 10 and 11, dealing with improved lighting and air conditioning, respectively.

Teams C and E have the poorest quality. Since team C is poor in all respects, this is not surprising, but team E's contradictory performances must be explained. Since team E has no problem girls and the production is good, it is more necessary to explain the high rejects than the high production. If this step is agreed upon, then the next step can be taken. If this step is not agreed upon, then it follows that the trend in data has been rejected because it is necessary to assume that team E is a good team in order to entertain the trend.

Let us assume for the purpose of further analysis that team E's low quality (high rejects) must be explained. Will poor lighting or poor ventilation explain the low quality better? Generally it is agreed that poor lighting accounts for team E's low quality more effectively than does poor ventilation.

The merits of improved lighting versus air conditioning solutions can be approached in a second way. It is usually agreed that poor lighting would affect rejects more than production, whereas poor ventilation would affect production more than rejects. If this is conceded, the trends for production and rejects may be compared. It is usually agreed that the exceptions found for the reject trend are less deviant than those for the production trend, thus favoring the solution of improved lighting.

FINAL EVALUATION

Solutions that survive the screening principles become the final topic of group discussion. The solutions that remain for consideration have a basis in the facts of the case, and even though they may vary in quality they should be superior to those that have been rejected by the negative principles and also to those that were not selected by the positive principles. This means that the final evaluation is concerned with an appraisal of solutions that have some grounding in the known facts.

These solutions may now be appraised in terms of the following five points of view: (1) cost and practical considerations; (2) the way in which they may be integrated; (3) a selection from among alternatives when two actions are incompatible; (4) an examination of the extent of support given by facts or interpretations; and (5) acceptability to group members. These considerations ordinarily enter into problem solving. In the screening process they are treated as unique stages in the final evaluation and become the crucial considerations in the final selection.

The first of these points of view deals with the ability to execute various solutions. A solution that (1) exceeds the financial ability of the organization, (2) is more costly than the anticipated returns, (3) exceeds the area of freedom of the group, or (4) requires facilities or materials not available may be unacceptable to the group.

The second point of view requires an examination of the surviving solutions in terms of whether some of them can be combined or integrated. Each of several alternatives might profit from an integration.

The third point of view deals with the process of selecting between solutions that cannot be integrated or combined in that they are mutually exclusive. For example, the solution to "discharge Bill" is in conflict with that to "train Bill," and both would have the same foundation in fact. Although a compromise might be formulated that included trying to train Bill and if that failed, to fire him, it might be found that a choice between these equally good alternatives (from the screening approach) might be made. It might also be added that such a choice would involve little risk since the alternatives are of equal value with respect to what is known.

The fourth point of view requires an examination of the number of supporting posts and of the degree of support given each solution. Two supporting posts are better than one, and two supporting posts spaced apart (based upon different kinds of facts) are better than two supporting posts that are close together (see Figure 8, page 223).

Finally, one must consider the fact that participants prefer some solutions over others. This point of view recognizes the human factor that enters into decision making. Decisions that are likely to hurt feelings tend to be unpopular, and when alternatives to these decisions are present, opportunities to make a choice should be permitted. The important thing is to face the reality of why one solu-

tion is favored over another. To reject the solution of discharging Bill because it goes contrary to one's value system
is a good reason, but to reject it by refusing to respect the
fact that he is a poor supervisor is not a sound reason. The
purpose of these considerations is to clarify reasons and
avoid rationalization.

Let us now examine the various solutions that survived
the screening principles. The recommended solutions that
remain for further consideration are solutions 2, 3, 4, 10,
and 17. Since solutions 2, 10, and 17 have one support each,
while solutions 3 and 4 have more than one, the latter two
actions would be ruled as the ones most likely to produce
results. Since solutions 3 and 4 are in conflict, they would
either have to be integrated, or a choice would have to be
made between them. Solutions 2 and 10 are relatively in-
expensive, and they might also be acceptable for that reason.
Solutions 4 and 17 would be related in that they could be
made a part of a single program, and this might result in
an integration. Thus the final decision rests with ways to
integrate or combine selected solutions in a practical and
acceptable manner.

The final evaluation should be a relatively free type of
discussion. At this stage, preferences and biases should be
permitted to operate. In working with the screening principles we have repeatedly been able to cause teams of
problem solvers who were in initial disagreement to change
their selection and settle for solutions 2, 4, and 10. Solution
3 is usually not accepted because blame is also placed on
Johnson, Bill's boss. Since solutions 3 and 4 are alternatives,
preference settles on solution 4. This degree of agreement
cannot be achieved through a general discussion of results.
Such discussions drift in various directions, and persons tend
to defend their initial decisions. Solution 10 rarely survives
when the screening principles are not used for selection
purposes, whereas solutions 5, 6, and 12 are among the
top favorites. Solutions 2 and 4 are selected regardless of
whether or not the screening principles are used. Thus the
screening process in this problem takes out at least three

solutions (5, 6, and 12) that are strong contenders and introduces one (solution 10) that usually is lost by informal group discussion.

SUMMARY OF THE SCREENING PROCESS

A good deal of discussion time is lost evaluating solutions in group problem solving because of difficulties created during the process of trying to solve an initial problem. These difficulties constitute a source of new problems, and these problems interfere with the solving of the original problem because they are purely artifacts created by interpersonal relations. Such factors as injured feelings, faulty communication, personal involvement, insecurity, and face saving can function so as to necessitate compromise solutions or the acceptance of solutions that arouse the least opposition. As a result the products of group thinking often lack objective quality.

This unproductive aspect of problem solving is particularly disturbing when facts are inadequate and freedom of thinking is not restricted by the need to conform to known realities. Often a person will unknowingly advocate a pet solution for a given situation because it solved an old problem or will solve another problem with which he is faced. For example, a works manager wanted to transfer a particular operation to a different factory, and this became his pet solution to all problems involving this group of workers.

Although good conference leadership can reduce these sources of interference, it is apparent that there is a need for other methods for improving solution quality. Obviously an acceptable evaluation process must be impersonal. The screening principles were developed to eliminate poor quality solutions and to select those with objective quality. The acceptance of this screening process by persons participating in group problem solving is evidenced by the fact that there is high agreement on merits of the solutions that survive the screening process.

The two negative principles that screen out solutions

may be stated as follows: (1) solutions transferred from other problems should be rejected; (2) solutions supported by facts or by interpretations of facts that are challenged by other members of a group should be rejected.

The two positive principles that select solutions for consideration may be stated as follows: (1) solutions founded upon any of the unchallenged facts or unchallenged interpretations of facts (taken from the problem situation) should be selected for consideration and evaluation; (2) when exceptions to a trend in results can be satisfactorily explained, solutions based upon the trend should be selected for further consideration.

Solutions that are selected by the positive principles are evaluated by group discussion in terms of (1) cost and practical considerations, (2) the way in which they may be integrated, (3) a selection from among alternatives when two actions are incompatible, (4) an examination of the extent of support given by facts or interpretations, and (5) acceptability to group members.

Solutions that are neither screened out nor selected are tabled and should be considered only when the positive principles have failed to select solutions.

It is apparent that the evaluation process makes use of group discussion, but only after the screening process has forced a thorough consideration of the facts in the situation. Facts cannot be used exclusively to evaluate the type of problems considered because they are deficient.

CHAPTER NINE

Summary of problem-solving principles

Throughout this volume use has been made of certain principles which serve to increase the productivity of group problem solving. By means of the application of these principles, it is possible for a discussion leader to increase the ability of a group of people to solve problems. Since these principles are scattered through the various chapters, it seems desirable to bring them together. No claim is made that the nine principles restated below make up a complete list, and it is also possible that the number may be reduced to fewer more fundamental principles. Some of the principles seem to overlap in certain respects. Nevertheless, the principles stated below are adequate in their present form to serve as a guide to the discussion leader.

PRINCIPLES FOR CREATIVE DISCUSSIONS

Principle 1—success in problem solving requires that effort be directed toward overcoming surmountable obstacles. In Chapter 3 the question of a problem's location was discussed in detail. If we think of a problem situation as being one in which obstacles block us from reaching a goal, it follows that some of these obstacles will be more readily overcome than others. As a matter of fact, a problem will be insoluble if attempts are made to reach the goal by means of an insurmountable obstacle. This means that persistent attempts to overcome some obstacles might be doomed to failure. Success in problem solving, therefore, depends on locating obstacles that can more readily be overcome.

It is the common tendency to persist in following an initial approach to a problem. In other words, a particular obstacle is selected and pursued despite the fact that it cannot be remedied. Usually this obstacle is the most obvious one or is one toward which previous experience directs one. For example, medical research reveals that inoculation with a serum to create immunity has been a successful approach for dealing with some diseases so it tends to be followed for others. In business it is not uncommon to approach new problems with approaches previously found successful. Yet difficult problems require new and unusual approaches; if they did not, they would not be difficult problems.

A common tendency that frequently leads to failure is associated with the attempt to solve a problem by locating a person or group that is at fault. For example, a solution to international problems that requires another nation to behave differently may meet with failure because the problem solvers cannot control the action they recommend. Lacking such control, when it is essential to the solution, represents an insurmountable obstacle. A solution that cannot be effectuated falls short of solving the problem and hence leads us only to the insurmountable obstacles. Successful solutions must be workable.

Principle 2—available facts should be used even when they are inadequate. In the previous chapter it was found that people tend to overgeneralize solutions. A solution that was effective in one situation becomes favored and is used in new situations even when there are no facts in support of a similarity between the old and the new situation. The assumption that the situations are the same tends to detract from a careful examination of the facts that are available.

When a good deal of information is available, problem solvers are more prone to work with the evidence. There is then enough information given to permit them to reject some solutions. However, in the absence of adequate information, it becomes more difficult to be selective, and as a consequence imagination and biases dominate the problem solving.

Principle 3—the starting point of a problem is richest in solution possibilities. In Chapter 4 the solution of a problem was described as a route from the starting point to the goal. The process of thinking about a solution is like proceeding along a particular route. Once one starts in a particular direction one moves away from certain alternatives, and this reduces the number of possible alternative directions that may be pursued.

Each route may confront one with obstacles. As discussion of a problem proceeds, successive obstacles present themselves. A group may have successfully bypassed two obstacles along the way and then find difficulty with others that face them at their advanced stage of progress. Because of this partial success in moving forward, it is difficult for them to revert and start all over again, yet a new start is the only way to increase the variety of solution possibilities. For example, a great deal of progress was made with propeller-driven planes; however, they had limitations. They were not able to fly above a certain height because of the lack of atmosphere. Increasing their power and design could raise the flying ceiling somewhat; nevertheless, the need for atmosphere limited the ceiling for propeller-driven craft. A plane with an entirely different power plant—the jet engine—represented a fresh start in aviation.

In the usual problem situation a person develops certain ideas about solutions. This means he moves from the starting point in a particular direction toward the goal. Thus the supervisor who wishes to improve phone-answering services in his office by eliminating or reducing personal calls finds it difficult to think of approaches that do not limit personal calls. Rather he thinks of different alternatives for limiting personal calls and loses sight of the original goal of improving phone-answering service. The solution reached now becomes confused with the problem. This is why statements of problems frequently contain suggestions of solutions. Obviously such statements of problems are so near the goal that they limit other solution possibilities. Such suggested solutions may be unacceptable and unimaginative.

In order to get a better appreciation of the starting point of a problem, a discussion leader should ask himself why he wishes or favors a certain solution: What purpose does my solution serve? Such a question may suggest the nature of the starting point of the problem. Spending time with the group to explain the prime objective, therefore, represents a procedure for finding the starting point.

All solutions represent methods for reaching a goal, but frequently sight is lost of the starting point. Rather the goal becomes an ideal toward which to strive. Practical consideration, however, requires that we reach a goal from the point at which we find ourselves. It may be unrealistic to get to an ideal goal from certain points. If one could start over again, more problems could be solved or more ideal goals could be reached, but this is not realistic problem solving. A solution always is a path *from* the starting point *to* a goal, and sight of this starting point should not be lost.

Principle 4—problem-mindedness should be increased while solution-mindedness is delayed. By nature people progress too rapidly toward a solution. This is what is meant by solution-mindedness. This tendency is similar to the phenomena known as the Zeigarnik[1] effect. Once a task is begun, psychological forces are set up to push the task to completion. The reader will understand how he himself resists being interrupted while engaged in a task and how he worries over unfinished activities. It is only natural, therefore, that since the goal of a problem is to find a solution, energy and activity toward accomplishing this end are set in motion.

This means that in almost any discussion the members' responses tend to interrupt the thinking process of one another, and this is often disturbing. It is only natural for a dominant person to push through his ideas, and when this person happens to be the leader, the value of group participation is lost.

In Chapter 5 evidence supporting the value of delaying the reaching of a solution and spending more time focusing on the problem was presented. Several experimental studies were cited which were designed to test the relevance of this principle. Common experience also may be cited.

It is not uncommon to find people disagreeing about solutions and later finding that they have not even agreed on the problem. The first prerequisite for reaching agreement on a solution would seem to be reaching agreement on the problem. The reader will also recall that when he asks his friends for help on a problem, they offer suggestions before he has finished his statement of the problem. It is also probable that part of the value of the developmental discussion (discussed in Chapters 2 and 7) lies in the fact that the procedure delays the solution.

It is apparent that a discussion leader can cause a group to be more problem-minded. Usually he is a strong force in encouraging solution-mindedness. He must not only inhibit this tendency, but encourage problem-mindedness in his

---

[1] B. Zeigarnik, Ueber das Behalten von erledigten und unerledigten Handlungen, *Psychol. Forsch.*, 1927, 9, 1–85. M. Ovsiankina, Die Wiederaufnahme unterbrochener Handlungen. *Psychol. Forsch.*, 1928, 11, 302–379.

group in the process of improving his discussion leadership.

Principle 5—disagreement can lead either to hard feelings or to innovation, depending on the discussion leadership. Two strong forces give rise to conformity: (1) fear of the leader's unfavorable judgment and (2) fear of unfavorable responses from the group to which one belongs. These factors unfortunately operate only too frequently in group discussion so that the leader must be prepared to deal with both of them. Experimental evidence in support of this conclusion is to be found largely in Chapter 5.

Almost everyone has learned that he can get into more trouble by disagreeing with his boss than by agreeing with him. This is the kind of learning that develops yes-men. In most organizations conferees need a great deal of encouragement to feel free to disagree with the boss. This does not mean that disagreeing is a virtue. Rather the subordinate must feel free to disagree if he is to contribute the best of his thinking. By withholding judgment, entertaining criticism, and trying to understand strange ideas, the leader takes the first steps toward reducing conformity.

The dangers of disagreeing with the majority members of one's own group or with society in general are less readily learned. The dissenter and the innovator sometimes find themselves popular and sometimes unpopular. For this reason, any hard feelings created by disagreement are not too apparent. However, an additional factor also operates. This is the security gained in going along with the crowd. When people are unsure of themselves, they are particularly prone to follow group opinion rather than risk a deviant opinion.[2] Conformity to group standards becomes unfortunate when it inhibits free expression or rejects the person who innovates without examining or understanding his contributions. A majority does not have to prove or justify itself because it does not have to change minds, but a minority can be laughed down and hence is denied the opportunity to prove itself. Original ideas are new, so the original person fre-

[2] E. L. Walker and R. W. Heyns, *An Anatomy for Conformity.* Prentice-Hall, Inc., Englewood Cliffs, N.J., 1962.

quently finds himself in a minority. This means that he may not only be a lonely person, but will have to justify many of his views.

When one person disagrees with another, the latter is inclined to feel that he has been attacked. As a consequence he feels hurt and defends himself or becomes angry and counterattacks. Such emotional reactions lead to interpersonal conflict, and this type of interaction tends to worsen. As a result, people avoid hurting others. "Good" group members therefore tend to be sensitive to group opinion and become careful in expressing their views. As a matter of fact, they may find that the easiest way to be careful is to avoid disagreeing. People who get along with other participants by conforming may be good group members, but they also become poor problem solvers.[3] Members cannot learn from one another by agreeing. They can avoid generating hard feelings, but eventually they may become bored. Satisfaction in group problem solving should come from accomplishment in one's physical environment; otherwise the group activity is primarily social.

We therefore are confronted with the fact that because disagreeing with others frequently leads to injured pride and interpersonal conflict, it is considered to be poor manners. In attempts to avoid trouble, people learn to refrain from disagreeing and hence move toward conformity. However, this alternative also is undesirable. The resolution of this dilemma is not only to prevent the suppression of disagreement, but to encourage a respect for disagreement and thereby turn it into a stimulant for new ideas. How is this to be done?

First of all, each individual can learn to be less defensive himself, even if he cannot expect this tolerance from others. This is not much of a gain, but it can be a personal

[3] L. R. Hoffman, Homogeneity of Member Personality and Its Effect on Group Problem-solving. *J. abnorm. soc. Psychol.*, 1959, **58**, 27–32. L. R. Hoffman and N. R. F. Maier, Quality and Acceptance of Problem Solutions by Members of Homogeneous and Heterogeneous Groups. *J. abnorm. soc. Psychol.*, 1961, **62**, 401–407.

one. A group leader, however, can accomplish a good deal in this respect. The leader of a group discussion can create a climate where disagreement is encouraged; he can use his position in the group to protect minority individuals; and he can turn disagreements among group members into situational problems. This is a second skill area for reducing the undesirable aspects of conformity; and in addition, this skill in group leadership increases innovation by using disagreement constructively.

Group thinking has a potential advantage over individual thinking in that the resources making for disagreement are greater in a group. Group thinking also has a potential disadvantage in that the dominant thinking may be that of the majority. The leader's responsibility is to capitalize on the advantages and avoid the disadvantages of group processes.

While organizations search for creative talent and attempt to develop it, the creative talent already present in the organization is being depressed at all levels. In a recent study [4] the solutions of four-person groups taken from four populations differing in organizational orientation were compared. The problem used involved an industrial situation in which the need for a change in work procedure was raised (see pages 25 ff.).

The results showed that the least creative solutions came from management groups, better solutions came from students in the school of business administration, still better ones from students in a college course on industrial psychology, while the greatest number of innovative solutions came from students in liberal arts courses. It appears that the farther the problem solvers were removed from organizational experience, the more innovative were their solutions. Unless something is done to prevent it, awareness of organization structure tends to suppress innovation. The key factor seems to be the perception of the role of the boss in introducing and gaining acceptance of change.

[4] N. R. F. Maier and L. R. Hoffman, Organization and Creative Problem Solving. *J. appl. Psychol.*, 1961, **45**, 277–280.

Principle 6—the idea-getting process should be separated from the idea-evaluation process because the latter inhibits the former. Idea evaluation involves the testing and the comparison of solutions in the light of what is known, their probability for succeeding, and other practical considerations. It is the practical side of problem solving and is the phase of problem solving when judgment is passed on solutions. Idea getting requires a willingness to break away from past experience. It is this process that requires an escape from the bonds of learning and demands that we search for unusual approaches and entertain new and untried ideas.

Robert Ingersoll once said, "Colleges polish the pebbles and dim the diamonds." This may be an overstatement, but it points up the dual aspect of learning. It is the creative potentials that are inhibited by knowledge. In so far as education teaches us what is known, it develops us and permits us to meet situations that have been previously met. In this way our problem solving is enhanced—our knowledge can generalize—and this is polish. However, in order to escape from the search into the past, new combinations of elements must be generated. The process of learning is to build associative bonds between elements of experience that are found and observed in conjunction with one another. Thus we learn names of things; we relate causes with effects; and we see and compare likenesses and differences. Creativity, however, requires the combination of elements and events that have never been experienced together—the generation of a new route from the starting point to the goal, made up of parts of old routes.

In other words, creativity requires the ability to fragment past experience and permit the formation of new spontaneous combinations. In contrast, learning requires the ability to combine or connect elements that have been contiguous to each other in our experience. Since these two abilities are basically different, they do not necessarily go together. One person may possess an unusual learning ability and be uncreative; another may be unusually creative but not be outstanding in learning ability. Both the abilities to learn and to fragment experience are necessary for good problem solving. However, the second of these has been largely overlooked because of our emphasis on the study of learning.[5]

In order to illustrate the difference between learning and fragmenting, let us return to our string problem discussed in Chapter 3. This problem requires that the ends of two strings hanging from the ceiling be tied together. They are spaced so that a person cannot reach one while holding the other. With the aid of strings or sticks one could readily solve this problem. However, the only tool available is a pair of pliers. Past experience has associated this tool with certain functional uses, and as a consequence it becomes less likely to be seen as a weight than would an ordinary piece of metal. The creative solution requires that a pendulum be constructed by using the pair of pliers as a pendulum weight. Thus the distant string can be made to swing within reach. To find this solution the old associative bonds must be broken in order to permit the pliers to become a pendulum bob. When this new connection is made (pliers fastened to the string) and the pendulum is discovered, there is a sharp change in functional meanings. It is this change in meaning that causes the experience of insight. Sudden insights are associated with creative discoveries because the new meaning is not gradually built up through experience but comes suddenly as a result of a spontaneous new combination.[6]

The acquisition of knowledge, such as college training, actually may give an individual a mental set that reduces his creativity in certain respects, even though such knowledge is valuable in other ways. This is because the educated

[5] N. R. F. Maier, "Selector-Integrator Mechanisms in Behavior," in B. Kaplan and S. Wapner (eds.), *Perspectives in Psychological Theory*. International Universities Press, New York, 1960.

[6] N. R. F. Maier, Reasoning in Humans: II. The Solution of a Problem and Its Appearance in Consciousness. *J. comp. Psychol.*, 1931, **12**, 181–194.

person may attempt to solve a problem by applying what he knows, and although this would be a successful approach on some occasions, it would not be a creative solution. This set prevents him from making up unique solutions and thereby developing a combination of parts that cannot be found in his past. Thus a potentially creative person (a diamond) might be dimmed (in Ingersoll's sense) by a knowledge of standard or known approaches to a problem.

Past learning, practical considerations, and evaluation all tend to depress flights of imagination—the forward leap that is based on a hunch (insufficient evidence). Creative thinking is a radical rather than a conservative look at a problem situation and requires encouragement if it is to be nurtured. To demand proof of new ideas at the time of their inception is to discourage the creative process.

However, creative ideas and insane ideas sometimes are difficult to distinguish. Both represent a departure from the common and traditional ways of thinking; both are new and unique to the person. But there is also a difference. The creative idea has a basis in objective reality, even though the evidence to convince others is inadequate; in contrast, the product of the insane mind is made up of elements derived largely from internal stimulation, such as hallucinations and imagined events.

The practical aspects of the separation of idea getting and idea evaluation are discussed in Chapter 6. The discussion leader can delay a group's criticism of an idea by asking for alternative contributions, and he can encourage variety in thinking by encouraging the search for something different, something new. Turning ideas upside down, backward, trying out different combinations of old ideas, all represent ways to encourage the expression and generation of new ideas.

Principle 7—choice situations should be turned into problem situations. As pointed out in Chapter 5, the characteristic of a choice situation is one of being confronted with two or more alternatives. As a consequence, behavior is blocked until one of the alternatives is selected. The char-

acteristic of a problem situation, on the other hand, is one
of being confronted with an obstacle that prevents the reaching of a goal. Behavior is blocked until the obstacle can be
removed or surmounted. Creative alternatives tend to be
overlooked in choice situations because a choice is made
between the obvious alternatives. The fact that such alternatives exist directs the energy toward making a choice and
thus detracts from the search for additional alternatives.

Creative or unusual alternatives, not being among the
obvious ones, are unlikely to characterize behavior in choice
situations because activity is directed toward a choice between existing alternatives. Something must be done to
delay this choice until the possibility of additional alternatives is explored. This is something the discussion leader
can do. Since the unusual alternatives are not readily apparent, it is necessary to encourage considerable searching.

The discovery or creation of solutions is inherent in the
nature of problem solving. This means that the discussion
leader should approach each choice situation as one in which
the possibility of additional alternatives exists. When he
encourages this searching behavior in group discussion, he
is turning a choice situation into a problem situation. Only
after other alternatives are found or invented should the
process of making a choice be undertaken.

*Principle 8—problem situations should be turned into
choice situations.* In Chapter 5 it also was pointed out that
because problem situations block behavior, the natural reaction is for people to act on the first solution that is obtained.
The objective in problem situations is to remove or get
around an obstacle. As a consequence, the discovery of the
first successful possibility tends to terminate the search. The
fact that one solution is found does not preclude the possibility that there may be others, yet people frequently
behave as though this were the case.

If the leader accepts the first solution as a possibility,
he may then proceed to ask the group members to see if
they can find another solution. If more solutions (even if
only one) are obtained, the problem situation will have been
turned into a choice situation. The opportunity to make a

choice must necessarily improve the final decision because a choice between alternatives is permitted and the better one can win out.

Research reported in Chapter 5 reveals that a second solution to a problem actually tends to be superior in quality to the first. This is not surprising when one realizes that a second solution requires further searching. Continued searching tends to lead to less obvious discoveries, and these are likely to be the more innovative possibilities. Other factors may also favor the superior quality of the second solution. An aggressive leader or certain vocal members may have pushed their ideas because of their ability to dominate, thereby discouraging the development of disagreement in the groups. Hoffman,[7] in reviewing a number of studies, believes that balanced conflict, in which opposing members are equally strong, favors creative solutions. Such conflict requires an innovative solution, he believes, because one point of view cannot dominate over another. Both alternatives are likely to be obvious alternatives for conflicting parties, and hence each might be overlooking something.

Turning problem situations into choice situations thus has two advantages. It leads to more unusual solutions, which would tend to be the more creative; and it permits the opportunity to select the best of the alternatives.

Decision making should involve choice behavior and problem-solving behavior. To identify decision making either with choice behavior or with problem solving is to restrict its function. Both activities go on in decision making, and since the two processes differ, it is desirable to make capital of the difference and thereby upgrade each.

Principle 9—solutions suggested by the leader are improperly evaluated and tend either to be accepted or rejected. When the discussion leader conducts a discussion with his subordinates, he is in a position of power so that his ideas receive a different reception than those coming from participants. This point is basic to the group decision process and has been raised in several chapters. In this

[7] L. R. Hoffman, Conditions for Creative Problem Solving. *J. Psychol.*, 1961, **52**, 429–444.

connection an experiment by Solem [8] nicely illustrates the principle. He found that discussion leaders acting as superiors had more successful conferences when they did not have a chance to study a problem beforehand. When they studied a problem and reached a decision before the discussion, they tended to express their ideas. As a result, the discussion was diverted into a reaction to their ideas so that alternatives were not generated. The tendency of members was either to show acceptance or rejection reactions to the leader's ideas. Thus the leader's previous study of a problem caused the group to reach less acceptable and poorer decisions.

Even when the discussion leader has no formal authority over the group, his position is seen as one of power. Actually such a leader exerts considerable power by merely approving or disapproving of ideas that are expressed. Thus a leader's suggestions are either blindly followed or resented rather than weighed.

The best way to avoid these two undesirable reactions is for the leader to refrain from introducing his views or passing judgment on the ideas expressed by participants. His job is to conduct the discussion and show his proficiency in this regard. In applying the principles in this chapter his position becomes analogous to that of a symphony orchestra conductor. He plays no instrument but makes use of the instruments of the participants. Similarly the discussion leader uses the minds of conferees and is interested in the best end results. At this point the analogy breaks down because the orchestra conductor has a particular outcome in mind, while the discussion leader strives for acceptable and high-quality solutions, not his particular one.

CONCLUSION

We began this volume with a consideration of *quality* and *acceptance* as essential dimensions in decision making.

[8] A. R. Solem, An Evaluation of Two Attitudinal Approaches to Delegation. *J. appl. Psychol.*, 1958, **22**, 36–39.

The quality dimension refers to the objective features of a decision—in other words, how does it square with the objective facts? The acceptance dimension refers to the degree to which the group that must execute the decision accepts it —in other words, how does the group feel about the decision? High quality and high acceptance are both needed for effective decisions. This means that group discussion must effectively deal with both facts and feelings.

A major problem is raised because the methods for dealing with facts are quite different from those for dealing with feelings. The skilled conference leader must recognize when he is dealing with facts and ideas and when he is confronted with feelings and biases. The difference is not always too apparent because feelings are often couched behind made-up reasons or rationalizations. Diagnostic skill therefore is one of his leadership requirements.

Once he is able to make diagnostic judgments, his next step is to effectively deal with facts and feelings. The skills for removing conference obstacles in the form of feelings and in the form of ideas are quite different, and each set of skills has its place.

The problem-solving principles discussed in this chapter are primarily relevant to handling the intellectual aspects of discussion. In dealing with emotional aspects the leader performs a more permissive function and serves largely in the role of a group counselor. Chapters 5 and 7 are primarily devoted to a consideration of these two qualitatively different kinds of discussion process.

Actually the skill requirements are not difficult to learn. The problem lies more with the interference caused by old habits. Once one can break away from these and get a fresh start, the battle is half won. The first step is to recognize the existence of qualitative distinctions. No one skill is best for all purposes. If the basic distinctions are made, progress in each area becomes relatively easy.

Index